Understanding Software Architecture

Understanding Software Architecture

Ryan McNeil

CLANRYE
INTERNATIONAL
www.clanryeinternational.com

Clanrye International,
750 Third Avenue, 9ᵗʰ Floor,
New York, NY 10017, USA

ISBN: 978-1-64726-110-8

Cataloging-in-Publication Data

Understanding software architecture / Ryan McNeil.
p. cm.
Includes bibliographical references and index.
ISBN: 978-1-64726-110-8
1. Software architecture. 2. Software architecture--Standards.
3. Software engineering. I. McNeil, Ryan.
QA76.754 .U53 2022
005.3--dc23

For information on all Clanrye International publications visit our website at www.clanryeinternational.com

TABLE OF CONTENTS

Permissions

Index

PREFACE

This book aims to help a broader range of students by exploring a wide variety of significant topics related to this discipline. It will help students in achieving a higher level of understanding of the subject and excel in their respective fields. This book would not have been possible without the unwavered support of my senior professors who took out the time to provide me feedback and help me with the process. I would also like to thank my family for their patience and support.

The creation of the fundamental structures of a software system is referred to as software architecture. The architecture of a software system functions as a blueprint for the system and the developing project. It details the tasks necessary to be executed during the designing. There are four core activities in software architecture design that are performed iteratively at different stages of the initial software development life cycle. These activities include architectural analysis, architectural synthesis, architectural evaluation and architectural evolution. Some common components of software architecture are software architecture description, architecture description languages, architecture viewpoints, architecture frameworks and software architecture erosion. This book contains some path-breaking studies in the field of software architecture. It traces the progress of this field and highlights some of its key concepts and applications. The extensive content of this textbook provides the readers with a thorough understanding of the subject.

A brief overview of the book contents is provided below:

Chapter – Introduction to Software Architecture

The discipline which is involved in the creation and study of the fundamental structures of a software system is known as software architecture. Some of the styles and models which are applied within this field are data-centered architecture and data flow architecture respectively. This chapter has been carefully written to provide an easy introduction to these facets of software architecture.

Chapter – Software Architectural Pattern and its Types

A concept which delineates and solves a few integral cohesive elements of a software architecture is known as an architectural pattern. N tier architecture, blackboard architecture, domain driven design and microkernel architecture are some of the popular types of architectural patterns. The diverse applications of these types of architectural patterns have been thoroughly discussed in this chapter.

Chapter – Software Architecture Description

The set of practices which are used for expressing, communicating and analyzing software architectures is termed as software architecture description. The topics elaborated in this chapter will help in gaining a better perspective about software architecture description and its diverse aspects such as software architecture recovery and view models.

Chapter – Software Architecture Description Languages

The computer language which is used to create a description of a software architecture is known as an architecture description language. Some of the popular languages are DUALLy, EAST-ADL, Darwin, Unified Modeling Language and ERIL. This chapter discusses in detail these architectural description languages to provide a thorough understanding of the subject.

Chapter – Software Development Processes

The splitting of software development work into separate phases for the purpose of improving the planning and management is known as software development process. Some of the techniques used in this field are software prototyping and continuous integration. This chapter closely examines these practices related to software development process to provide an extensive understanding of the subject.

Ryan McNeil

Introduction to Software Architecture

- **Principles**
- **Data Flow Architecture**
- **Data-Centered Architecture**
- **Hierarchical Architecture**

The discipline which is involved in the creation and study of the fundamental structures of a software system is known as software architecture. Some of the styles and models which are applied within this field are data-centered architecture and data flow architecture respectively. This chapter has been carefully written to provide an easy introduction to these facets of software architecture.

The architecture of a system describes its major components, their relationships (structures), and how they interact with each other. Software architecture and design includes several contributory factors such as Business strategy, quality attributes, human dynamics, design, and IT environment.

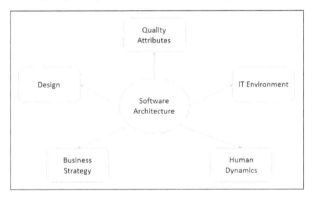

We can segregate Software Architecture and Design into two distinct phases: Software Architecture and Software Design. In Architecture, nonfunctional decisions are cast and separated by the functional requirements. In Design, functional requirements are accomplished.

Software Architecture

Architecture serves as a blueprint for a system. It provides an abstraction to manage the system complexity and establish a communication and coordination mechanism among components:

- It defines a structured solution to meet all the technical and operational requirements, while optimizing the common quality attributes like performance and security.

- Further, it involves a set of significant decisions about the organization related to software development and each of these decisions can have a considerable impact on quality, maintainability, performance, and the overall success of the final product. These decisions comprise of:

    ○ Selection of structural elements and their interfaces by which the system is composed.

    ○ Behavior as specified in collaborations among those elements.

    ○ Composition of these structural and behavioral elements into large subsystem.

    ○ Architectural decisions align with business objectives.

    ○ Architectural styles guide the organization.

Software Design

Software design provides a design plan that describes the elements of a system, how they fit, and work together to fulfill the requirement of the system. The objectives of having a design plan are as follows:

- To negotiate system requirements, and to set expectations with customers, marketing, and management personnel.

- Act as a blueprint during the development process.

- Guide the implementation tasks, including detailed design, coding, integration, and testing.

It comes before the detailed design, coding, integration, and testing and after the domain analysis, requirements analysis, and risk analysis.

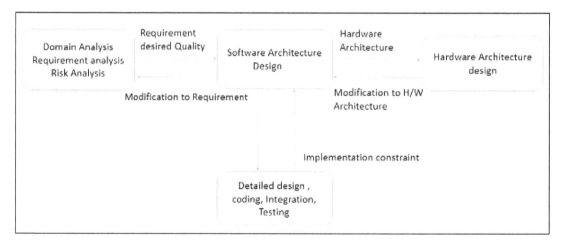

Goals of Architecture

The primary goal of the architecture is to identify requirements that affect the structure of the application. A well-laid architecture reduces the business risks associated with building a technical solution and builds a bridge between business and technical requirements.

Some of the other goals are as follows:

- Expose the structure of the system, but hide its implementation details.
- Realize all the use-cases and scenarios.
- Try to address the requirements of various stakeholders.
- Handle both functional and quality requirements.
- Reduce the goal of ownership and improve the organization's market position.
- Improve quality and functionality offered by the system.
- Improve external confidence in either the organization or system.

Limitations

Software architecture is still an emerging discipline within software engineering. It has the following limitations:

- Lack of tools and standardized ways to represent architecture.
- Lack of analysis methods to predict whether architecture will result in an implementation that meets the requirements.
- Lack of awareness of the importance of architectural design to software development.
- Lack of understanding of the role of software architect and poor communication among stakeholders.
- Lack of understanding of the design process, design experience and evaluation of design.

Role of Software Architect

A Software Architect provides a solution that the technical team can create and design for the entire application. A software architect should have expertise in the following areas:

Design Expertise

- Expert in software design, including diverse methods and approaches such as object-oriented design, event-driven design, etc.
- Lead the development team and coordinate the development efforts for the integrity of the design.
- Should be able to review design proposals and tradeoff among themselves.

Domain Expertise

- Expert on the system being developed and plan for software evolution.
- Assist in the requirement investigation process, assuring completeness and consistency.
- Coordinate the definition of domain model for the system being developed.

Technology Expertise

- Expert on available technologies that helps in the implementation of the system.
- Coordinate the selection of programming language, framework, platforms, databases, etc.

Methodological Expertise

- Expert on software development methodologies that may be adopted during SDLC (Software Development Life Cycle).
- Choose the appropriate approaches for development that helps the entire team.

Hidden Role of Software Architect

- Facilitates the technical work among team members and reinforcing the trust relationship in the team.
- Information specialist who shares knowledge and has vast experience.
- Protect the team members from external forces that would distract them and bring less value to the project.

Deliverables of the Architect

- A clear, complete, consistent, and achievable set of functional goals.
- A functional description of the system, with at least two layers of decomposition.
- A concept for the system.
- A design in the form of the system, with at least two layers of decomposition.
- A notion of the timing, operator attributes, and the implementation and operation plans.
- A document or process which ensures functional decomposition is followed, and the form of interfaces is controlled.

Quality Attributes

Quality is a measure of excellence or the state of being free from deficiencies or defects. Quality attributes are the system properties that are separate from the functionality of the system.

Implementing quality attributes makes it easier to differentiate a good system from a bad one. Attributes are overall factors that affect runtime behavior, system design, and user experience. They can be classified as:

Static Quality Attributes

Reflect the structure of a system and organization, directly related to architecture, design, and source code. They are invisible to end-user, but affect the development and maintenance cost, e.g.: modularity, testability, maintainability, etc.

Dynamic Quality Attributes

Reflect the behavior of the system during its execution. They are directly related to system's architecture, design, source code, configuration, deployment parameters, environment, and platform.

They are visible to the end-user and exist at runtime, e.g. throughput, robustness, scalability, etc.

Quality Scenarios

Quality scenarios specify how to prevent a fault from becoming a failure. They can be divided into six parts based on their attribute specifications:

- Source – An internal or external entity such as people, hardware, software, or physical infrastructure that generate the stimulus.

- Stimulus – A condition that needs to be considered when it arrives on a system.

- Environment – The stimulus occurs within certain conditions.

- Artifact – A whole system or some part of it such as processors, communication channels, persistent storage, processes etc.

- Response – An activity undertaken after the arrival of stimulus such as detect faults, recover from fault, disable event source etc.

- Response measure – Should measure the occurred responses so that the requirements can be tested.

Common Quality Attributes

Table: The following table lists the common quality attributes a software architecture must have.

Category	Quality Attribute	Description
Design Qualities	Conceptual Integrity	Defines the consistency and coherence of the overall design. This includes the way components or modules are designed.
	Maintainability	Ability of the system to undergo changes with a degree of ease.
	Reusability	Defines the capability for components and subsystems to be suitable for use in other applications.
Run-time Qualities	Interoperability	Ability of a system or different systems to operate successfully by communicating and exchanging information with other external systems written and run by external parties.
	Manageability	Defines how easy it is for system administrators to manage the application.
	Reliability	Ability of a system to remain operational over time.
	Scalability	Ability of a system to either handle the load increase without impacting the performance of the system or the ability to be readily enlarged.
	Security	Capability of a system to prevent malicious or accidental actions outside of the designed usages.
	Performance	Indication of the responsiveness of a system to execute any action within a given time interval.

	Availability	Defines the proportion of time that the system is functional and working. It can be measured as a percentage of the total system downtime over a predefined period.
System Qualities	Supportability	Ability of the system to provide information helpful for identifying and resolving issues when it fails to work correctly.
	Testability	Measure of how easy it is to create test criteria for the system and its components.
User Qualities	Usability	Defines how well the application meets the requirements of the user and consumer by being intuitive.
Architecture Quality	Correctness	Accountability for satisfying all the requirements of the system.
	Portability	Ability of the system to run under different computing environment.
Non-runtime Quality	Integrality	Ability to make separately developed components of the system work correctly together.
	Modifiability	Ease with which each software system can accommodate changes to its software.
Business quality attributes	Cost and schedule	Cost of the system with respect to time to market, expected project lifetime & utilization of legacy.
	Marketability	Use of system with respect to market competition.

Principles

Software architecture is described as the organization of a system, where the system represents a set of components that accomplish the defined functions.

Architectural Style

The architectural style, also called as architectural pattern, is a set of principles which shapes an application. It defines an abstract framework for a family of system in terms of the pattern of structural organization.

The architectural style is responsible to:

- Provide a lexicon of components and connectors with rules on how they can be combined.

- Improve partitioning and allow the reuse of design by giving solutions to frequently occurring problems.

- Describe a particular way to configure a collection of components (a module with well-defined interfaces, reusable, and replaceable) and connectors (communication link between modules).

The software that is built for computer-based systems exhibit one of many architectural styles. Each style describes a system category that encompasses:

- A set of component types which perform a required function by the system.

- A set of connectors (subroutine call, remote procedure call, data stream, and socket) that enable communication, coordination, and cooperation among different components.

- Semantic constraints which define how components can be integrated to form the system.

- A topological layout of the components indicating their runtime interrelationships.

Common Architectural Design

Table: The following table lists architectural styles that can be organized by their key focus area.

Category	Architectural Design	Description
Communication	Message bus	Prescribes use of a software system that can receive and send messages using one or more communication channels.
	Service–Oriented Architecture (SOA)	Defines the applications that expose and consume functionality as a service using contracts and messages.
Deployment	Client/server	Separate the system into two applications, where the client makes requests to the server.
	3-tier or N-tier	Separates the functionality into separate segments with each segment being a tier located on a physically separate computer.
Domain	Domain Driven Design	Focused on modeling a business domain and defining business objects based on entities within the business domain.
Structure	Component Based	Breakdown the application design into reusable functional or logical components that expose well-defined communication interfaces.
	Layered	Divide the concerns of the application into stacked groups (layers).
	Object oriented	Based on the division of responsibilities of an application or system into objects, each containing the data and the behavior relevant to the object.

Types of Architecture

There are four types of architecture from the viewpoint of an enterprise and collectively, these architectures are referred to as enterprise architecture:

- Business architecture – Defines the strategy of business, governance, organization, and key business processes within an enterprise and focuses on the analysis and design of business processes.

- Application (software) architecture – Serves as the blueprint for individual application systems, their interactions, and their relationships to the business processes of the organization.

- Information architecture – Defines the logical and physical data assets and data management resources.

- Information technology (IT) architecture – Defines the hardware and software building blocks that make up the overall information system of the organization.

Architecture Design Process

The architecture design process focuses on the decomposition of a system into different components and their interactions to satisfy functional and nonfunctional requirements. The key inputs to software architecture design are:

- The requirements produced by the analysis tasks.

- The hardware architecture (the software architect in turn provides requirements to the system architect, who configures the hardware architecture).

The result or output of the architecture design process is an architectural description. The basic architecture design process is composed of the following steps:

Understand the Problem

- This is the most crucial step because it affects the quality of the design that follows.

- Without a clear understanding of the problem, it is not possible to create an effective solution.

- Many software projects and products are considered failures because they did not actually solve a valid business problem or have a recognizable return on investment (ROI).

Identify Design Elements and their Relationships

- In this phase, build a baseline for defining the boundaries and context of the system.

- Decomposition of the system into its main components based on functional requirements. The decomposition can be modeled using a design structure matrix (DSM), which shows the dependencies between design elements without specifying the granularity of the elements.

- In this step, the first validation of the architecture is done by describing a number of system instances and this step is referred as functionality based architectural design.

Evaluate the Architecture Design

- Each quality attribute is given an estimate so in order to gather qualitative measures or quantitative data, the design is evaluated.

- It involves evaluating the architecture for conformance to architectural quality attributes requirements.

- If all estimated quality attributes are as per the required standard, the architectural design process is finished.

- If not, the third phase of software architecture design is entered: architecture transformation. If the observed quality attribute does not meet its requirements, then a new design must be created.

Transform the Architecture Design

- This step is performed after an evaluation of the architectural design. The architectural design must be changed until it completely satisfies the quality attribute requirements.

- It is concerned with selecting design solutions to improve the quality attributes while preserving the domain functionality.

- A design is transformed by applying design operators, styles, or patterns. For transformation, take the existing design and apply design operator such as decomposition, replication, compression, abstraction, and resource sharing.

- The design is again evaluated and the same process is repeated multiple times if necessary and even performed recursively.

- The transformations (i.e. quality attribute optimizing solutions) generally improve one or some quality attributes while they affect others negatively.

Key Architecture Principles

Following are the key principles to be considered while designing an architecture:

Build to Change Instead of Building to Last

Consider how the application may need to change over time to address new requirements and challenges, and build in the flexibility to support this.

Reduce Risk and Model to Analyze

Use design tools, visualizations, modeling systems such as UML to capture requirements and design decisions. The impacts can also be analyzed. Do not formalize the model to the extent that it suppresses the capability to iterate and adapt the design easily.

Use Models and Visualizations as a Communication and Collaboration Tool

Efficient communication of the design, the decisions, and ongoing changes to the design is critical to good architecture. Use models, views, and other visualizations of the architecture to communicate and share the design efficiently with all the stakeholders. This enables rapid communication of changes to the design.

Identify and understand key engineering decisions and areas where mistakes are most often made. Invest in getting key decisions right the first time to make the design more flexible and less likely to be broken by changes.

Use an Incremental and Iterative Approach

Start with baseline architecture and then evolve candidate architectures by iterative testing to improve the architecture. Iteratively add details to the design over multiple passes to get the big or right picture and then focus on the details.

Key Design Principles

Following are the design principles to be considered for minimizing cost, maintenance requirements, and maximizing extendibility, usability of architecture:

Separation of Concerns

Divide the components of system into specific features so that there is no overlapping among the components functionality. This will provide high cohesion and low coupling. This approach avoids the interdependency among components of system which helps in maintaining the system easy.

Single Responsibility Principle

Each and every module of a system should have one specific responsibility, which helps the user to clearly understand the system. It should also help with integration of the component with other components.

Principle of Least Knowledge

Any component or object should not have the knowledge about internal details of other components. This approach avoids interdependency and helps maintainability.

Minimize Large Design Upfront

Minimize large design upfront if the requirements of an application are unclear. If there is a possibility of modifying requirements, then avoid making a large design for whole system.

Do not Repeat the Functionality

Do not repeat functionality specifies that functionality of components should not to be repeated and hence a piece of code should be implemented in one component only. Duplication of functionality within an application can make it difficult to implement changes, decrease clarity, and introduce potential inconsistencies.

Prefer Composition over Inheritance while Reusing the Functionality

Inheritance creates dependency between children and parent classes and hence it blocks the free use of the child classes. In contrast, the composition provides a great level of freedom and reduces the inheritance hierarchies.

Identify Components and Group them in Logical Layers

Identity components and the area of concern that are needed in system to satisfy the requirements. Then group these related components in a logical layer, which will help the user to understand the structure of the system at a high level. Avoid mixing components of different type of concerns in same layer.

Define the Communication Protocol between Layers

Understand how components will communicate with each other which requires a complete knowledge of deployment scenarios and the production environment.

Define Data Format for a Layer

Various components will interact with each other through data format. Do not mix the data formats so that applications are easy to implement, extend, and maintain. Try to keep data format same for a layer, so that various components need not code/decode the data while communicating with each other. It reduces a processing overhead.

System Service Components should be Abstract

Code related to security, communications, or system services like logging, profiling, and configuration should be abstracted in the separate components. Do not mix this code with business logic, as it is easy to extend design and maintain it.

Design Exceptions and Exception Handling Mechanism

Defining exceptions in advance, helps the components to manage errors or unwanted situation in an elegant manner. The exception management will be same throughout the system.

Naming Conventions

Naming conventions should be defined in advance. They provide a consistent model that helps the users to understand the system easily. It is easier for team members to validate code written by others, and hence will increase the maintainability.

Data Flow Architecture

- Data Flow Architecture is transformed input data by a series of computational or manipulative components into output data.

- It is a computer architecture which do not have a program counter and therefore the execution is unpredictable which means behavior is indeterministic.

- Data flow architecture is a part of Von-neumann model of computation which consists of a single program counter, sequential execution and control flow which determines fetch, execution, commit order.

- This architecture has been successfully implemented.

- Data flow architecture reduces development time and can move easily between design and implementation.

- It has main objective is to achieve the qualities of reuse and modifiability.

- In data flow architecture, the data can be flow in the graph topology with cycles or in a linear structure without cycles.

There are three types of execution sequences between modules:

- Batch Sequential

- Pipe and Filter

- Process Control

Batch Sequential

- Batch sequential compilation was regarded as a sequential process in 1970.

- In Batch sequential, separate programs are executed in order and the data is passed as an aggregate from one program to the next.

- It is a classical data processing model.

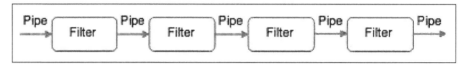

The above diagram shows the flow of batch sequential architecture. It provides simpler divisions on subsystems and each subsystem can be an independent program working on input data and produces output data.

- The main disadvantage of batch sequential architecture is that, it does not provide concurrency and interactive interface. It provides high latency and low throughput.

Pipe and Filter

Pipe:

- Pipe is a connector which passes the data from one filter to the next.

- Pipe is a directional stream of data implemented by a data buffer to store all data, until the next filter has time to process it.

- It transfers the data from one data source to one data sink.

- Pipes are the stateless data stream.

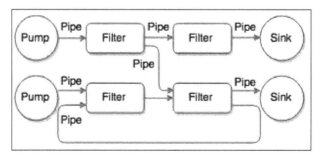

The above figure shows the pipe-filter sequence. All filters are the processes that run at the same time, it means that they can run as different threads, coroutines or be located on different machines entirely.

Each pipe is connected to a filter and has its own role in the function of the filter. The filters are robust where pipes can be added and removed at runtime.

Filter reads the data from its input pipes and performs its function on this data and places the result on all output pipes. If there is insufficient data in the input pipes, the filter simply waits.

Filters:

- Filter is a component.
- It has interfaces from which a set of inputs can flow in and a set of outputs can flow out.
- It transforms and refines input data.
- Filters are the independent entities.

There are two strategies to construct a filter:

- Active Filter
  - Active filter derives the data flow on the pipes.
- Passive Filter
  - Passive filter is driven by the data flow on the pipes.
- Filter does not share state with other filters.
- They don't know the identity to upstream and downstream filters.
- Filters are implemented by separate threads. These may be either hardware or software threads or coroutines.

Advantages of Pipes and Filters

- Pipe-filter provides concurrency and high throughput for excessive data processing.
- It simplifies the system maintenance and provides reusability.
- It has low coupling between filters and flexibility by supporting both sequential and parallel execution.

Disadvantages of Pipe and Filter

- Pipe and Filter are not suitable for dynamic interactions.
- It needs low common denominator for transmission of data in ASCII format.
- It is difficult to configure Pipe-filter architecture dynamically.

Process Control

- Process Control Architecture is a type of Data Flow Architecture, where data is neither batch sequential nor pipe stream.
- In process control architecture, the flow of data comes from a set of variables which controls the execution of process.
- This architecture decomposes the entire system into subsystems or modules and connects them.

- Process control architecture is suitable in the embedded system software design, where the system is manipulated by process control variable data and in the Real time system software, process control architecture is used to control automobile anti-lock brakes, nuclear power plants etc.

- This architecture is applicable for car-cruise control and building temperature control system.

Data-Centered Architecture

An information focused architecture, the information is concentrated and gotten to every now and again by different parts, which alter information. The fundamental motivation behind this style is to accomplish integrality of information. Information focused architecture comprises of various parts that convey through shared information vaults. The segments get to a common information structure and are generally free, in that, they associate just through the information store.

The most surely understood cases of the information focused design is a database architecture, in which the regular database construction is made with information definition convention – for instance, an arrangement of related tables with fields and information types in a RDBMS.

Another case of information focused structures is the web architecture which has a typical information composition (i.e. meta-structure of the Web) and takes after hypermedia information model and procedures impart using shared online information administrations.

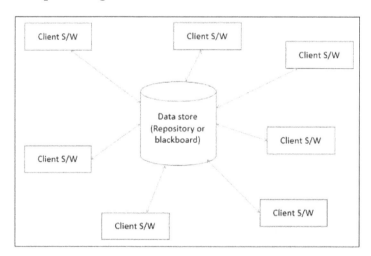

Types of Components

There are two types of segments:

- A focal information structure or information store or information vault, which is in charge of giving perpetual information stockpiling. It speaks to the present state.

- A information accessor or an accumulation of autonomous parts that work on the focal information store, perform calculations, and might return the outcomes.

Connections or correspondence between the information accessors is just through the information store. The information is the main methods for correspondence among customers. The stream of control separates the architecture into two classes as Repository Architecture Style and Blackboard Architecture Style. A short insight about both the classes is given underneath:

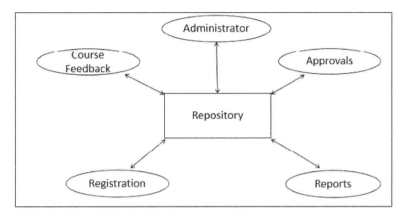

In Repository Architecture Style, the information store is inactive and the customers (Software segments or operators) of the information store are dynamic, which control the rationale stream. The taking an interest segments check the information store for changes.

A customer sends a demand to the system to perform activities (e.g. embed information). The computational procedures are autonomous and activated by approaching solicitations. On the off chance that the types of exchanges in an info stream of exchanges trigger determination of procedures to execute, at that point it is conventional database or storehouse design, or detached vault. This approach is broadly utilized as a part of DBMS, library data system, the interface archive in CORBA, compilers, and CASE (PC supported Software designing) situations.

Advantages

Storehouse Architecture Style has following favorable circumstances:

- Provides information trustworthiness, reinforcement and reestablish highlights.
- Provides adaptability and reusability of operators as they don't have coordinate correspondence with each other.
- Reduces overhead of transient information between Software parts.

Disadvantages

Due to being more helpless against disappointment and information replication or duplication, Repository Architecture Style has following inconveniences:

- High reliance between information structure of information store and its specialists.
- Changes in information structure exceedingly influence the customers.
- Evolution of information is troublesome and costly.
- Cost of moving information on organizes for circulated information.

Blackboard Architecture Styles

In Blackboard Architecture Style, the information store is dynamic and its customers are inactive. In this way the sensible stream is dictated by the present information status in information store. It has a writing board segment, going about as a focal information store, and an interior portrayal is constructed and followed up on by various computational components.

Further, various segments that demonstration freely on the basic information structure are put away in the writing board. In this style, the parts collaborate just through the chalkboard. The information store alarms the customers at whatever point there is an information store changes. The present condition of the arrangement is put away in the board and handling is activated by the condition of the slate.

At the point when changes happen in the information, the system sends the notices known as trigger and information to the customers. This approach is found in certain AI applications and complex applications, for example, discourse acknowledgment, picture acknowledgment, security system, and business asset administration systems and so on.

In the event that the present condition of the focal information structure is the fundamental trigger of choosing procedures to execute, the store can be a chalkboard and this mutual information source is a dynamic specialist.

A noteworthy contrast with customary database systems is that the conjuring of computational components in chalkboard architecture is activated by the present condition of the slate, and not by outside sources of info.

Parts of Blackboard Model

The chalkboard show is typically given three noteworthy parts:

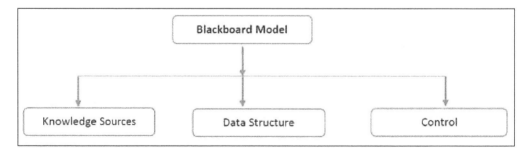

Knowledge Sources (KS)

Information Sources, otherwise called Listeners or Subscribers are particular and free units. They take care of parts of an issue and total fractional outcomes. Connection among learning sources happens exceptionally through the slate.

Blackboard Data Structure

The critical thinking state information is sorted out into an application-subordinate progression. Information sources roll out improvements to the slate that lead incrementally to an answer for the issue.

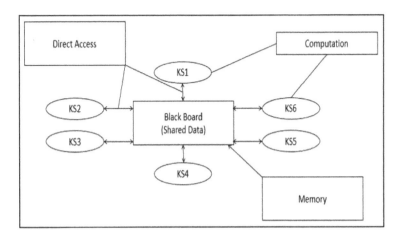

Control

Control oversees undertakings and checks the work state.

Advantages

Slate Model gives simultaneousness that permits all information sources to work in parallel as they free of each other. Its adaptability include encourages simple strides to include or refresh learning source. Further, it bolsters experimentation for theories and reusability of learning source specialists.

Disadvantages

The auxiliary difference in board may significantly affect the greater part of its specialists, as close reliance exists amongst writing board and information source. Board demonstrates is required to create surmised arrangement; nonetheless, now and again, it winds up noticeably hard choosing when to end the thinking.

Further, this model endures a few issues in synchronization of different specialists, subsequently; it faces challenge in outlining and testing of the system.

Hierarchical Architecture

Hierarchical architecture is a form of control system. It includes a set of devices and controlling software arranged in a hierarchical tree. Hierarchical architecture is used in organization of the class libraries such as .NET class library in namespace hierarchy.

Styles Included in the Hierarchical Architecture

In hierarchical architecture, the software system is decomposed into logical modules or subsystems at different levels in the hierarchy. This architecture is used in designing system software such as network protocols and operating system.

There are the three types of hierarchical architecture:

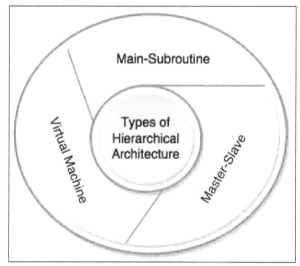

Types of hierarchical architecture.

Main-subroutine

- Main-subroutine is a style of hierarchical architecture which dominates the software design methodologies for a very long time.

- Main-subroutine reuses the subroutines and have individual subroutines developed independently.

- Using main-subroutine, a software system is decomposed into subroutines hierarchically refined according to the desired functionality of the system and each module reads input files and writes output files.

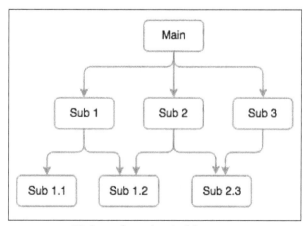

Main –subroutine Architecture.

- Main-subroutine has a benefit, it is easy to decompose the system based on the definition of the tasks in a top-down refinement manner.

- Main-subroutine has a limitation because of tight coupling it may cause more ripple effects of changes as compared to object-oriented design.

Master-slave

- Master-slave is a modification of the main-subroutine architecture.

- Master-slave architecture provides fault tolerance and system reliability.

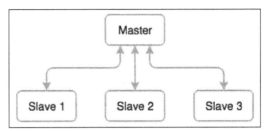

Master-slave architecture.

- In master-slave architecture, slave provides duplicate services to the master and the master chooses a particular result between slaves by a certain selection strategy.

- It provides replicated services to the master.

- Master-slave architecture is suitable for applications where reliability of software is critical issue and can be implemented to minimize semantic errors.

- This architecture has faster computation and easy scalability.

- Master-slave architecture has limitations also, it is hard to implement, not all problems can be divided and has portability issue.

- Slave performs the same functional task by different algorithms and methods or totally different functionality.

Virtual Machine

- Virtual machine architecture provides a virtual abstraction, a set of attributes and operations.

- This architecture appears similar to emulator software, for eg. JVM, Virtual Box.

- It pretends some functionality, which is not native to the hardware or software on which it is implemented.

- Virtual machine architecture is suitable for solving a problem by simulation or translation if there is no direct solution.

- It includes interpreters of microprogramming, XML processing, script command language execution, Smalltalk and Java interpreter typed programming language.

- The examples of virtual machines are rule-based system, syntactic shells and command language processors.

- It introduces modifications at runtime and provides flexibility through the ability to interrupt.

- It provides portability and machine platform independency.

- Virtual machine architecture has disadvantage, it slows execution of the interpreter due to the interpreter nature and it incurs extra performance cost because of the additional computation involved in execution.

Layered Style

- In Layered style, it decomposes the system into a number of higher and lower layers and each layer has its responsibility.

- Using layered architecture, applications involve distinct classes of services that can be organized hierarchically and have clear divisions between core services, critical services, user interface services etc.

- Layered architecture design is based on incremental levels of abstraction.

- It is implemented by using component-based technology which makes the system much easier to allow for plug-and-play of new components.

- Using layered architecture, It is easy to decompose the system based on the definition of the tasks in a top-down refinement manner.

References

- Introduction, software-architecture-design: tutorialspoint.com, Retrieved 6 March, 2019

- Key-principles, software-architecture-design: tutorialspoint.com, Retrieved 7 April, 2019

- Data-flow-architecture, software-architecture-and-design: tutorialride.com, Retrieved 8 May, 2019

- Data-centered-architecture-26204, software-architecture-and-design-tutorial-2531, e-university: wisdomjobs.com, Retrieved 9 June, 2019

- Hierarchical-architecture, software-architecture-and-design: tutorialride.com, Retrieved 10 July, 2019

Software Architectural Pattern and its Types

2

- **Architecture Pattern**
- **N-Tier Architecture**
- **Domain Driven Design**
- **Microkernel**
- **Blackboard**
- **Model-View-Controller**
- **Model-View-Adapter**
- **Model-View-Presenter**
- **Action Domain Responder**
- **Active Record Pattern**
- **Multiuse-Model View**
- **Model-View-View Model**

A concept which delineates and solves a few integral cohesive elements of a software architecture is known as an architectural pattern. N tier architecture, blackboard architecture, domain driven design and microkernel architecture are some of the popular types of architectural patterns. The diverse applications of these types of architectural patterns have been thoroughly discussed in this chapter.

Architecture Pattern

Patterns for system architecting are very much in their infancy. They have been introduced into TOGAF essentially to draw them to the attention of the systems architecture community as an emerging important resource, and as a placeholder for hopefully more rigorous descriptions and references to more plentiful resources in future versions of TOGAF.

They have not (as yet) been integrated into TOGAF. However, in the following, we attempt to indicate the potential value to TOGAF, and to which parts of the TOGAF Architecture Development Method (ADM) they might be relevant.

A "pattern" has been defined as: "an idea that has been useful in one practical context and will probably be useful in others".

In TOGAF, patterns are considered to be a way of putting building blocks into context; for example, to describe a re-usable solution to a problem. Building blocks are what you use: patterns can tell you how you use them, when, why, and what trade-offs you have to make in doing so.

Patterns offer the promise of helping the architect to identify combinations of Architecture and/or Solution Building Blocks (ABBs/SBBs) that have been proven to deliver effective solutions in the past, and may provide the basis for effective solutions in the future.

Pattern techniques are generally acknowledged to have been established as a valuable architectural design technique by Christopher Alexander.

Content of a Pattern

Several different formats are used in the literature for describing patterns, and no single format has achieved widespread acceptance. However, there is broad agreement on the types of things that a pattern should contain.The elements described below will be found in most patterns, even if different headings are used to describe them.

Name

A meaningful and memorable way to refer to the pattern, typically a single word or short phrase.

Problem

A description of the problem indicating the intent in applying the pattern - the intended goals and objectives to be reached within the context and forces described below (perhaps with some indication of their priorities).

Context

The preconditions under which the pattern is applicable - a description of the initial state before the pattern is applied.

Forces

A description of the relevant forces and constraints, and how they interact/conflict with each other and with the intended goals and objectives. The description should clarify the intricacies of the problem and make explicit the kinds of trade-offs that must be considered. (The need for such trade-offs is typically what makes the problem difficult, and generates the need for the pattern in the first place.) The notion of "forces" equates in many ways to the "qualities" that architects seek to optimize, and the concerns they seek to address, in designing architectures. For example:

- Security, robustness, reliability, fault-tolerance.

- Manageability.

- Efficiency, performance, throughput, bandwidth requirements, space utilization.

- Scalability (incremental growth on-demand).

- Extensibility, evolvability, maintainability.

- Modularity, independence, re-usability, openness, composability (plug-and-play), portability.

- Completeness and correctness.

- Ease-of-construction.

- Ease-of-use, etc.

A description, using text and/or graphics, of how to achieve the intended goals and objectives. The description should identify both the solution's static structure and its dynamic behavior - the people and computing actors, and their collaborations. The description may include guidelines for implementing the solution. Variants or specializations of the solution may also be described.

Resulting Context

The post-conditions after the pattern has been applied. Implementing the solution normally requires trade-offs among competing forces. This element describes which forces have been resolved and how, and which remain unresolved. It may also indicate other patterns that may be applicable in the new context. (A pattern may be one step in accomplishing some larger goal.)

Examples

One or more sample applications of the pattern which illustrate each of the other elements: a specific problem, context, and set of forces; how the pattern is applied; and the resulting context.

Rationale

An explanation/justification of the pattern as a whole, or of individual components within it, indicating how the pattern actually works, and why - how it resolves the forces to achieve the desired goals and objectives, and why this is "good". The Solution element of a pattern describes the external structure and behavior of the solution: the Rationale provides insight into its internal workings.

Related Patterns

The relationships between this pattern and others. These may be predecessor patterns, whose resulting contexts correspond to the initial context of this one; or successor patterns, whose initial contexts correspond to the resulting context of this one; or alternative patterns, which describe a different solution to the same problem, but under different forces; or co-dependent patterns, which may/must be applied along with this pattern.

Known Uses

Known applications of the pattern within existing systems, verifying that the pattern does indeed describe a proven solution to a recurring problem. Known Uses can also serve as Examples.

Patterns may also begin with an Abstract providing an overview of the pattern and indicating the types of problems it addresses. The Abstract may also identify the target audience and what assumptions are made of the reader.

Architecture Patterns and Design Patterns

The term "design pattern" is often used to refer to any pattern which addresses issues of software architecture, design, or programming implementation. Three types of patterns as follows:

- An Architecture Pattern expresses a fundamental structural organization or schema for software systems. It provides a set of predefined subsystems, specifies their responsibilities, and includes rules and guidelines for organizing the relationships between them.

- A Design Pattern provides a scheme for refining the subsystems or components of a software system, or the relationships between them. It describes a commonly recurring structure of communicating components that solves a general design problem within a particular context.

- An Idiom is a low-level pattern specific to a programming language. An idiom describes how to implement particular aspects of components or the relationships between them using the features of the given language.

These distinctions are useful, but it is important to note that architecture patterns in this context still refers solely to software architecture. Software architecture is certainly an important part of the focus of TOGAF, but it is not its only focus.

Patterns for enterprise system architecture are analogous to software architecture and design patterns, and borrow many of their concepts and terminology, but focus on providing re-usable models and methods specifically for the architecting of enterprise information systems - comprising software, hardware, networks, and people - as opposed to purely software systems.

Patterns and the Architecture Continuum

Although architecture patterns have not (as yet) been integrated into TOGAF, each of the first four main phases of the ADM (Phases A through D) gives an indication of the stage at which relevant re-usable architecture assets from the enterprise's Architecture Continuum should be considered for use. Architecture patterns are one such asset.

An enterprise that adopts a formal approach to use and re-use of architecture patterns will normally integrate their use into the enterprise's Architecture Continuum.

Patterns and Views

Architecture views are selected parts of one or more models representing a complete system architecture, focusing on those aspects that address the concerns of one or more stakeholders. Patterns can provide help in designing such models, and in composing views based on them.

Patterns and Business Scenarios

Relevant architecture patterns may well be identified in the work on business scenarios.

N-Tier Architecture

An N-Tier Application program is one that is distributed among three or more separate computers in a distributed network.

The most common form of n-tier is the 3-tier Application, and it is classified into three categories:

- User interface programming in the user's computer,

- Business logic in a more centralized computer,

- Required data in a computer that manages a database.

This architecture model provides Software Developers to create Reusable application/systems with maximum flexibility.

In N-tier, "N" refers to a number of tiers or layers are being used like – 2-tier, 3-tier or 4-tier, etc. It is also called "Multi-Tier Architecture".

The n-tier architecture is an industry-proven software architecture model. It is suitable to support enterprise level client-server applications by providing solutions to scalability, security, fault tolerance, reusability, and maintainability. It helps developers to create flexible and reusable applications.

N-Tier Architecture

A diagrammatic representation of an n-tier system depicts here – presentation, application, and database layers.

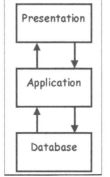

N Tier Architecture Diagram.

These three layers can be further subdivided into different sub-layers depending on the requirements.

Some of the popular sites who have applied this architecture are:

- MakeMyTrip.com,

- Sales Force enterprise application,

- Indian Railways – IRCTC,

- Amazon.com, etc.

Some common terms to remember, so as to understand the concept more clearly:

Distributed Network: It is a network architecture, where the components located at network computers coordinate and communicate their actions only by passing messages. It is a collection of multiple systems situated at different nodes but appears to the user as a single system.

- It provides a single data communication network which can be managed separately by different networks.

- An example of Distributed Network– where different clients are connected within LAN architecture on one side and on the other side they are connected to high-speed switches along with a rack of servers containing service nodes.

Client-Server Architecture: It is an architecture model where the client (one program) requests a service from a server (another program) i.e. It is a request-response service provided over the internet or through an intranet.

In this model, Client will serve as one set of program/code which executes a set of actions over the network. While Server, on the other hand, is a set of another program, which sends the result sets to the client system as requested.

- In this, client computer provides an interface to an end user to request a service or a resource from a server and on the other hand server then processes the request and displays the result to the end user.

- An example of Client-Server Model– an ATM machine. A bank is the server for processing the application within the large customer databases and ATM machine is the client having a user interface with some simple application processing.

Platform: In computer science or software industry, a platform is a system on which applications program can run. It consists of a combination of hardware and software that have a built-in instruction for a processors/microprocessors to perform specific operations.

- In more simple words, the platform is a system or a base where any applications can run and execute to obtain a specific task.

- An example of Platform – A personal machine loaded with Windows 2000 or Mac OS X as examples of 2 different platforms.

Database: It is a collection of information in an organized way so that it can be easily accessed, managed and updated.

- Examples of Database – MySQL, SQL Server, and Oracle Database are some common Db's.

Types of N-Tier Architectures

There are different types of N-Tier Architectures, like 3-tier Architecture, 2-Tier Architecture and 1- Tier Architecture.

3-Tier Architecture

By looking at the below diagram, you can easily identify that 3-tier architecture has three different layers.

- Presentation layer.
- Business Logic layer.
- Database layer.

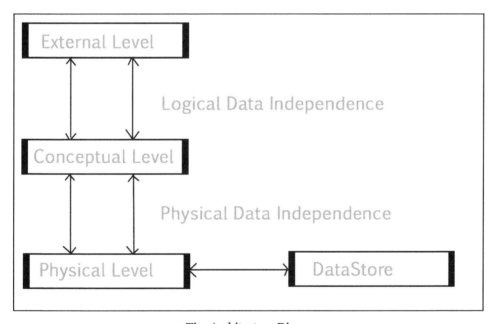

3 Tier Architecture Diagram.

Here we have taken a simple example of student form to understand all these three layers. It has information about a student like – Name, Address, Email, and Picture.

User Interface Layer or Presentation Layer

Students Information				
ID	Name	Address	Email	Picture

Presentation Layer

```
private void DataGrid1_SelectedIndexChanged(object sender, System.EventArgs e)
{
// Object of the Property layer
clsStudent objproperty=new clsStudent();
// Object of the business layer
clsStudentInfo objbs=new clsStudentInfo();
// Object of the dataset in which we receive the data sent by the business layer
DataSet ds=new DataSet();
// here we are placing the value in the property using the object of the
//property layer
objproperty.id=int.Parse(DataGrid1.SelectedItem.Cells.Text.ToString());
// In this following code we are calling a function from the business layer and
// passing the object of the property layer which will carry the ID till the
database.
ds=objbs.GetAllStudentBsIDWise(objproperty);
// What ever the data has been returned by the above function into the dataset
//is being populate through the presentation laye.
txtId.Text=ds.Tables.Rows.ToString();
txtFname.Text=ds.Tables.Rows.ToString();
txtAddress.Text=ds.Tables.Rows.ToString();
txtemail.Text=ds.Tables.Rows.ToString();
```

Code Explanation

- The above code defines the basic designing of a front end view of applications as well as calling of the functions of other layers so that they can be integrated with each other.

Business Access Layer

This is the function of the business layer which accepts the data from the application layer and passes it to the data layer.

- Business logic acts as an interface between Client layer and Data Access Layer.

- All business logic – like validation of data, calculations, data insertion/modification are written under business logic layer.

- It makes communication faster and easier between the client and data layer.

- Defines a proper workflow activity that is necessary to complete a task.

```
// this is the function of the business layer which accepts the data from the
//application layer and passes it to the data layer.
public class clsStudentInfo
{
    public DataSet GetAllStudentBsIDWise(clsStudent obj)
    {
      DataSet ds=new DataSet();
      ds=objdt.getdata_dtIDWise(obj);// Calling of Data layer function
      return ds;
    }
}
```

Explanation of Code

The code is using the function of business layer, which will accept the data for the application layer and passed it to the data layer. The Business layer codes act as a mediator between the functions defined in the presentation layer and data layer and calling the functions vice -versa.

Data Access Layer

This is the data layer function, which receives the data from the business layer and performs the necessary operation into the database.

```
// this is the datalayer function which is receiving the data from the business
//layer and performing the required operation into the database
public class clsStudentData // Data layer class
{
    // object of property layer class
    public DataSet getdata_dtIDUise(clsStudent obj)
    {
      DataSet ds;
      string sql;
      sql="select * from student where StudentId=" +obj.id+ "order by Stu-
dentId;
```

```
     ds=new DataSet();

     //this is the datalayer function which accepts the sql query and performs
the

     //corresponding operation

          ds=objdt.ExecuteSql(sql);

          return ds;

     }

}
```

Explanation of Code

The code defines in dataset layer above accepts the entire request: requested by the system and performing the required operations into the database.

2-Tier Architecture

It is like Client-Server architecture, where communication takes place between client and server.

In this type of software architecture, the presentation layer or user interface layer runs on the client side while dataset layer gets executed and stored on server side.

There is no Business logic layer or immediate layer in between client and server.

Single Tier or 1-Tier Architecture

It is the simplest one as it is equivalent to running the application on the personal computer. All of the required components for an application to run are on a single application or server.

Presentation layer, Business logic layer, and data layer are all located on a single machine.

Advantages and Disadvantages of Multi-Tier Architectures

Advantages	Disadvantages
• Scalability	• Increase in Effort
• Data Integrity	• Increase in Complexity
• Reusability	
• Reduced Distribution	
• Improved Security	
• Improved Availability	

Hence, it is a part of a program which encrypts real-world business problems and determines how data can be updated, created, stored, or changed to get the complete task done.

N-Tier Architecture Tips and Development

Considering the software professionals must have a full control on all the layers of the architecture, tips on n-tier architecture are given as below:

- Try to decouple layers from another layer as much as possible by using a technique like soap XML.

- Use some automated tools to generate a mapping between a business logic layer and a relational database layer (data layer). Tools that can help in modeling these mapping techniques are – Entity Framework and Hibernate for .Net etc.

- In client presenter layer, put a common code for all the clients in a separate library as much as possible. This will maximize the code reusability for all types of clients.

- A cache layer can be added into an existing layer to speed up the performance.

Domain Driven Design

Domain-driven design (DDD) is an approach to software development for complex needs by connecting the implementation to an evolving model.

Domain-driven design is predicated on the following goals:

- Placing the project's primary focus on the core domain and domain logic;

- Basing complex designs on a model of the domain;

- Initiating a creative collaboration between technical and domain experts to iteratively refine a conceptual model that addresses particular domain problems.

Concepts of the model include:

- Context: The setting in which a word or statement appears that determines its meaning;

- Domain: A sphere of knowledge (ontology), influence, or activity. The subject area to which the user applies a program is the domain of the software;

- Model: A system of abstractions that describes selected aspects of a domain and can be used to solve problems related to that domain;

- Ubiquitous Language: A language structured around the domain model and used by all team members to connect all the activities of the team with the software.

Strategic Domain-Driven Design

Ideally, it would be preferable to have a single, unified model. While this is a noble goal, in reality it typically fragments into multiple models. It is useful to recognize this fact of life and work with it.

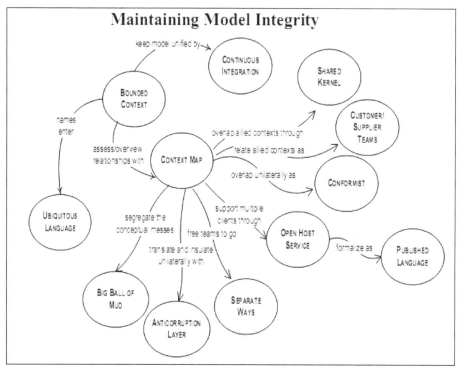

Semantic network of patterns in strategic domain-driven design.

Strategic Design is a set of principles for maintaining model integrity, distilling the Domain Model, and working with multiple models.

Bounded Context

Multiple models are in play on any large project. Yet when code based on distinct models is combined, software becomes buggy, unreliable, and difficult to understand. Communication among team members becomes confusing. It is often unclear in what context a model should not be applied.

Therefore: Explicitly define the context within which a model applies. Explicitly set boundaries in terms of team organization, usage within specific parts of the application, and physical manifestations such as code bases and database schemas. Keep the model strictly consistent within these bounds, but don't be distracted or confused by issues outside.

Continuous Integration

When a number of people are working in the same bounded context, there is a strong tendency for the model to fragment. The bigger the team, the bigger the problem, but as few as three or four people can encounter serious problems. Yet breaking down the system into ever-smaller contexts eventually loses a valuable level of integration and coherency.

Therefore: Institute a process of merging all code and other implementation artifacts frequently, with automated tests to flag fragmentation quickly. Relentlessly exercise the ubiquitous language to hammer out a shared view of the model as the concepts evolve in different people's heads.

Context Map

An individual bounded context leaves some problems in the absence of a global view. The context of other models may still be vague and in flux.

People on other teams won't be very aware of the context bounds and will unknowingly make changes that blur the edges or complicate the interconnections. When connections must be made between different contexts, they tend to bleed into each other.

Therefore: Identify each model in play on the project and define its bounded context. This includes the implicit models of non-object-oriented subsystems. Name each bounded context, and make the names part of the ubiquitous language. Describe the points of contact between the models, outlining explicit translation for any communication and highlighting any sharing. Map the existing terrain.

Building Blocks

- Entity: An object that is not defined by its attributes, but rather by a thread of continuity and its identity.

  Example: Most airlines distinguish each seat uniquely on every flight. Each seat is an entity in this context. However, Southwest Airlines, EasyJet and Ryanair do not distinguish between every seat; all seats are the same. In this context, a seat is actually a value object.

- Value object: An object that contains attributes but has no conceptual identity. They should be treated as immutable.

  Example: When people exchange business cards, they generally do not distinguish between each unique card; they are only concerned about the information printed on the card. In this context, business cards are value objects.

- Aggregate: A collection of objects that are bound together by a root entity, otherwise known as an aggregate root. The aggregate root guarantees the consistency of changes being made within the aggregate by forbidding external objects from holding references to its members.

  Example: When you drive a car, you do not have to worry about moving the wheels forward, making the engine combust with spark and fuel, etc.; you are simply driving the car. In this context, the car is an aggregate of several other objects and serves as the aggregate root to all of the other systems.

- Domain Event: A domain object that defines an event (something that happens). A domain event is an event that domain experts care about.

- Service: When an operation does not conceptually belong to any object. Following the natural contours of the problem, you can implement these operations in services.

- Repository: Methods for retrieving domain objects should delegate to a specialized Repository object such that alternative storage implementations may be easily interchanged.

- Factory: Methods for creating domain objects should delegate to a specialized Factory object such that alternative implementations may be easily interchanged.

Disadvantages

In order to help maintain the model as a pure and helpful language construct, the team must typically implement a great deal of isolation and encapsulation within the domain model. Consequently, a system based on domain-driven design can come at a relatively high cost. While domain-driven design provides many technical benefits, such as maintainability, Microsoft recommends that it be applied only to complex domains where the model and the linguistic processes provide clear benefits in the communication of complex information, and in the formulation of a common understanding of the domain.

Relationship to other Ideas

- Object-oriented analysis and design:

  Although, in theory, the general idea of DDD need not be restricted to object-oriented approaches, in practice DDD seeks to exploit the advantages that object-oriented techniques make possible. These include entities/aggregate roots as receivers of commands/method invocations and the encapsulation of state within foremost aggregate roots and on a higher architectural level, bounded contexts.

- Model-driven engineering (MDE) and Model-driven architecture (MDA):

  While DDD is compatible with MDA/MDE (where MDE can be regarded as a superset of MDA) the intent of the two concepts is somewhat different. MDA is concerned more with the means of translating a model into code for different technology platforms than with the practice of defining better domain models. The techniques provided by MDE (to model domains, to create DSLs to facilitate the communication between domain experts and developers) facilitate the application of DDD in practice and help DDD practitioners to get more out of their models. Thanks to the model transformation and code generation techniques of MDE, the domain model can be used not only to represent the domain but also to generate the actual software system that will be used to manage it. This picture shows a possible representation of DDD and MDE combined.

- Plain Old Java Objects (POJOs) and Plain Old CLR Objects (POCOs):

  POJOs and POCOs are technical implementation concepts, specific to Java and the .NET framework respectively. However, the emergence of the terms POJO and POCO reflect a growing view that, within the context of either of those technical platforms, domain objects should be defined purely to implement the business behaviour of the corresponding domain concept, rather than be defined by the requirements of a more specific technology framework.

- The naked objects pattern:

  Based on the premise that if you have a good enough domain model, the user interface can simply be a reflection of this domain model; and that if you require the user interface to be a direct reflection of the domain model then this will force the design of a better domain model.

- Domain-specific modeling (DSM):

DSM is DDD applied through the use of Domain-specific languages.

- Domain-specific language (DSL):

DDD does not specifically require the use of a DSL, though it could be used to help define a DSL and support methods like domain-specific multimodeling.

- Aspect-oriented programming (AOP):

AOP makes it easy to factor out technical concerns (such as security, transaction management, logging) from a domain model, and as such makes it easier to design and implement domain models that focus purely on the business logic.

- Command Query Responsibility Segregation (CQRS):

CQRS is an architectural pattern for separation of reads from writes, where the former is a Query and the latter is a Command. Commands mutate state and are hence approximately equivalent to method invocation on aggregate roots/entities. Queries query state but do not mutate it. CQRS is a derivative architectural pattern from the design pattern called Command and Query Separation (CQS) which was coined by Bertrand Meyer. While CQRS does not require DDD, domain-driven design makes the distinction between commands and queries, explicit, around the concept of an aggregate root. The idea is that a given aggregate root has a method that corresponds to a command and a command handler invokes the method on the aggregate root. The aggregate root is responsible for performing the logic of the operation and yielding either a number of events or a failure (exception or execution result enumeration/number) response OR (if Event Sourcing (ES) is not used) just mutating its state for a persister implementation such as an ORM to write to a data store, while the command handler is responsible for pulling in infrastructure concerns related to the saving of the aggregate root's state or events and creating the needed contexts (e.g. transactions).

- Event Sourcing (ES):

An architectural pattern which warrants that your entities (as per Eric Evans' definition) do not track their internal state by means of direct serialization or O/R mapping, but by means of reading and committing events to an event store. Where ES is combined with CQRS and DDD, aggregate roots are responsible for thoroughly validating and applying commands (often by means having their instance methods invoked from a Command Handler), and then publishing a single or a set of events which is also the foundation upon which the aggregate roots base their logic for dealing with method invocations. Hence, the input is a command and the output is one or many events which are transactionally (single commit) saved to an event store, and then often published on a message broker for the benefit of those interested (often the views are interested; they are then queried using Query-messages). When modeling your aggregate roots to output events, you can isolate the internal state even further than would be possible when projecting read-data from your entities, as is done in standard n-tier data-passing architectures. One significant benefit from this is that tooling such as axiomatic theorem provers (e.g. Microsoft Contracts or CHESS) are easier to apply, as the aggregate root comprehensively hides its internal state. Events are often persisted based on the version of the aggregate root instance, which yields a domain model that synchronizes in distributed systems around the concept of optimistic concurrency.

Tools

- Actifsource is a plug-in for Eclipse which enables software development combining DDD with model-driven engineering and code generation.

- ECO (Domain Driven Design): Framework with database, class, code and state machine generation from UML diagrams by CapableObjects.

- OpenMDX: Open source, Java based, MDA Framework supporting Java SE, Java EE, and .NET. OpenMDX differs from typical MDA frameworks in that "use models to directly drive the runtime behavior of operational systems".

- OpenXava: Generates an AJAX application from JPA entities. You only need to write the domain classes to obtain a ready to use application.

- Restful Objects is a standard for a Restful API onto a domain object model (where the domain objects may represent entities, view models, or services). Two open source frameworks (one for Java, one for .NET) can create a Restful Objects API from a domain model automatically, using reflection.

- CubicWeb is an open source semantic web framework entirely driven by a data model. High-level directives allow to refine the data model iteratively, release after release. Defining the data model is enough to get a functioning web application. Further work is required to define how the data is displayed when the default views are not sufficient.

- Context Mapper provides a Domain-specific language (DSL) to create Context Maps based on strategic Domain-driven Design (DDD). The tool supports context refactoring and PlantUML generation.

- Cell-based Architecture is a Reference Architecture based on decentralization which focused on architecture blocks (Cells). DDD can use to define cells and create cell boundaries. Cell-based architecture takes DDD into practice.

Microkernel

In computer science, a microkernel (often abbreviated as μ-kernel) is the near-minimum amount of software that can provide the mechanisms needed to implement an operating system (OS). These mechanisms include low-level address space management, thread management, and inter-process communication (IPC).

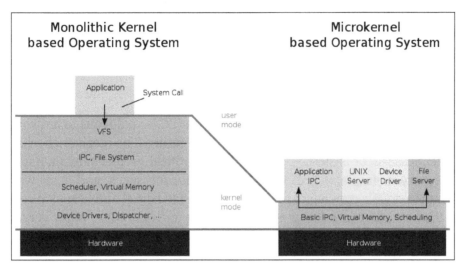

Structure of monolithic and microkernel-based operating systems, respectively

If the hardware provides multiple rings or CPU modes, the microkernel may be the only software executing at the most privileged level, which is generally referred to as supervisor or kernel mode. Traditional operating system functions, such as device drivers, protocol stacks and file systems, are typically removed from the microkernel itself and are instead run in user space.

In terms of the source code size, microkernels are often smaller than monolithic kernels. The MINIX 3 microkernel, for example, has approximately 12,000 lines of code.

Early operating system kernels were rather small, partly because computer memory was limited. As the capability of computers grew, the number of devices the kernel had to control also grew. Throughout the early history of Unix, kernels were generally small, even though they contained various device drivers and file system implementations. When address spaces increased from 16 to 32 bits, kernel design was no longer constrained by the hardware architecture, and kernels began to grow larger.

The Berkeley Software Distribution (BSD) of Unix began the era of larger kernels. In addition to operating a basic system consisting of the CPU, disks and printers, BSD added a complete TCP/IP networking system and a number of "virtual" devices that allowed the existing programs to work 'invisibly' over the network. This growth continued for many years, resulting in kernels with millions of lines of source code. As a result of this growth, kernels were prone to bugs and became increasingly difficult to maintain.

The microkernel was intended to address this growth of kernels and the difficulties that resulted. In theory, the microkernel design allows for easier management of code due to its division into user space services. This also allows for increased security and stability resulting from the reduced amount of code running in kernel mode. For example, if a networking service crashed due to buffer overflow, only the networking service's memory would be corrupted, leaving the rest of the system still functional.

Inter-process Communication

Inter-process communication (IPC) is any mechanism which allows separate processes to communicate with each other, usually by sending messages. Shared memory is strictly speaking also an inter-process communication mechanism, but the abbreviation IPC usually only refers to message passing, and it is the latter that is particularly relevant to microkernels. IPC allows the operating system to be built from a number of small programs called servers, which are used by other programs on the system, invoked via IPC. Most or all support for peripheral hardware is handled in this fashion, with servers for device drivers, network protocol stacks, file systems, graphics, etc.

IPC can be synchronous or asynchronous. Asynchronous IPC is analogous to network communication: the sender dispatches a message and continues executing. The receiver checks (polls) for the availability of the message, or is alerted to it via some notification mechanism. Asynchronous IPC requires that the kernel maintains buffers and queues for messages, and deals with buffer overflows; it also requires double copying of messages (sender to kernel and kernel to receiver). In synchronous IPC, the first party (sender or receiver) blocks until the other party is ready to perform the IPC. It does not require buffering or multiple copies, but the implicit rendezvous can make programming tricky. Most programmers prefer asynchronous send and synchronous receive.

First-generation microkernels typically supported synchronous as well as asynchronous IPC, and suffered from poor IPC performance. Jochen Liedtke assumed the design and implementation of the IPC mechanisms to be the underlying reason for this poor performance. In his L4 microkernel he pioneered methods that lowered IPC costs by an order of magnitude. These include an IPC system call that supports a send as well as a receive operation, making all IPC synchronous, and passing as much data as possible in registers. Furthermore, Liedtke introduced the concept of the *direct process switch*, where during an IPC execution an (incomplete) context switch is performed from the sender directly to the receiver. If, as in L4, part or all of the message is passed in registers, this transfers the in-register part of the message without any copying at all. Furthermore, the overhead of invoking the scheduler is avoided; this is especially beneficial in the common case where IPC is used in an RPC-type fashion by a client invoking a server. Another optimization, called *lazy scheduling*, avoids traversing scheduling queues during IPC by leaving threads that block during IPC in the ready queue. Once the scheduler is invoked, it moves such threads to the appropriate waiting queue. As in many cases a thread gets unblocked before the next scheduler invocation, this approach saves significant work. Similar approaches have since been adopted by QNX and MINIX 3.

In a series of experiments, Chen and Bershad compared memory cycles per instruction (MCPI) of monolithic Ultrix with those of microkernel Mach combined with a 4.3BSD Unix server running in user space. Their results explained Mach's poorer performance by higher MCPI and demonstrated that IPC alone is not responsible for much of the system overhead, suggesting that optimizations focused exclusively on IPC will have limited impact. Liedtke later refined Chen and Bershad's results by making an observation that the bulk of the difference between Ultrix and Mach MCPI was caused by capacity cache-misses and concluding that drastically reducing the cache working set of a microkernel will solve the problem.

In a client-server system, most communication is essentially synchronous, even if using asynchronous primitives, as the typical operation is a client invoking a server and then waiting for a reply. As it also lends itself to more efficient implementation, most microkernels generally followed L4's lead and only provided a synchronous IPC primitive. Asynchronous IPC could be implemented on top by using helper threads. However, experience has shown that the utility of synchronous IPC is dubious: synchronous IPC forces a multi-threaded design onto otherwise simple systems, with the resulting synchronization complexities. Moreover, an RPC-like server invocation sequentializes client and server, which should be avoided if they are running on separate cores. Versions of L4 deployed in commercial products have therefore found it necessary to add an asynchronous notification mechanism to better support asynchronous communication. This signal-like mechanism does not carry data and therefore does not require buffering by the kernel. By having two forms of IPC, they have nonetheless violated the principle of minimality. Other versions of L4 have switched to asynchronous IPC completely.

As synchronous IPC blocks the first party until the other is ready, unrestricted use could easily lead to deadlocks. Furthermore, a client could easily mount a denial-of-service attack on a server by sending a request and never attempting to receive the reply. Therefore, synchronous IPC must provide a means to prevent indefinite blocking. Many microkernels provide timeouts on IPC calls, which limit the blocking time. In practice, choosing sensible timeout values is difficult, and systems almost inevitably use infinite timeouts for clients and zero timeouts for servers. As a consequence, the trend is towards not providing arbitrary timeouts, but only a flag which indicates that the IPC should fail immediately if the partner is not ready. This approach effectively provides a choice of the two timeout values of zero and infinity. Recent versions of L4 and MINIX have gone down this path (older versions of L4 used timeouts). QNX avoids the problem by requiring the client to specify the reply buffer as part of the message send call. When the server replies the kernel copies the data to the client's buffer, without having to wait for the client to receive the response explicitly.

Servers

Microkernel servers are essentially daemon programs like any others, except that the kernel grants some of them privileges to interact with parts of physical memory that are otherwise off limits to most programs. This allows some servers, particularly device drivers, to interact directly with hardware.

A basic set of servers for a general-purpose microkernel includes file system servers, device driver servers, networking servers, display servers, and user interface device servers. This set of servers (drawn from QNX) provides roughly the set of services offered by a Unix monolithic kernel. The necessary servers are started at system startup and provide services, such as file, network, and device access, to ordinary application programs. With such servers running in the environment of a user application, server development is similar to ordinary application development, rather than the build-and-boot process needed for kernel development.

Additionally, many "crashes" can be corrected by simply stopping and restarting the server. However, part of the system state is lost with the failing server, hence this approach requires applications to cope with failure. A good example is a server responsible for TCP/IP connections: If this server is restarted, applications will experience a "lost" connection, a normal occurrence in a networked system. For other services, failure is less expected and may require changes to application code. For QNX, restart capability is offered as the QNX High Availability Toolkit.

Device Drivers

Device drivers frequently perform direct memory access (DMA), and therefore can write to arbitrary locations of physical memory, including various kernel data structures. Such drivers must therefore be trusted. It is a common misconception that this means that they must be part of the kernel. In fact, a driver is not inherently more or less trustworthy by being part of the kernel.

While running a device driver in user space does not necessarily reduce the damage a misbehaving driver can cause, in practice it is beneficial for system stability in the presence of buggy (rather than malicious) drivers: memory-access violations by the driver code itself (as opposed to the device) may still be caught by the memory-management hardware. Furthermore, many devices are not DMA-capable, their drivers can be made untrusted by running them in user space. Recently, an increasing number of computers feature IOMMUs, many of which can be used to restrict a device's access to physical memory. This also allows user-mode drivers to become untrusted.

User-mode drivers actually predate microkernels. The Michigan Terminal System (MTS), in 1967, supported user space drivers (including its file system support), the first operating system to be designed with that capability. Historically, drivers were less of a problem, as the number of devices was small and trusted anyway, so having them in the kernel simplified the design and avoided potential performance problems. This led to the traditional driver-in-the-kernel style of Unix, Linux, and Windows NT. With the proliferation of various kinds of peripherals, the amount of driver code escalated and in modern operating systems dominates the kernel in code size.

Essential Components and Minimality

As a microkernel must allow building arbitrary operating system services on top, it must provide some core functionality. At a minimum, this includes:

- Some mechanisms for dealing with address spaces, required for managing memory protection.

- Some execution abstraction to manage CPU allocation, typically threads or scheduler activations.

- Inter-process communication, required to invoke servers running in their own address spaces.

This minimal design was pioneered by Brinch Hansen's Nucleus and the hypervisor of IBM's VM. It has since been formalised in Liedtke's minimality principle:

A concept is tolerated inside the microkernel only if moving it outside the kernel, i.e., permitting competing implementations, would prevent the implementation of the system's required functionality.

Everything else can be done in a usermode program, although device drivers implemented as user programs may on some processor architectures require special privileges to access I/O hardware.

Related to the minimality principle, and equally important for microkernel design, is the separation of mechanism and policy, it is what enables the construction of arbitrary systems on top of a minimal kernel. Any policy built into the kernel cannot be overwritten at user level and therefore limits the generality of the microkernel. Policy implemented in user-level servers can be changed by replacing the servers (or letting the application choose between competing servers offering similar services).

For efficiency, most microkernels contain schedulers and manage timers, in violation of the minimality principle and the principle of policy-mechanism separation.

Start up (booting) of a microkernel-based system requires device drivers, which are not part of the kernel. Typically this means that they are packaged with the kernel in the boot image, and the kernel supports a bootstrap protocol that defines how the drivers are located and started; this is the traditional bootstrap procedure of L4 microkernels. Some microkernels simplify this by placing some key drivers inside the kernel (in violation of the minimality principle), LynxOS and the original Minix are examples. Some even include a file system in the kernel to simplify booting. A microkernel-based system may boot via multiboot compatible boot loader. Such systems usually load statically-linked servers to make an initial bootstrap or mount an OS image to continue bootstrapping.

A key component of a microkernel is a good IPC system and virtual-memory-manager design that allows implementing page-fault handling and swapping in usermode servers in a safe way. Since all services are performed by usermode programs, efficient means of communication between programs are essential, far more so than in monolithic kernels. The design of the IPC system makes or breaks a microkernel. To be effective, the IPC system must not only have low overhead, but also interact well with CPU scheduling.

Performance

On most mainstream processors, obtaining a service is inherently more expensive in a microkernel-based system than a monolithic system. In the monolithic system, the service is obtained by a single system call, which requires two mode switches (changes of the processor's ring or CPU mode). In the microkernel-based system, the service is obtained by sending an IPC message to a server, and obtaining the result in another IPC message from the server. This requires a context switch if the drivers are implemented as processes, or a function call if they are implemented as procedures. In addition, passing actual data to the server and back may incur extra copying overhead, while in a monolithic system the kernel can directly access the data in the client's buffers.

Performance is therefore a potential issue in microkernel systems. Indeed, the experience of first-generation microkernels such as Mach and ChorusOS showed that systems based on them performed very poorly. However, Jochen Liedtke showed that Mach's performance problems were the result of poor design and implementation, specifically Mach's excessive cache footprint. Liedtke demonstrated with his own L4 microkernel that through careful design and implementation, and especially by following the minimality principle, IPC costs could be reduced by more than an order of magnitude compared to Mach. L4's IPC performance is still unbeaten across a range of architectures.

While these results demonstrate that the poor performance of systems based on first-generation microkernels is not representative for second-generation kernels such as L4, this constitutes no proof that microkernel-based systems can be built with good performance. It has been shown that a monolithic Linux server ported to L4 exhibits only a few percent overhead over native Linux. However, such a single-server system exhibits few, if any, of the advantages microkernels are supposed to provide by structuring operating system functionality into separate servers.

A number of commercial multi-server systems exist, in particular the real-time systems QNX and Integrity. No comprehensive comparison of performance relative to monolithic systems has been published for those multiserver systems. Furthermore, performance does not seem to be the overriding concern for those commercial systems, which instead emphasize reliably quick interrupt handling response times (QNX) and simplicity for the sake of robustness. An attempt to build a high-performance multiserver operating system was the IBM Sawmill Linux project. However, this project was never completed.

It has been shown in the meantime that user-level device drivers can come close to the performance of in-kernel drivers even for such high-throughput, high-interrupt devices as Gigabit Ethernet. This seems to imply that high-performance multi-server systems are possible.

Security

The security benefits of microkernels have been frequently discussed. In the context of security the minimality principle of microkernels is, some have argued, a direct consequence of the principle of least privilege, according to which all code should have only the privileges needed to provide required functionality. Minimality requires that a system's trusted computing base (TCB) should be kept minimal. As the kernel (the code that executes in the privileged mode of the hardware) has unvetted access to any data and can thus violate its integrity or confidentiality, the kernel is always part of the TCB. Minimizing it is natural in a security-driven design.

Consequently, microkernel designs have been used for systems designed for high-security applications, including KeyKOS, EROS and military systems. In fact common criteria (CC) at the highest assurance level (Evaluation Assurance Level (EAL) 7) has an explicit requirement that the target of evaluation be "simple", an acknowledgment of the practical impossibility of establishing true trustworthiness for a complex system. Unfortunately, again, the term "simple" is misleading and ill-defined. At least the Department of Defense Trusted Computer System Evaluation Criteria introduced somewhat more precise verbiage at the B3/A1 classes:

The TCB shall [implement] complete, conceptually simple protection mechanisms with precisely defined semantics. Significant system engineering shall be directed toward minimizing the complexity of the TCB, as well as excluding from the TCB those modules that are not protection-critical.

Third Generation

More recent work on microkernels has been focusing on formal specifications of the kernel API, and formal proofs of the API's security properties and implementation correctness. The first example of this is a mathematical proof of the confinement mechanisms in EROS, based on a simplified model of the EROS API. More recently (in 2007) a comprehensive set of machine-checked proofs was performed of the properties of the protection model of seL4, a version of L4.

This has led to what is referred to as third-generation microkernels, characterised by a security-oriented API with resource access controlled by capabilities, virtualization as a first-class concern, novel approaches to kernel resource management, and a design goal of suitability for formal analysis, besides the usual goal of high performance. Examples are Coyotos, seL4, Nova, Redox and Fiasco.OC.

In the case of seL4, complete formal verification of the implementation has been achieved, i.e. a mathematical proof that the kernel's implementation is consistent with its formal specification.

This provides a guarantee that the properties proved about the API actually hold for the real kernel, a degree of assurance which goes beyond even CC EAL7. It was followed by proofs of security-enforcement properties of the API, and a proof demonstrating that the executable binary code is a correct translation of the C implementation, taking the compiler out of the TCB. Taken together, these proofs establish an end-to-end proof of security properties of the kernel.

Nanokernel

The term nanokernel or picokernel historically referred to:

- A kernel where the total amount of kernel code, i.e. code executing in the privileged mode of the hardware, is very small. The term picokernel was sometimes used to further emphasize small size. The term nanokernel was coined by Jonathan S. Shapiro in the paper The KeyKOS NanoKernel Architecture. It was a sardonic response to Mach, which claimed to be a microkernel while Shapiro considered it monolithic, essentially unstructured, and slower than the systems it sought to replace. Subsequent reuse of and response to the term, including the picokernel coinage, suggest that the point was largely missed. Both nanokernel and picokernel have subsequently come to have the same meaning expressed by the term microkernel.

- A virtualization layer underneath an operating system, which is more correctly referred to as a hypervisor.

- A hardware abstraction layer that forms the lowest-level part of a kernel, sometimes used to provide real-time functionality to normal operating systems, like Adeos.

There is also at least one case where the term nanokernel is used to refer not to a small kernel, but one that supports a nanosecond clock resolution.

Blackboard

The blackboard pattern is a behavioral design pattern that provides a computational framework for the design and implementation of systems that integrate large and diverse specialized modules, and implement complex, non-deterministic control strategies.

This pattern was identified by the members of the HEARSAY-II project and first applied to speech recognition.

Structure

The blackboard model defines three main components:

- Blackboard - a structured global memory containing objects from the solution space.

- Knowledge sources - specialized modules with their own representation.

- Control component - selects, configures and executes modules.

Implementation

The first step is to design the solution space (i.e. potential solutions) that leads to the blackboard structure. Then, knowledge sources are identified. These two activities are closely related.

The next step is to specify the control component; it generally takes the form of a complex scheduler that makes use of a set of domain-specific heuristics to rate the relevance of executable knowledge sources.

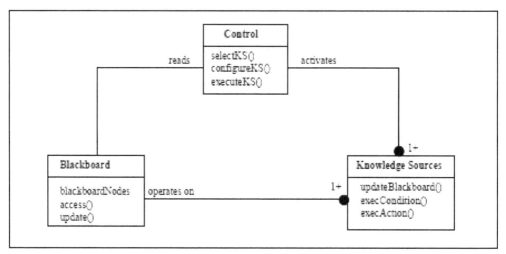

System Structure

Applications

Usage-domains include:

- Speech recognition,
- Vehicle identification and tracking,
- Protein structure identification,
- Sonar signals interpretation.

Consequences

The blackboard pattern provides effective solutions for designing and implementing complex systems where heterogeneous modules have to be dynamically combined to solve a problem. This provides non-functional properties such as:

- Reusability
- Changeability
- Robustness

The blackboard pattern allows multiple processes to work closer together on separate threads, polling and reacting when necessary.

Model-View-Controller

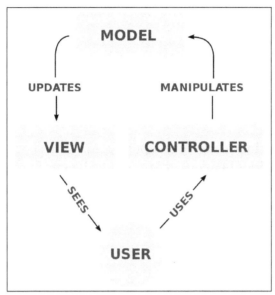

Diagram of interactions within the MVC pattern.

Model–View–Controller (usually known as MVC) is a software design pattern commonly used for developing user interfaces which divides the related program logic into three interconnected elements. This is done to separate internal representations of information from the ways information is presented to and accepted from the user. Following the MVC architectural pattern decouples these major components allowing for code reuse and parallel development.

Traditionally used for desktop graphical user interfaces (GUIs), this pattern has become popular for designing web applications. Popular programming languages like JavaScript, Python, Ruby, PHP, Java, and C# have MVC frameworks that are used in web application development straight out of the box.

Components

- Model: The central component of the pattern. It is the application's dynamic data structure, independent of the user interface. It directly manages the data, logic and rules of the application.

- View: Any representation of information such as a chart, diagram or table. Multiple views of the same information are possible, such as a bar chart for management and a tabular view for accountants.

- Controller: Accepts input and converts it to commands for the model or view.

In addition to dividing the application into these components, the model–view–controller design defines the interactions between them.

- The model is responsible for managing the data of the application. It receives user input from the controller.

- The view means presentation of the model in a particular format.

- The controller responds to the user input and performs interactions on the data model objects. The controller receives the input, optionally validates it and then passes the input to the model.

As with other software patterns, MVC expresses the "core of the solution" to a problem while allowing it to be adapted for each system. Particular MVC designs can vary significantly.

Use in Web Applications

Although originally developed for desktop computing, MVC has been widely adopted as a design for World Wide Web applications in major programming languages. Several web frameworks have been created that enforce the pattern. These software frameworks vary in their interpretations, mainly in the way that the MVC responsibilities are divided between the client and server.

Some web MVC frameworks take a thin client approach that places almost the entire model, view and controller logic on the server. This is reflected in frameworks such as Django, Rails and ASP. NET MVC. In this approach, the client sends either hyperlink requests or form submissions to the controller and then receives a complete and updated web page (or other document) from the view; the model exists entirely on the server. Other frameworks such as AngularJS, EmberJS, JavaScriptMVC and Backbone allow the MVC components to execute partly on the client.

Goals of MVC

Simultaneous Development

Because MVC decouples the various components of an application, developers are able to work in parallel on different components without affecting or blocking one another. For example, a team might divide their developers between the front-end and the back-end. The back-end developers can design the structure of the data and how the user interacts with it without requiring the user interface to be completed. Conversely, the front-end developers are able to design and test the layout of the application prior to the data structure being available.

Code Reuse

The same (or similar) view for one application can be refactored for another application with different data because the view is simply handling how the data is being displayed to the user. Unfortunately this does not work when that code is also useful for handling user input. For example, DOM code (including the application's custom abstractions to it) is useful for both graphics display and user input. (Despite the name Document Object Model, the DOM is actually not an MVC model, because it is the application's interface to the user).

To address these problems, MVC (and patterns like it) are often combined with a component architecture that provides a set of UI elements. Each UI element is a single higher-level component that combines the 3 required MVC components into a single package. By creating these higher-level components that are independent of each other, developers are able to reuse components quickly and easily in other applications.

Advantages and Disadvantages

Advantages

- Simultaneous development – Multiple developers can work simultaneously on the model, controller and views.

- High cohesion – MVC enables logical grouping of related actions on a controller together. The views for a specific model are also grouped together.

- Loose coupling – The very nature of the MVC framework is such that there is low coupling among models, views or controllers.

- Ease of modification – Because of the separation of responsibilities, future development or modification is easier.

- Multiple views for a model – Models can have multiple views.

Disadvantages

The disadvantages of MVC can be generally categorized as overhead for incorrectly factored software:

- Code navigability – The framework navigation can be complex because it introduces new layers of abstraction and requires users to adapt to the decomposition criteria of MVC.

- Multi-artifact consistency – Decomposing a feature into three artifacts causes scattering. Thus, requiring developers to maintain the consistency of multiple representations at once.

- Undermined by inevitable clustering – Applications tend to have heavy interaction between what the user sees and what the user uses. Therefore each feature's computation and state tends to get clustered into one of the 3 program parts, erasing the purported advantages of MVC.

- Excessive boilerplate – Due to the application computation and state being typically clustered into one of the 3 parts, the other parts degenerate into either boilerplate shims or code-behind that exists only to satisfy the MVC pattern.

- Pronounced learning curve – Knowledge on multiple technologies becomes the norm. Developers using MVC need to be skilled in multiple technologies.

- Lack of incremental benefit – UI applications are already factored into components, and achieving code reuse and independence via the component architecture, leaving no incremental benefit to MVC.

Model-View-Adapter

Model–view–adapter (MVA) or mediating-controller MVC is a software architectural pattern and multitier architecture. In complex computer applications that present large amounts of data to users, developers often wish to separate data (model) and user interface (view) concerns so that changes to the user interface will not affect data handling and that the data can be reorganized without changing the user interface. MVA and traditional MVC both attempt to solve this same problem, but with two different styles of solution. Traditional MVC arranges model (e.g., data structures and storage), view (e.g., user interface), and controller (e.g., business logic) in a triangle, with model, view, and controller as vertices, so that some information flows between the model and views outside of the controller's direct control. The model–view–adapter solves this rather differently from the model–view–controller by arranging model, adapter or mediating controller and view linearly without any connections whatsoever directly between model and view.

View and Model do not Communicate Directly

The view is completely decoupled from the model such that view and the model can interact only via the mediating controller or adapter between the view and the model. Via this arrangement, only the adapter or mediating controller has knowledge of both the model and the view, because it is the responsibility of solely the adapter or mediating controller to adapt or mediate between the model and the view—hence the names adapter and mediator. The model and view are kept intentionally oblivious of each other. In traditional MVC, the model and view are made aware of each other, which might permit disadvantageous coupling of view (e.g., user interface) concerns into the model (e.g., database) and vice versa, when the architecture might have been better served by the schema of the database and the presentation of information in the user-interface being divorced entirely from each other and allowed to diverge from each other radically. For example, in a text editor, the model might best be a piece table (instead of, say, a gap buffer or a linked list of lines). But, the user interface should present the final resting state of the edits on the file, not some direct information-overload presentation of the piece-table's meticulous raw undo-redo deltas and incremental operations on that file since the current editing session began.

Model is Intentionally Oblivious of Views

This separation of concerns permits a wide variety of different views to indirectly access the same model either via exactly the same adapter or via the same class of adapters. For example, one underlying data-storage model and schema and technology could be accessed via different views—e.g., Qt GUI, Microsoft MFC GUI, GTK+ GUI, Microsoft .NET GUI, Java Swing GUI, Silverlight website, and AJAX website—where (unlike traditional MVC) the model is kept completely oblivious of what information flows toward these user interfaces. The adapter or class of adapters keeps the model completely oblivious that it is supporting multiple of the user interfaces and perhaps even supporting this variety concurrently. To the model, these multiple types of user interface would look like multiple instances of a generic user oblivious of type of technology.

View is Intentionally Oblivious of Models

Likewise, any one user interface can be kept intentionally oblivious of a wide variety of different models that may underlie the mediating controller or adapter. For example, the same website can be kept oblivious of the fact that it can be served (A) by an SQL database server such as PostgreSQL, Sybase SQL Server, or Microsoft SQL Server that has business logic built into the database server via stored procedures and that has transactions that the server may roll back or (B) by an SQL database server such as MySQL that lacks one or more of these capabilities, or (C) by a nonSQL RDF database, because the website interacts only with the mediating controller or adapter and never directly with the model.

Multiple Adapters between the Same Model-View Pair

Additionally, multiple adapters may be created to change the way one view presents data for a given model. For example, different governments (either among different states of the United States or different nation-states internationally) may impose different codes of law, that in turn impose different business logic for the same underlying database and for the same outwardly presented website. In this scenario, a class of various adapters or mediating controllers can represent the variations in business logic among these jurisdictions in between the same database model and the same website view.

Model-View-Presenter

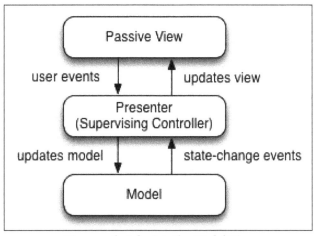

Diagram that depicts the Model View
Presenter (MVP) GUI design pattern.

Model–view–presenter (MVP) is a derivation of the model–view–controller (MVC) architectural pattern, and is used mostly for building user interfaces.

In MVP, the *presenter* assumes the functionality of the "middle-man". In MVP, all presentation logic is pushed to the presenter.

MVP is a user interface architectural pattern engineered to facilitate automated unit testing and improve the separation of concerns in presentation logic:

- The model is an interface defining the data to be displayed or otherwise acted upon in the user interface.

- The view is a passive interface that displays data (the model) and routes user commands (events) to the presenter to act upon that data.

- The presenter acts upon the model and the view. It retrieves data from repositories (the model), and formats it for display in the view.

Normally, the view implementation instantiates the concrete presenter object, providing a reference to itself. The following C# code demonstrates a simple view constructor, where ConcreteDomainPresenter implements the IDomainPresenter interface:

```
public class DomainView : IDomainView

{

 private IDomainPresenter domainPresenter = null;

 ///<summary>Constructor</summary>

 public DomainView()

 {

 domainPresenter = new ConcreteDomainPresenter(this);

 }

}
```

The degree of logic permitted in the view varies among different implementations. At one extreme, the view is entirely passive, forwarding all interaction operations to the presenter. In this formulation, when a user triggers an event method of the view, it does nothing but invoke a method of the presenter that has no parameters and no return value. The presenter then retrieves data from the view through methods defined by the view interface. Finally, the presenter operates on the model and updates the view with the results of the operation. Other versions of model-view-presenter allow some latitude with respect to which class handles a particular interaction, event, or command. This is often more suitable for web-based architectures, where the view, which executes on a client's browser, may be the best place to handle a particular interaction or command.

From a layering point of view, the presenter class might be considered as belonging to the application layer in a multilayered architecture system, but it can also be seen as a presenter layer of its own between the application layer and the user interface layer.

Implementation in .NET

The .NET environment supports the MVP pattern much like any other development environment. The same model and presenter class can be used to support multiple interfaces, such as an ASP. NET Web application, a Windows Forms application, or a Silverlight application. The presenter gets and sets information from/to the view through an interface that can be accessed by the interface (view) component.

In addition to manually implementing the pattern, a model-view-presenter framework may be used to support the MVP pattern in a more automated fashion.

Implementation in Java

In a Java (AWT/Swing/SWT) application, the MVP pattern can be used by letting the user interface class implement a view interface.

The same approach can be used for Java web-based applications, since modern Java component-based Web frameworks allow development of client-side logic using the same component approach as thick clients.

Implementing MVP in Google Web Toolkit requires only that some component implement the view interface. The same approach is possible using Vaadin or the Echo2 Web framework.

Java frameworks include the following:

- JavaFX
- Echo2
- Google Web Toolkit
- JFace
- Swing
- Vaadin
- ZK

Implementation in PHP

As of PHP's flexible runtime environment, there are wide possibilities of approaches of an application logic. Implementation of model layer is left on the end application programmer.

PHP frameworks include the following:

- Nette Framework

Implementation in Kotlin

Kotlin focuses on multi-platform compatibility and so are the frameworks based on it. The purpose is to focus only once on the business logic and implement it thanks to a framework made to be compatible to each platform. Kodein Framework is a good example of that.

Action Domain Responder

Action domain responder (ADR) is a software architectural pattern that was proposed by Paul M. Jones as a refinement of Model–view–controller (MVC) that is better suited for web applications. ADR was devised to match the request-response flow of HTTP communications more closely than MVC, which was originally designed for desktop software applications. Similar to MVC, the pattern is divided into three parts.

Components

- The action takes HTTP requests (URLs and their methods) and uses that input to interact with the domain, after which it passes the domain's output to one and only one responder.

- The domain can modify state, interacting with storage and/or manipulating data as needed. It contains the business logic.

- The responder builds the entire HTTP response from the domain's output which is given to it by the action.

Comparison to MVC

ADR should not be mistaken for a renaming of MVC; however, some similarities do exist:

- The MVC model is very similar to the ADR domain. The difference is in behavior: in MVC, the view can send information to or modify the model, whereas in ADR, the domain only receives information from the action, not the responder.

- In web-centric MVC, the view is merely used by the controller to generate the content of a response, which the controller could then manipulate before sending as output. In ADR, execution control passes to the responder after the action finishes interacting with the domain, and thus the responder is entirely responsible for generating all output. The responder can then use any view or template system that it needs to.

- MVC controllers usually contain several methods that, when combined in a single class, require additional logic to handle properly, like pre- and post-action hooks. Each ADR action, however, is represented by separate classes or closures. In terms of behavior, the action interacts with the domain in the same way that the MVC controller interacts with the model, except that the action does not then interact with a view or template system, but rather passes control to the responder which handles that.

Active Record Pattern

The active record pattern is an architectural pattern found in software that stores in-memory object data in relational databases. It was named by martin fowler the interface of an object conforming to this pattern would include functions such as insert, update, and delete, plus properties that correspond more or less directly to the columns in the underlying database table.

The active record pattern is an approach to accessing data in a database. A database table or view is wrapped into a class. Thus, an object instance is tied to a single row in the table. After creation of an object, a new row is added to the table upon save. Any object loaded gets its information from the database. When an object is updated, the corresponding row in the table is also updated. The wrapper class implements accessor methods or properties for each column in the table or view.

This pattern is commonly used by object persistence tools and in object-relational mapping (orm). Typically, foreign key relationships will be exposed as an object instance of the appropriate type via a property.

Implementations

Implementations of the concept can be found in various frameworks for many programming environments. For example, if in a database there is a table parts with columns name (string type) and price (number type), and the Active Record pattern is implemented in the class Part, the pseudo-code:

```
part = new Part()

part.name = "Sample part"

part.price = 123.45

part.save()
```

will create a new row in the parts table with the given values, and is roughly equivalent to the SQL command

```
INSERT INTO parts (name, price) VALUES ('Sample part', 123.45);
```

Conversely, the class can be used to query the database:

```
b = Part.find_first("name", "gearbox")
```

This will find a new `Part` object based on the first matching row from the `parts` table whose `name` column has the value "gearbox". The SQL command used might be similar to the following, depending on the SQL implementation details of the database:

```
SELECT * FROM parts WHERE name = 'gearbox' LIMIT 1; -- MySQL or PostgreSQL
```

Multiuse-Model View

The Multiuse-Model View (MMV) is an architectural pattern used in software engineering that came about as an enhancement to the MVVM design pattern. The pattern is specific for Windows Presentation Foundation (WPF) and Windows Communication Foundation (WCF) applications. While keeping the logical separation of user interface (View) versus logic (Model), MMV's primary objective is to address the shortcomings of the MVVM pattern. The Multiuse-Model of MMV typically relies on reflection to facilitate object building in order to easily integrate logic-centric object models with view-centric object models minimizing the amount of duplicate code. MMV was designed to make use of specific functions in C#, WPF and WCF to better facilitate the reuse of code between the server and the client.

Pattern Description

The Multiuse-Model View pattern attempts to leverage the advantages of separation of logic as well as the advantages of XAML and the Windows Presentation Foundation just like MVVM does, however, it also attempts to deal with most of the disadvantages of MVVM including promoting a more object oriented class design, reducing the amount of duplicate code required, simplifying maintenance and reducing the amount of metadata generated. To accomplish this MMV relies on a set of base classes which provide generic functionality for sending data from/to the client and displaying data on the UI.

Model-View-View Model

The Model-View-View Model (MVVM) pattern helps to cleanly separate the business and presentation logic of an application from its user interface (UI). Maintaining a clean separation between application logic and the UI helps to address numerous development issues and can make an application easier to test, maintain, and evolve. It can also greatly improve code reuse opportunities and allows developers and UI designers to more easily collaborate when developing their respec-tive parts of an app.

The MVVM Pattern

There are three core components in the MVVM pattern: the model, the view, and the view model. Each serves a distinct purpose. Figure shows the relationships between the three components.

The MVVM pattern.

In addition to understanding the responsibilities of each component, it's also important to understand how they interact with each other. At a high level, the view "knows about" the view model, and the view model "knows about" the model, but the model is unaware of the view model, and the view model is unaware of the view. Therefore, the view model isolates the view from the model, and allows the model to evolve independently of the view.

The benefits of using the MVVM pattern are as follows:

- If there's an existing model implementation that encapsulates existing business logic, it can be difficult or risky to change it. In this scenario, the view model acts as an adapter for the model classes and enables you to avoid making any major changes to the model code.

- Developers can create unit tests for the view model and the model, without using the view. The unit tests for the view model can exercise exactly the same functionality as used by the view.

- The app UI can be redesigned without touching the code, provided that the view is implemented entirely in XAML. Therefore, a new version of the view should work with the existing view model.

- Designers and developers can work independently and concurrently on their components during the development process. Designers can focus on the view, while developers can work on the view model and model components.

The key to using MVVM effectively lies in understanding how to factor app code into the correct classes, and in understanding how the classes interact. Following are the responsibilities of each of the classes in the MVVm pattern.

View

The view is responsible for defining the structure, layout, and appearance of what the user sees on screen. Ideally, each view is defined in XAML, with a limited code-behind that does not contain business logic. However, in some cases, the code-behind might contain UI logic that implements visual behavior that is difficult to express in XAML, such as animations.

In a Xamarin.Forms application, a view is typically a Page-derived or ContentView-derived class. However, views can also be represented by a data template, which specifies the UI elements to be used to visually represent an object when it's displayed. A data template as a view does not have any code-behind, and is designed to bind to a specific view model type.

There are several options for executing code on the view model in response to interactions on the view, such as a button click or item selection. If a control supports commands, the control's Command property can be data-bound to an ICommand property on the view model. When the control's command is invoked, the code in the view model will be executed. In addition to commands, behaviors can be attached to an object in the view and can listen for either a command to be invoked or event to be raised. In response, the behavior can then invoke an ICommand on the view model or a method on the view model.

View Model

The view model implements properties and commands to which the view can data bind to, and notifies the view of any state changes through change notification events. The properties and commands that the view model provides define the functionality to be offered by the UI, but the view determines how that functionality is to be displayed.

The view model is also responsible for coordinating the view's interactions with any model classes that are required. There's typically a one-to-many relationship between the view model and the model classes. The view model might choose to expose model classes directly to the view so that controls in the view can data bind directly to them. In this case, the model classes will need to be designed to support data binding and change notification events.

Each view model provides data from a model in a form that the view can easily consume. To accomplish this, the view model sometimes performs data conversion. Placing this data conversion in the view model is a good idea because it provides properties that the view can bind to. For example, the view model might combine the values of two properties to make it easier for display by the view.

In order for the view model to participate in two-way data binding with the view, its properties must raise the PropertyChanged event. View models satisfy this requirement by implementing the INotifyPropertyChanged interface, and raising the PropertyChanged event when a property is changed.

For collections, the view-friendly ObservableCollection <T> is provided. This collection implements collection changed notification, relieving the developer from having to implement the INotifyCollectionChanged interface on collections.

Model

Model classes are non-visual classes that encapsulate the app's data. Therefore, the model can be thought of as representing the app's domain model, which usually includes a data model along with business and validation logic. Examples of model objects include data transfer objects (DTOs), Plain Old CLR Objects (POCOs), and generated entity and proxy objects.

Model classes are typically used in conjunction with services or repositories that encapsulate data access and caching.

Connecting View Models to Views

View models can be connected to views by using the data-binding capabilities of Xamarin. Forms. There are many approaches that can be used to construct views and view models and associate them at runtime. These approaches fall into two categories, known as view first composition, and view model first composition. Choosing between view first composition and view model first composition is an issue of preference and complexity. However, all approaches share the same aim, which is for the view to have a view model assigned to its BindingContext property.

With view first composition the app is conceptually composed of views that connect to the view models they depend on. The primary benefit of this approach is that it makes it easy to construct loosely coupled, unit testable apps because the view models have no dependence on the views themselves. It's also easy to understand the structure of the app by following its visual structure, rather than having to track code execution to understand how classes are created and associated. In addition, view first construction aligns with the Xamarin.Forms navigation system that's responsible for constructing pages when navigation occurs, which makes a view model first composition complex and misaligned with the platform.

With view model first composition the app is conceptually composed of view models, with a service being responsible for locating the view for a view model. View model first composition feels more natural to some developers, since the view creation can be abstracted away, allowing them to focus on the logical non-UI structure of the app. In addition, it allows view models to be created by other view models. However, this approach is often complex and it can become difficult to understand how the various parts of the app are created and associated.

Following are the main approaches to connecting view models to view:

Creating a View Model Declaratively

The simplest approach is for the view to declaratively instantiate its corresponding view model in XAML. When the view is constructed, the corresponding view model object will also be constructed. This approach is demonstrated in the following code example:

XAML

```
<ContentPage ... xmlns:local="clr-namespace:eShop">
    <ContentPage.BindingContext>
```

```
<local:LoginViewModel />

</ContentPage.BindingContext>

...
```

`</ContentPage>`

When the ContentPage is created, an instance of the LoginViewModel is automatically constructed and set as the view's BindingContext.

This declarative construction and assignment of the view model by the view has the advantage that it's simple, but has the disadvantage that it requires a default (parameter-less) constructor in the view model.

Creating a View Model Programmatically

A view can have code in the code-behind file that results in the view model being assigned to its BindingContext property. This is often accomplished in the view's constructor, as shown in the following code example:

```C#
public LoginView()
{
  InitializeComponent();

  BindingContext = new LoginViewModel(navigationService);
}
```

The programmatic construction and assignment of the view model within the view's code-behind has the advantage that it's simple. However, the main disadvantage of this approach is that the view needs to provide the view model with any required dependencies. Using a dependency injection container can help to maintain loose coupling between the view and view model.

Creating a View Defined as a Data Template

A view can be defined as a data template and associated with a view model type. Data templates can be defined as resources, or they can be defined inline within the control that will display the view model. The content of the control is the view model instance, and the data template is used to visually represent it. This technique is an example of a situation in which the view model is instantiated first, followed by the creation of the view.

Automatically Creating a View Model with a View Model Locator

A view model locator is a custom class that manages the instantiation of view models and their association to views. In the eShopOnContainers mobile app, the ViewModelLocator class has an attached property, AutoWireViewModel, that's used to associate view models with views. In the view's XAML, this attached property is set to true to indicate that the view model should be automatically connected to the view, as shown in the following code example:

XAML

```
viewModelBase:ViewModelLocator.AutoWireViewModel="true"
```

The AutoWireViewModel property is a bindable property that's initialized to false, and when its value changes the OnAutoWireViewModelChanged event handler is called. This method resolves the view model for the view. The following code example shows how this is achieved:

C#

```
private static void OnAutoWireViewModelChanged(BindableObject bindable, object
oldValue, object newValue)
{
    var view = bindable as Element;
    if (view == null)
    {
    return;
    }
    var viewType = view.GetType();
    var viewName = viewType.FullName.Replace(".Views.", ".ViewModels.");
    var viewAssemblyName = viewType.GetTypeInfo().Assembly.FullName;
    var viewModelName = string.Format(
    CultureInfo.InvariantCulture, "{0}Model, {1}", viewName, viewAssemblyName);
    var viewModelType = Type.GetType(viewModelName);
    if (viewModelType == null)
    {
    return;
    }
    var viewModel = _container.Resolve(viewModelType);
    view.BindingContext = viewModel;
}
```

The OnAutoWireViewModelChanged method attempts to resolve the view model using a convention-based approach. This convention assumes that:

- View models are in the same assembly as view types.

- Views are in a .Views child namespace.

- View models are in a .ViewModels child namespace.

- View model names correspond with view names and end with "ViewModel".

Finally, the OnAutoWireViewModelChanged method sets the BindingContext of the view type to the resolved view model type.

This approach has the advantage that an app has a single class that is responsible for the instantiation of view models and their connection to views.

Updating Views in Response to Changes in the Underlying View Model or Model

All view model and model classes that are accessible to a view should implement the INotifyPropertyChanged interface. Implementing this interface in a view model or model class allows the class to provide change notifications to any data-bound controls in the view when the underlying property value changes.

Apps should be architected for the correct use of property change notification, by meeting the following requirements:

- Always raising a PropertyChanged event if a public property's value changes. Do not assume that raising the PropertyChanged event can be ignored because of knowledge of how XAML binding occurs.

- Always raising a PropertyChanged event for any calculated properties whose values are used by other properties in the view model or model.

- Always raising the PropertyChanged event at the end of the method that makes a property change, or when the object is known to be in a safe state. Raising the event interrupts the operation by invoking the event's handlers synchronously. If this happens in the middle of an operation, it might expose the object to callback functions when it is in an unsafe, partially updated state. In addition, it's possible for cascading changes to be triggered by PropertyChanged events. Cascading changes generally require updates to be complete before the cascading change is safe to execute.

- Never raising a PropertyChanged event if the property does not change. This means that you must compare the old and new values before raising the PropertyChanged event.

- Never raising the PropertyChanged event during a view model's constructor if you are initializing a property. Data-bound controls in the view will not have subscribed to receive change notifications at this point.

- Never raising more than one PropertyChanged event with the same property name argument within a single synchronous invocation of a public method of a class. For example, given a NumberOfItems property whose backing store is the _numberOfItems field, if a method increments _numberOfItems fifty times during the execution of a loop, it should only raise property change notification on the NumberOfItems property once, after all the work is complete. For asynchronous methods, raise the PropertyChanged event for a given property name in each synchronous segment of an asynchronous continuation chain.

The eShopOnContainers mobile app uses the ExtendedBindableObject class to provide change notifications, which is shown in the following code example:

C#

```csharp
public abstract class ExtendedBindableObject : BindableObject
{
    public void RaisePropertyChanged<T>(Expression<Func<T>> property)
    {
    var name = GetMemberInfo(property).Name;
    OnPropertyChanged(name);
    }
    private MemberInfo GetMemberInfo(Expression expression)
    {
      ...
    }
}
```

Xamarin.Form's BindableObject class implements the INotifyPropertyChanged interface, and provides an OnPropertyChanged method. The ExtendedBindableObject class provides the RaisePropertyChanged method to invoke property change notification, and in doing so uses the functionality provided by the BindableObject class.

Each view model class in the eShopOnContainers mobile app derives from the ViewModelBase class, which in turn derives from the ExtendedBindableObject class. Therefore, each view model class uses the RaisePropertyChanged method in the ExtendedBindableObject class to provide property change notification. The following code example shows how the eShopOnContainers mobile app invokes property change notification by using a lambda expression:

C#

```csharp
public bool IsLogin
{
    get
    {
      return _isLogin;
    }
    set
    {
```

```
        _isLogin = value;

        RaisePropertyChanged(() => IsLogin);

    }

}
```

Note that using a lambda expression in this way involves a small performance cost because the lambda expression has to be evaluated for each call. Although the performance cost is small and would not normally impact an app, the costs can accrue when there are many change notifications. However, the benefit of this approach is that it provides compile-time type safety and refactoring support when renaming properties.

UI Interaction using Commands and Behaviors

In mobile apps, actions are typically invoked in response to a user action, such as a button click, that can be implemented by creating an event handler in the code-behind file. However, in the MVVM pattern, the responsibility for implementing the action lies with the view model, and placing code in the code-behind should be avoided.

Commands provide a convenient way to represent actions that can be bound to controls in the UI. They encapsulate the code that implements the action, and help to keep it decoupled from its visual representation in the view. Xamarin.Forms includes controls that can be declaratively connected to a command, and these controls will invoke the command when the user interacts with the control.

Behaviors also allow controls to be declaratively connected to a command. However, behaviors can be used to invoke an action that's associated with a range of events raised by a control. Therefore, behaviors address many of the same scenarios as command-enabled controls, while providing a greater degree of flexibility and control. In addition, behaviors can also be used to associate command objects or methods with controls that were not specifically designed to interact with commands.

Implementing Commands

View models typically expose command properties, for binding from the view, that are object instances that implement the ICommand interface. A number of Xamarin.Forms controls provide a Command property, which can be data bound to an ICommand object provided by the view model. The ICommand interface defines an Execute method, which encapsulates the operation itself, a CanExecute method, which indicates whether the command can be invoked, and a CanExecuteChanged event that occurs when changes occur that affect whether the command should execute. The Command and Command<T> classes, provided by Xamarin. Forms, implement the ICommand interface, where T is the type of the arguments to Execute and CanExecute.

Within a view model, there should be an object of type Command or Command <T> for each public property in the view model of type ICommand. The Command or Command <T> constructor requires an Action callback object that's called when the ICommand.Execute method is invoked. The CanExecute method is an optional constructor parameter, and is a Func that returns a bool.

The following code shows how a Command instance, which represents a register command, is constructed by specifying a delegate to the Register view model method:

C#

```
public ICommand RegisterCommand => new Command(Register);
```

The command is exposed to the view through a property that returns a reference to an ICommand. When the Execute method is called on the Command object, it simply forwards the call to the method in the view model via the delegate that was specified in the Command constructor.

An asynchronous method can be invoked by a command by using the async and await keywords when specifying the command's Execute delegate. This indicates that the callback is a Task and should be awaited. For example, the following code shows how a Command instance, which represents a sign-in command, is constructed by specifying a delegate to the SignInAsync view model method:

C#

```
public ICommand SignInCommand => new Command(async () => await SignInAsync());
```

Parameters can be passed to the Execute and CanExecute actions by using the Command<T> class to instantiate the command. For example, the following code shows how a Command<T> instance is used to indicate that the NavigateAsync method will require an argument of type string:

C#

```
public ICommand NavigateCommand => new Command<string>(NavigateAsync);
```

In both the Command and Command<T> classes, the delegate to the CanExecute method in each constructor is optional. If a delegate isn't specified, the Command will return true for CanExecute. However, the view model can indicate a change in the command's CanExecute status by calling the ChangeCanExecute method on the Command object. This causes the CanExecuteChanged event to be raised. Any controls in the UI that are bound to the command will then update their enabled status to reflect the availability of the data-bound command.

Invoking Commands from a View

The following code example shows how a Grid in the LoginView binds to the RegisterCommand in the LoginViewModel class by using a TapGestureRecognizer instance:

XAML

```
<Grid Grid.Column="1" HorizontalOptions="Center">

    <Label Text="REGISTER" TextColor="Gray"/>

    <Grid.GestureRecognizers>

        <TapGestureRecognizer Command="{Binding RegisterCommand}" NumberOfTaps-
Required="1" />
```

```
</Grid.GestureRecognizers>
```

```
</Grid>
```

A command parameter can also be optionally defined using the CommandParameter property. The type of the expected argument is specified in the Execute and CanExecute target methods. The TapGestureRecognizer will automatically invoke the target command when the user interacts with the attached control. The command parameter, if provided, will be passed as the argument to the command's Execute delegate.

Implementing Behaviors

Behaviors allow functionality to be added to UI controls without having to subclass them. Instead, the functionality is implemented in a behavior class and attached to the control as if it was part of the control itself. Behaviors enable you to implement code that you would normally have to write as code-behind, because it directly interacts with the API of the control, in such a way that it can be concisely attached to the control, and packaged for reuse across more than one view or app. In the context of MVVM, behaviors are a useful approach for connecting controls to commands.

A behavior that's attached to a control through attached properties is known as an attached behavior. The behavior can then use the exposed API of the element to which it is attached to add functionality to that control, or other controls, in the visual tree of the view. The eShopOnContainers mobile app contains the LineColorBehavior class, which is an attached behavior.

A Xamarin.Forms behavior is a class that derives from the Behavior or Behavior <T> class, where T is the type of the control to which the behavior should apply. These classes provide OnAttachedTo and OnDetachingFrom methods, which should be overridden to provide logic that will be executed when the behavior is attached to and detached from controls.

In the eShopOnContainers mobile app, the BindableBehavior <T> class derives from the Behavior <T> class. The purpose of the BindableBehavior <T> class is to provide a base class for Xamarin.Forms behaviors that require the BindingContext of the behavior to be set to the attached control.

The BindableBehavior <T> class provides an overridable OnAttachedTo method that sets the BindingContext of the behavior, and an overridable OnDetachingFrom method that cleans up the BindingContext. In addition, the class stores a reference to the attached control in the AssociatedObject property.

The eShopOnContainers mobile app includes an EventToCommandBehavior class, which executes a command in response to an event occurring. This class derives from the BindableBehavior <T> class so that the behavior can bind to and execute an ICommand specified by a Command property when the behavior is consumed. The following code example shows the EventToCommandBehavior class:

C#

```
public class EventToCommandBehavior : BindableBehavior<View>
```

```
{
```

```
   ...
   protected override void OnAttachedTo(View visualElement)
   {
base.OnAttachedTo(visualElement);
var events = AssociatedObject.GetType().GetRuntimeEvents().ToArray();
if (events.Any())
{
_eventInfo = events.FirstOrDefault(e => e.Name == EventName);
if (_eventInfo == null)
throw new ArgumentException(string.Format(
"EventToCommand: Can't find any event named '{0}' on attached type",
EventName));
AddEventHandler(_eventInfo, AssociatedObject, OnFired);
}
}
protected override void OnDetachingFrom(View view)
{
if (_handler != null)
_eventInfo.RemoveEventHandler(AssociatedObject, _handler);
base.OnDetachingFrom(view);
}
private void AddEventHandler(
EventInfo eventInfo, object item, Action<object, EventArgs> action)
{
...
}
private void OnFired(object sender, EventArgs eventArgs)
{
...
}
}
```

The OnAttachedTo and OnDetachingFrom methods are used to register and deregister an event handler for the event defined in the EventName property. Then, when the event fires, the OnFired method is invoked, which executes the command.

The advantage of using the EventToCommandBehavior to execute a command when an event fires, is that commands can be associated with controls that weren't designed to interact with commands. In addition, this moves event-handling code to view models, where it can be unit tested.

Invoking Behaviors from a View

The EventToCommandBehavior is particularly useful for attaching a command to a control that doesn't support commands. For example, the ProfileView uses the EventToCommandBehavior to execute the OrderDetailCommand when the ItemTapped event fires on the ListView that lists the user's orders, as shown in the following code:

XAML

```
<ListView>

    <ListView.Behaviors>

        <behaviors:EventToCommandBehavior

            EventName="ItemTapped"

            Command="{Binding OrderDetailCommand}"

            EventArgsConverter="{StaticResource ItemTappedEventArgsConverter}" />

    </ListView.Behaviors>

    ...

</ListView>
```

At runtime, the EventToCommandBehavior will respond to interaction with the ListView. When an item is selected in the ListView, the ItemTapped event will fire, which will execute the OrderDetailCommand in the ProfileViewModel. By default, the event arguments for the event are passed to the command. This data is converted as it's passed between source and target by the converter specified in the EventArgsConverter property, which returns the Item of the ListView from the ItemTappedEventArgs. Therefore, when the OrderDetailCommand is executed, the selected Order is passed as a parameter to the registered Action.

References

- Evans, Eric (2004). Domain-Driven Design: Tackling Complexity in the Heart of Software. Addison-Wesley. ISBN 978-032-112521-7. Retrieved 2012-08-12

- N-tier-architecture-system-concepts-tips: guru99.com, Retrieved 11 August, 2019

- Elkaduwe, Dhammika; Derrin, Philip; Elphinstone, Kevin (April 2008). "Kernel design for isolation and assurance of physical memory". 1st Workshop on Isolation and Integration in Embedded Systems. Glasgow, UK. Doi:10.1145/1435458

- Enterprise-application-patterns, xamarin-forms, xamarin, en-us: microsoft.com, Retrieved 12 January, 2019

- Thiruvathukal, George K.; Läufer, Konstantin (2018), "Managing Concurrency in Mobile User Interfaces with Examples in Android", Topics in Parallel and Distributed Computing, Springer, Cham, pp. 243–285, doi:10.1007/978-3-319-93109-8-9, ISBN 9783319931081

Software Architecture Description

3

- **Architecture Description Language**
- **View Model**
- **Software Architecture Recovery**
- **General Methods for Software Architecture Recovery**
- **Software Architecture Erosion**

The set of practices which are used for expressing, communicating and analyzing software architectures is termed as software architecture description. The topics elaborated in this chapter will help in gaining a better perspective about software architecture description and its diverse aspects such as software architecture recovery and view models.

The architectural description tells us what components we need. The component design effort builds those components in conformance to the architecture and specification. The components will in general include both hardware—FPGAs, boards, and so on—and software modules.

Some of the components will be ready-made. The CPU, for example, will be a standard component in almost all cases, as will memory chips and many other components. In the moving map, the GPS receiver is a good example of a specialized component that will nonetheless be a predesigned, standard component. We can also make use of standard software modules. One good example is the topographic database. Standard topographic databases exist, and you probably want to use standard routines to access the database—not only are the data in a predefined format, but also they are highly compressed to save storage. Using standard software for these access functions not only saves us design time, but it may also give us a faster implementation for specialized functions such as the data decompression phase.

You will have to design some components yourself. Even if you are using only standard integrated circuits, you may have to design the printed circuit board that connects them. You will probably have to do a lot of custom programming as well. When creating these embedded software modules, you must of course make use of your expertise to ensure that the system runs properly in real time and that it does not take up more memory space than is allowed. The power consumption of the moving map software example is particularly important. You may need to be very careful about how you read and write memory to minimize power—for example, because memory accesses are a major source of power consumption, memory transactions must be carefully planned to avoid reading the same data several times.

Working with Architecture

Running an enterprise inevitably involves putting these structures in place, either consciously or just as they emerge in daily business. Processes, roles and responsibilities, information exchange, and some kind of office space are elements you will find in any organization. Their importance in individual cases depends on various factors such as the individual industry, the number of actors involved, or the size of the organization.

Enterprise relationships captured in architectural descriptions form a complex and intertwined structure of structures, undergoing constant change. Individual substructures cannot be viewed and addressed as static constructs in isolation, since they are difficult to separate and largely depend on each other to work—changing one means affecting others as well. Many formal structures in the enterprise, like social and organizational configurations, tend to change very quickly. Any attempt to capture a holistic enterprise-wide architecture can only capture a moment in this development or lay out the direction of this transformation, by modeling a current or a desired state.

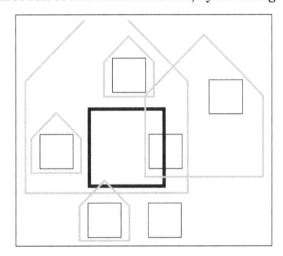

For those reasons, any work on architecture deals primarily with the complexity and ambiguity that comes with the large elaborate structures in constant transition that you typically find in an enterprise. While it is impossible to control such a system as a whole, initiatives aiming to shap e architecture have to influence it by establishing controlled substructures, understanding the linkages between them, and managing change and development.

As the set of structures driving all execution, architecture is intrinsically subject to all transformation processes in an enterprise. To be aligned with strategic intent and vision, it needs to be understood as it emerges dynamically, and consciously transformed to fulfill the purpose of the enterprise. This is true even if the goal of this transformation is to maintain the status quo of the enterprise by adapting to changed conditions.

To understand these structures and inform management, decision making and governance, architecture models are used to describe or visualize all structures in the enterprise. They show stakeholders both a view on the current situation and alternative developments to be considered. The instrument of choice for this is Enterprise Architecture, a discipline that aims to make architecture visible to stakeholders involved in or impacted by a transformation.

An Architecture Viewpoint for Modeling Dynamically Configurable Software Systems.

Metamodel for Runtime Adaptability Viewpoint

In figure we show the conceptual model for architectural view modeling. In fact, the conceptual model is based on the ISO/IEC recommended standard for architectural description but it enhances the standard to explicitly depict quality concerns and defines their relation to architectural views. The left part of the figure shows basically the definition of the architectural drivers. A system has one or more stakeholders who have interest in the system with respect to one or more concerns. Concerns can be functional or quality related. The right part of the figure focuses on the architectural views for the different concerns. Each system has an architecture, which is described by an architectural description. The architectural description consists of a set of views that correspond to their viewpoints. Viewpoints aim to address the stakeholder's concerns. Functional concerns will define the dominant decomposition along architectural units that are mainly functional in nature. On the other hand, quality concerns will define the dominant decomposition of the architecture along architectural units that explicitly represent quality concerns. Runtime adaptability is a specific quality concern that is addressed by runtime adaptability view. Run-adaptability is not directly considered in the other viewpoints.

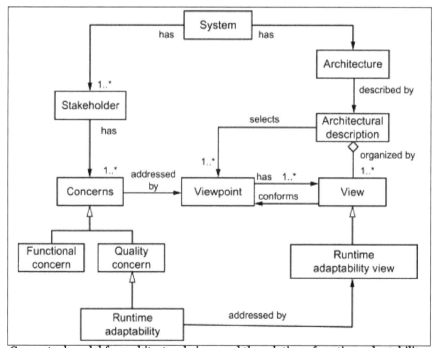

Conceptual model for architectural views and the relation of runtime adaptability.

To define the foundation for the runtime adaptability viewpoint we have performed a domain analysis regarding architectural frameworks introduced for dynamic configurability. These frameworks employ different adaptation mechanisms. We have reviewed these mechanisms and we focus on the adaptation capabilities that they can provide. For providing adaptability, one also needs to decide on the type of adaptation mechanism. However, we decided not to integrate this in the viewpoint because we aim to provide a generic viewpoint in which we address only *what* can be adapted. We did not wish to fix the mechanisms. The viewpoint is agnostic to the adaptation mechanisms and as such could be used together with existing adaptation frameworks. However, our approach allows the extension of the viewpoint to include also the mechanisms for adaptation.

Existing frameworks assume either a component-based architecture or service-oriented architecture (SOA). So, reconfigured architectural elements are components, connectors, or services. We have observed that the majority of the existing approaches mainly focus on the C&C view to depict the runtime structure and reason about dynamic adaptation. Hence, the proposed viewpoint mainly relies on the C&C viewpoint as defined by the V&B approach. The following figure depicts a metamodel of the viewpoint as described in this approach.

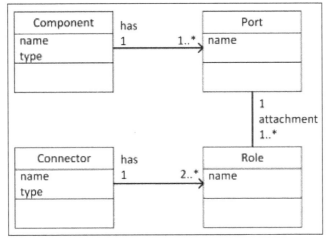

A metamodel of the C&C viewpoint.

In the C&C viewpoint, there are two basic types of elements: component types that represent principal processing units and data stores, and connector types that represent interaction mechanisms. Each of these elements has two properties: a name that suggests its functionality, and a type that determines the general functionality and constraints for the element. Every component has one or more ports. These ports have names that suggest the corresponding interface of the component. On the other hand, every connector has two or more roles. These roles have names that suggest the interacting parties. There is an attachment relation defined between a port and one or more roles.

As stated in the V&B approach many C&C styles allow C&Cs to be created or destroyed as the system is running. For example, in client-server based systems new server instances might be created as the number of client requests increases. In a peer-to-peer system, new components may dynamically join or leave the peer-to-peer network. In principle, any C&C style supports the dynamic creation and destruction of elements.

In addition to the C&C views, allocation views are also highly relevant for runtime adaptability. These views document a mapping between software elements and nonsoftware elements in the context of the system. In particular, deployment views constitute a type of allocation view, which describes a mapping between software elements and hardware elements in the computing platform. These views conform to the deployment style and they are relevant for dynamic reconfiguration because the allocation of software elements can be dynamic. Three types of dynamic relations are defined for deployment views in the V&B approach: (1) migrates-to: a software element can move from one processor to another processor, (2) copy-migrates-to: a software element can be copied to another processor and different copies can execute on different processors at the same time, (3) execution-migrates-to: a software element can be copied to another processor, where only one of the copies can be executed at a time. The corresponding metamodel is depicted in figure. Migration relations are mainly triggered by changing application profiles and operational context for supporting quality concerns such as performance, availability, reliability, and security. For example, performance improvements can be achieved by deploying some components together when the frequency of intercommunication is increased. Some components can be migrated for isolating them from the other components to improve reliability or security. Resource utilization and hardware faults can also trigger a migration.

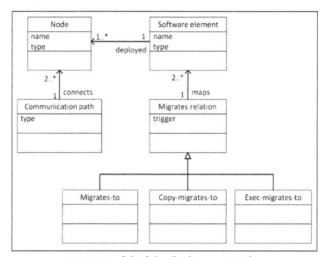

A metamodel of the deployment style.

To support the viewpoint for runtime adaptability and dynamic configurability we have integrated the metamodels of figures and as shown in figure.

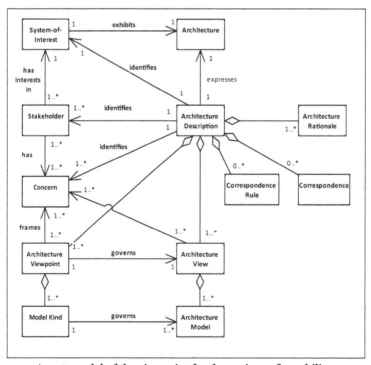

A metamodel of the viewpoint for dynamic configurability.

Dynamic configurability is facilitated in three ways (1) adaptation of elements by change of mode, state, parameters, (2) replacement of elements leading to a structural change, (3) migration of elements to different nodes. In general, formal specifications for dynamic software architectures utilize the second one; they define reconfigurations as a series of C&C addition/removal operations. To differentiate between elements that can be subject to configurability, we have introduced adaptable components and adaptable connectors. Such a distinction is also being made in existing frameworks. In some of the existing approaches, communication is assumed to be asynchronous and architectural elements are assumed to be stateless and independent. However, in some other approaches, architectural elements can be interdependent and they can be stateful. This makes a difference because adaptable components that are stateful provide means for loading and storing state information. In principle, connectors can also involve rich semantics just like components. For this reason, we also distinguished between stateful and stateless connectors in our viewpoint as depicted in the metamodel.

Architecture Description Language

Architecture description languages (ADLs) are used in several disciplines: system engineering, software engineering, and enterprise modelling and engineering.

The system engineering community uses an architecture description language as a language and/ or a conceptual model to describe and represent system architectures.

The software engineering community uses an architecture description language as a computer language to create a description of a software architecture. In the case of a so-called technical architecture, the architecture must be communicated to software developers; a functional architecture is communicated to various stakeholders and users. Some ADLs that have been developed are: Acme (developed by CMU), AADL (standardized by the SAE), C2 (developed by UCI), SBC-ADL (developed by National Sun Yat-Sen University), Darwin (developed by Imperial College London), and Wright (developed by CMU).

The ISO/IEC/IEEE 42010 document, Systems and software engineering—Architecture description, defines an architecture description language as "any form of expression for use in architecture descriptions" and specifies minimum requirements on ADLs.

The enterprise modelling and engineering community have also developed architecture description languages catered for at the enterprise level. Examples include ArchiMate (now a standard of The Open Group), DEMO, ABACUS (developed by the University of Technology, Sydney). These languages do not necessarily refer to software components, etc. Most of them, however, refer to an application architecture as the architecture that is communicated to the software engineers.

Most of the writing below refers primarily to the perspective from the software engineering community.

A standard notation (ADL) for representing architectures helps promote mutual communication, the embodiment of early design decisions, and the creation of a transferable abstraction of a system. Architectures in the past were largely represented by box-and-line drawing annotated with such things as the nature of the component, properties, semantics of connections, and overall system behavior. ADLs result from a linguistic approach to the formal representation of architectures, and as such they address its shortcomings. Also important, sophisticated ADLs allow for early analysis and feasibility testing of architectural design decisions.

ADLs have been classified into three broad categories: box-and-line informal drawings, formal architecture description language, and UML (Unified Modeling Language)-based notations.

Box-and-line have been for a long time the most predominant means for describing SAs. While providing useful documentation, the level of informality limited the usefulness of the architecture description. A more rigorous way for describing SAs was required. Quoting Allen and Garlan, "while these [box-and-line] descriptions may provide useful documentation, the current level of informality limits their usefulness. Since it is generally imprecise what is meant by such architectural descriptions, it may be impossible to analyze an architecture for consistency or determine non-trivial properties of it. Moreover, there is no way to check that a system implementation is faithful to its architectural design." A similar conclusion is drawn in Perry and Wolf, which reports that: "Aside from providing clear and precise documentation, the primary purpose of specifications is to provide automated analysis of the documents and to expose various kinds of problems that would otherwise go undetected."

Since then, a thread of research on formal languages for SA description has been carried out. Tens of formal ADLs have been proposed, each characterized by different conceptual architectural elements, different syntax or semantics, focusing on a specific operational domain, or only suitable for different analysis techniques. For example, domain-specific ADLs have been presented to deal with embedded and real-time systems (such as AADL, EAST-ADL, and EADL), control-loop applications (DiaSpec), product line architectures (Koala), and dynamic systems (Π-ADL)). Analysis-specific ADLs have been proposed to deal with availability, reliability, security, resource consumption, data quality and real-time performance analysis (AADL, behavioral analysis (Fractal)), and trustworthiness analysis (TADL).

However, these efforts have not seen the desired adoption by industrial practice. Some reasons for this lack of industry adoption have been analyzed by Woods and Hilliard, Pandey, Clements, and others: formal ADLs have been rarely integrated in the software life-cycle, they are seldom supported by mature tools, scarcely documented, focusing on very specific needs, and leaving no space for extensions enabling the addition of new features.

As a way to overcome some of those limitations, UML has been indicated as a possible successor of existing ADLs. Many proposals have been presented to use or extend the UML to more properly model software architectures.

In fact, as highlighted in a recent study conducted with practitioners, whilst practitioners are generally satisfied with the design capabilities provided by the languages they use, they are dissatisfied with the architectural language analysis features and their abilities to define extra-functional properties; architectural languages used in practice mostly originate from industrial development instead of from academic research; more formality and better usability are required of an architectural language.

Characteristics of Architecture Description Language

There is a large variety in ADLs developed by either academic or industrial groups. Many languages were not intended to be an ADL, but they turn out to be suitable for representing and analyzing an architecture. In principle ADLs differ from requirements languages, because ADLs are rooted in the solution space, whereas requirements describe problem spaces. They differ from programming languages, because ADLs do not bind architectural abstractions to specific point solutions. Modeling languages represent behaviors, where ADLs focus on representation of components. However, there are domain specific modeling languages (DSMLs) that focus on representation of components.

Minimal Requirements

The language must:

- Be suitable for communicating an architecture to all interested parties.

- Support the tasks of architecture creation, refinement and validation.

- Provide a basis for further implementation, so it must be able to add information to the ADL specification to enable the final system specification to be derived from the ADL.

- Provide the ability to represent most of the common architectural styles.

- Support analytical capabilities or provide quick generating prototype implementations.

ADLs have in common:

- Graphical syntax with often a textual form and a formally defined syntax and semantics.

- Features for modeling distributed systems.

- Little support for capturing design information, except through general purpose annotation mechanisms.

- Ability to represent hierarchical levels of detail including the creation of substructures by instantiating templates.

ADLs differ in their ability to:

- Handle real-time constructs, such as deadlines and task priorities, at the architectural level.

- Support the specification of different architectural styles. Few handle object oriented class inheritance or dynamic architectures.

- Support the analysis of the architecture.

- Handle different instantiations of the same architecture, in relation to product line architectures.

Positive Elements of ADL

- ADLs are a formal way of representing architecture.

- ADLs are intended to be both human and machine readable.

- ADLs support describing a system at a higher level than previously possible.

- ADLs permit analysis and assessment of architectures, for completeness, consistency, ambiguity, and performance.

- ADLs can support automatic generation of software systems.

Negative Elements of ADL

- There is no universal agreement on what ADLs should represent, particularly as regards the behavior of the architecture.

- Representations currently in use are relatively difficult to parse and are not supported by commercial tools.

- Most ADLs tend to be very vertically optimized toward a particular kind of analysis.

Common Concepts of Architecture

The ADL community generally agrees that Software Architecture is a set of components and the connections among them. But there are different kind of architectures like:

Object Connection Architecture

- Configuration consists of the interfaces and connections of an object-oriented system.

- Interfaces specify the features that must be provided by modules conforming to an interface.

- Connections represented by interfaces together with call graph.

- Conformance usually enforced by the programming language.

  - Decomposition — associating interfaces with unique modules.

  - Interface conformance — static checking of syntactic rules.

  - Communication integrity — visibility between modules.

Interface Connection Architecture

- Expands the role of interfaces and connections:

  - Interfaces specify both "required" and "provided" features.

  - Connections are defined between "required" features and "provided" features.

- Consists of interfaces, connections and constraints:

  - Constraints restrict behavior of interfaces and connections in an architecture.

  - Constraints in an architecture map to requirements for a system.

Most ADLs implement an interface connection architecture.

Architecture vs. Design

Architecture, in the context of software systems, is roughly divided into categories, primarily software architecture, network architecture, and systems architecture. Within each of these categories, there is a tangible but fuzzy distinction between architecture and design. To draw this distinction as universally and clearly as possible, it is best to consider design as a noun rather than as a verb, so that the comparison is between two nouns.

Design is the abstraction and specification of patterns and organs of functionality that have been or will be implemented. Architecture is a degree higher in both abstraction and granularity. Consequentially, architecture is also more topological in nature than design, in that it specifies where major components meet and how they relate to one another. Architecture focuses on the partitioning of major regions of functionality into high level components, where they will physically or virtually reside, what off-the-shelf components may be employed effectively, in general what interfaces each component will expose, what protocols will be employed between them, and what practices and high level patterns may best meet extensibility, maintainability, reliability, durability, scalability, and other non-functional objectives. Design is a detailing of these choices and a more concrete clarification of how functional requirements will be met through the delegation of pieces of that functionality to more granular components and how these smaller components will be organized within the larger ones.

Oftentimes, a portion of architecture is done during the conceptualization of an application, system, or network and may appear in the non-functional sections of requirement documentation. Canonically, design is not specified in requirements, but is rather driven by them.

The process of defining an architecture may involve heuristics, acquired by the architect or architectural team through experience within the domain. As with design, architecture often evolves through a series of iterations, and just as the wisdom of a high level design is often tested when low level design and implementation occurs, the wisdom of an architecture is tested during the specification of a high level design. In both cases, if the wisdom of the specification is called into question during detailing, another iteration of either architecture or design, as the case may be, may become necessary.

In summary, the primary differences between architecture and design are ones of granularity and abstraction, and (consequentially) chronology. (Architecture generally precedes design, although overlap and circular iteration is a common reality.)

View Model

A view model or viewpoints framework in systems engineering, software engineering, and enterprise engineering is a framework which defines a coherent set of views to be used in the construction of a system architecture, software architecture, or enterprise architecture. A view is a representation of a whole system from the perspective of a related set of concerns.

Since the early 1990s there have been a number of efforts to prescribe approaches for describing and analyzing system architectures. These recent efforts define a set of views (or viewpoints). They are sometimes referred to as architecture frameworks or enterprise architecture frameworks, but are usually called "view models".

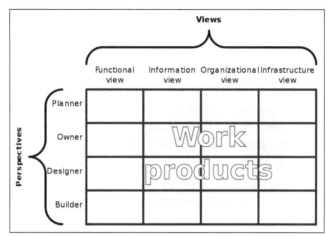

The TEAF Matrix of Views and Perspectives.

Usually a view is a work product that presents specific architecture data for a given system. However, the same term is sometimes used to refer to a view definition, including the particular viewpoint and the corresponding guidance that defines each concrete view. The term view model is related to view definitions.

The purpose of views and viewpoints is to enable humans to comprehend very complex systems, to organize the elements of the problem and the solution around domains of expertise and to separate concerns. In the engineering of physically intensive systems, viewpoints often correspond to capabilities and responsibilities within the engineering organization.

Most complex system specifications are so extensive that no single individual can fully comprehend all aspects of the specifications. Furthermore, we all have different interests in a given system and different reasons for examining the system's specifications. A business executive will ask different questions of a system make-up than would a system implementer. The concept of viewpoints framework, therefore, is to provide separate viewpoints into the specification of a given complex system in order to facilitate communication with the stakeholders. Each viewpoint satisfies an audience with interest in a particular set of aspects of the system. Each viewpoint may use a specific viewpoint language that optimizes the vocabulary and presentation for the audience of that viewpoint. Viewpoint modeling has become an effective approach for dealing with the inherent complexity of large distributed systems.

Architecture description practices, as described in IEEE Std 1471-2000, utilize multiple views to address several areas of concerns, each one focusing on a specific aspect of the system. Examples of architecture frameworks using multiple views include Kruchten's "4+1" view model, the Zachman Framework, TOGAF, DoDAF, and RM-ODP.

View Model Topics

View

A view of a system is a representation of the system from the perspective of a viewpoint. This viewpoint on a system involves a perspective focusing on specific concerns regarding the system, which suppresses details to provide a simplified model having only those elements related to the concerns of the viewpoint. For example, a security viewpoint focuses on security concerns and a security viewpoint model contains those elements that are related to security from a more general model of a system.

A view allows a user to examine a portion of a particular interest area. For example, an Information View may present all functions, organizations, technology, etc. that use a particular piece of information, while the Organizational View may present all functions, technology, and information of concern to a particular organization. In the Zachman Framework views comprise a group of work products whose development requires a particular analytical and technical expertise because they focus on either the "what," "how," "who," "where," "when," or "why" of the enterprise. For example, Functional View work products answer the question "how is the mission carried out?" They are most easily developed by experts in functional decomposition using process and activity modeling. They show the enterprise from the point of view of functions. They also may show organizational and information components, but only as they relate to functions.

Viewpoints

In systems engineering, a viewpoint is a partitioning or restriction of concerns in a system. Adoption of a viewpoint is usable so that issues in those aspects can be addressed separately. A good selection of viewpoints also partitions the design of the system into specific areas of expertise.

Viewpoints provide the conventions, rules, and languages for constructing, presenting and analysing views. In ISO/IEC 42010:2007 (IEEE-Std-1471-2000) a viewpoint is a specification for an individual view. A view is a representation of a whole system from the perspective of a viewpoint. A view may consist of one or more architectural models. Each such architectural model is developed using the methods established by its associated architectural system, as well as for the system as a whole.

Modeling Perspectives

Modeling perspectives is a set of different ways to represent pre-selected aspects of a system. Each perspective has a different focus, conceptualization, dedication and visualization of what the model is representing.

In information systems, the traditional way to divide modeling perspectives is to distinguish the structural, functional and behavioral/processual perspectives. This together with rule, object, communication and actor and role perspectives is one way of classifying modeling approaches.

Viewpoint Model

In any given viewpoint, it is possible to make a model of the system that contains only the objects that are visible from that viewpoint, but also captures all of the objects, relationships and constraints that are present in the system and relevant to that viewpoint. Such a model is said to be a viewpoint model, or a view of the system from that viewpoint.

A given view is a specification for the system at a particular level of abstraction from a given viewpoint. Different levels of abstraction contain different levels of detail. Higher-level views allow the engineer to fashion and comprehend the whole design and identify and resolve problems in the large. Lower-level views allow the engineer to concentrate on a part of the design and develop the detailed specifications.

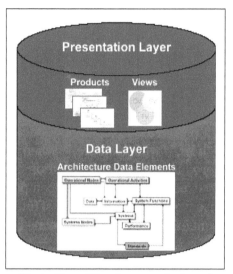

Illustration of the views, products and
data in Architecture Framework.

In the system itself, however, all of the specifications appearing in the various viewpoint models must be addressed in the realized components of the system. And the specifications for any given component may be drawn from many different viewpoints. On the other hand, the specifications induced by the distribution of functions over specific components and component interactions will typically reflect a different partitioning of concerns than that reflected in the original viewpoints. Thus additional viewpoints, addressing the concerns of the individual components and the bottom-up synthesis of the system, may also be useful.

Architecture Description

An architecture description is a representation of a system architecture, at any time, in terms of its component parts, how those parts function, the rules and constraints under which those parts function, and how those parts relate to each other and to the environment. In an architecture description the architecture data is shared across several views and products.

At the data layer are the architecture data elements and their defining attributes and relationships. At the presentation layer are the products and views that support a visual means to communicate and understand the purpose of the architecture, what it describes, and the various architectural analyses performed. Products provide a way for visualizing architecture data as graphical, tabular, or textual representations. Views provide the ability to visualize architecture data that stem across products, logically organizing the data for a specific or holistic perspective of the architecture.

Types of System View Models

Three-schema Approach

The Three-schema approach for data modeling, introduced in 1977, can be considered one of the first view models. It is an approach to building information systems and systems information management, that promotes the conceptual model as the key to achieving data integration. The Three schema approach defines three schemas and views:

- External schema for user views.

- Conceptual schema integrates external schemata.

- Internal schema that defines physical storage structures.

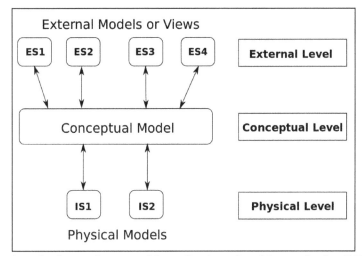

The notion of a three-schema model was first introduced in 1977 by the ANSI/X3/ SPARC three-level architecture, which determined three levels to model data.

At the center, the conceptual schema defines the ontology of the concepts as the users think of them and talk about them. The physical schema describes the internal formats of the data stored in the database, and the external schema defines the view of the data presented to the application programs. The framework attempted to permit multiple data models to be used for external schemata.

Over the years, the skill and interest in building information systems has grown tremendously. However, for the most part, the traditional approach to building systems has only focused on defining data from two distinct views, the "user view" and the "computer view". From the user view, which will be referred to as the "external schema," the definition of data is in the context of reports and screens designed to aid individuals in doing their specific jobs. The required structure of data from a usage view changes with the business environment and the individual preferences of the user. From the computer view, which will be referred to as the "internal schema," data is defined in terms of file structures for storage and retrieval. The required structure of data for computer storage depends upon the specific computer technology employed and the need for efficient processing of data.

4+1 View Model of Architecture

4+1 is a view model designed by Philippe Kruchten in 1995 for describing the architecture of software-intensive systems, based on the use of multiple, concurrent views. The views are used to describe the system in the viewpoint of different stakeholders, such as end-users, developers and project managers. The four views of the model are logical, development, process and physical view.

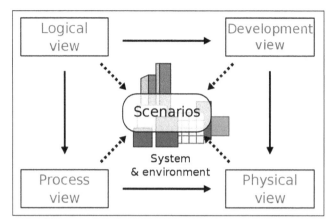

Illustration of the 4+1 view model or architecture.

The four views of the model are concerned with:

- Logical view is concerned with the functionality that the system provides to end-users.

- Development view illustrates a system from a programmers perspective and is concerned with software management.

- Process view deals with the dynamic aspect of the system, explains the system processes and how they communicate, and focuses on the runtime behavior of the system.

- Physical view depicts the system from a system engineer's point of view. It is concerned with the topology of software components on the physical layer, as well as communication between these components.

In addition selected use cases or scenarios are utilized to illustrate the architecture. Hence the model contains 4+1 views.

Software Architecture Recovery

Software architecture recovery is a set of methods for the extraction of architectural information from lower level representations of a software system, such as source code. The abstraction process to generate architectural elements frequently involves clustering source code entities (such as files, classes, functions etc.) into subsystems according to a set of criteria that can be application dependent or not. Architecture recovery from legacy systems is motivated by the fact that these systems do not often have an architectural documentation, and when they do, this documentation is many times out of synchronization with the implemented system. Software architecture recovery may be required as part of software retrofits.

Approaches

Most approaches to software architecture recovery has been exploring the static analysis of systems. When considering object-oriented software, which employs a lot of polymorphism and dynamic binding mechanisms, dynamic analysis becomes an essential technique to comprehend the system behavior, object interactions, and hence to reconstruct its architecture. In this work, the criteria used to determine how source code entities should be clustered in architectural elements are mainly based on the dynamic analysis of the system, taking into account the occurrences of interaction patterns and types (classes and interfaces) in use-case realizations.

General Methods for Software Architecture Recovery

Software architecture recovery is the process of inspecting software systems and ex- tracting representations of their artefacts (e.g., call graphs, file dependency graphs, etc.) for the purpose of documenting the software architecture. Software architecture recovery research has seen increased attention in the last few years from multiple perspectives. For example, an established body of work in this area flourishes in the form of EU projects such as REMICS4 and ARTIST5. Also, considerable standardisation efforts exist such as the OMG Architecture-Driven Modernisation taskforce. Finally, there has been research on discovering the Ground-Truth of architectures, such as Medvidovic et al.

Nevertheless, as recent results show, one limitation in the state of the art is that there is no single approach or technology that can be considered general, that is, systematically usable for recovering software architectures for any kind of system (e.g., a mission-critical system vs. an old web appli- cation), for any kind of purpose (e.g., for modernisation as opposed to re- documentation) or under any circumstance (e.g., without assuming artefacts other than sources).

What is more, most available approaches for software architecture recovery are inaccurate and frequently quite expensive. Furthermore, existing approaches do not provide a way to estimate the costs of the recovery effort so that an effective business case can be made, and an evaluation of expected ROI can be done. For these reasons, project managers are often hesitant to invest in such efforts. Finally, many existing approaches target just a single *view* of an architecture, for example a "component and connector" view of the running system, or a module view.

Here, we offer an architecture recovery approach that, basing its root around GT: (a) may be general by design; (b) can be made reliable at will, since it allows recovery of software architectures by construction from the very basic elements they represent (code artefacts, their structure, and modularisation), hence, multiple observers may be able to retrieve high-quality software architecture artefacts by triangulation, while the reliability of their observations can also be assessed with classical inter-coder reliability metrics; (c) can be, and in fact was, partially automated ; and whose *cost* can be estimated *up-front* and depends strictly on the number and size of artefacts for the system under analysis. This approach stems from an industrial research and development project called RTE6, recently unclassified by the European Space Agency (ESA). The key goal behind RTE was that of "delivering an effective round-trip engineering technology for heterogeneous legacy space software systems". As part of this project we elaborated an approach that combined: (a) Grounded Theory, the prince of Qualitative Re- search approaches; (b) Model-Driven Architecture (MDA) principles and tools, e.g., model transformation technology; and (c) reverse-engineering technology.

The key idea behind RTE is simple: manual inspection of code is unavoidable to retrieve high-ly-reliable, if not ground-truth software architectures but code, at its simplest, is nothing more than structured text embodying a theory. So, why not realise architecture recovery with a research method aimed at manual inspection and analysis of text and theory generation? This is where Grounded Theory (GT) comes into play. Grounded Theory is a systematic, incremental and iterative qualitative research methodology developed in the late 1960s and employed in many research domains, including software engineering. Granted, this approach is labor intensive; however, counterbalancing the cost are two benefits: a) we can accurately predict an upper bound on the expense, and b) we have techniques to help manage that expense.

The approach resulting from the RTE project came to be known as "Round- trip Engineering Methodology (REM)" and is the key contribution of this pa- per. The REM has many unique features: (a) may in fact be general - REM, following GT, makes no assumptions as to the nature of the text that needs to be analysed (e.g., in the scope of our project REM was applied to testing specifications as well as Java code) (b) REM involves the manual inspection of source code files using a structured GT methodology which is meant for the generation of a theory grounded in factual evidence and whose reliability can be increased with multiple observers by triangulation and assessed with classical inter rater reliability metrics; (c) REM can be, and was in fact, partially automated using MDA model transformation technology; (d) REM can be instrumented for cost-estimation which is required to build business cases around recovery expenses - REM could do this by associating an inspection cost with every source artefact available and evaluating analysis costs through GT phases. Several approaches exist to assist this estimation or to elaborate ad-hoc estimation techniques, e.g., by Thompson. Finally, REM does not substitute current analysis and reverse-engineering techniques. Rather, REM may be used in combination with approaches that provide a high-level view, or those that reverse-engineer code-level facts. Both of these provide a starting-point from which REM engineers can begin their reading of the code.

As a proof of concept to test the REM generality hypothesis, the method- ology was applied to a large mission-critical software system called FARC (File ARChive, part of the ESA MYCONYS Mission Control Software7). MY- CONYS provides a secure, highly available and dependable distributed file- system for all ESA stations (e.g., satellite observation posts or launching sites) across the world, and the data they produce and exchange.

Novelty, Limitations and Conclusions. As a result of the above proof- of-concept study, we argue that REM is a novel approach with profound potential. On one hand, we observed that the instruments we used to partially automate REM are sturdy and inextricably linked to the RTE scenario. On the other hand, we found that a measurable baseline needs to be created around approaches such as REM to provide quantification instruments for appraisal of precision, convenience, as well as testing the generality of the approach further. Finally, we recognise that the great potential of recovering highly-reliable soft- ware architectures comes at a great cost. Therefore, approaches such as REM should, for the moment, be considered as *last-resort* mechanisms, applicable wherefore all other approaches are inadequate. For example, our case study was a *last-resort* scenario, presented to us by ESA, where their heterogeneous code, operations, and maintenance scripts made all existing approaches infeasible. Similarly, the precision of approaches such as REM are still an open working hypothesis and seem to heavily depend by the case at hand.

In conclusion, this manuscript outlines and tests REM, a qualitative analysis- inspired semi-automated recovery approach. Although we claim that REM is a general approach, we cannot currently *prove* this yet. Rather, the industrial case study showcased in this manuscript shows that the approach does in fact *work* with no assumptions over systems under analysis and motivates further research in this direction to actually seize and demonstrate this opportunity towards generality. This paper is a humble bootstrap of the research line above; we offer a well-articulated but limited point of evidence that is consistent with our claim of generality, resting upon the foundations of GT.

GT-based Architecture Recovery

Grounded Theory

Grounded Theory is arguably the most widely-used and perhaps the most effective structured qualitative data analysis methodology ever created. GT was created by two researchers in sociology—Barney Glaser and Anselm Strauss— in late 1967. Although the method was initially designed for the analysis of structured text, recent evolutions and interpretations of the method have extended its usage to video, audio, web and other forms of content. GT is generally split into three phases:

Open Coding: during this phase the primary sources of data (usually text or qualitative data of some sort) are read or viewed and each portion of the text is constantly compared to "codes", i.e. labels for portions of text that represent the concepts expressed. For example, some source code or a code-inspection report discussing code review results may be labelled with the code "COD-REV" or several portions of the same code might be labelled with: (a) "REV-CONT" for content of the review, (b) with "REV-METH" for the method of the review, and so on. This process is known as text micro- analysis. If the elements in the text express concepts that cannot be mapped to an existing code, then an additional code is created. Moreover, the researcher applying the method is constantly noting down observations in the form of "memos", i.e. brief textual notes describing an idea or observation made on the data so far or on the portion of text just analysed. Following our code review example, for the "REV-METH" code researchers may note in a memo that these reviews seem to follow a similar method for interfaces and a slightly different method for private classes. This process of memoing is constant; for example, when new codes are created memos capture the rationale for creation. The end result of open coding is a set of categories, creating a taxonomy of codes.

Selective Coding: during this phase the codes are constantly compared with each other (rather than with other pieces of data) until the categories are saturated into clusters of core-categories. For example, the code category "REV-METH" is merged with category "REV-LIST-TYP" that identifies the types of code review guidelines applied in review exercises. Both codes are merged into a core-category of "REVIEW- PERF" identifying the prerequisites for performing code reviews. This process is typically instrumental to devise relations between two or more categories. For example, notice the relation between "REV-METH" and "REV-LIST- TYP". This is a process of selection of the core elements that the analyst can identify, but the process is also guided by the entity of merged concepts. The biggest and "denser" clusters of codes are usually selected first, since they clearly represent valuable clusters.

Theoretical Coding: during this phase the codes and core-categories are sorted and tentatively modelled (a process sometimes known as Theoretical Modelling). A Grounded Theory is generated by letting it emerge from one (or more) theory views or available data models, usually by observation, e.g., through theory-inference focus groups. For example, a focus-group of expert code reviewers may visually inspect, confirm, and refine all the relations inferred by researchers through open- and selective-coding.

Alternatively, the theory is "forced" by comparison with an initial set of hypotheses. For example, researchers may have previously generated a series of hypotheses regarding what they expect to find in code reviews. These hypotheses can then be tested against the generated theory.

At this point, one might consider applying further analysis techniques, such as the 6C causality modelling framework for GT, where six types of codes (Context, Cause, Consequence, Contingency, Covariance, Conditions) are tentatively related together to infer causal relations.

Figure shows the series of steps to be applied sequentially and iteratively as part of a GT-based analysis. Essentially, observers of a phenomenon are required to label any piece of evidence with a label, indicating the meaning of that piece of evidence (e.g., a method call, an entire method, an entire Java Class, depending on the desired accuracy – a class could be labelled with class purpose or functional role). These labels can then be analysed and clustered according to the emergent categorization. Subsequently, codes can be merged, e.g., according to semantic similarity principles. As labels (or better, codes) are merged, categories become enriched with further details (e.g., some labels likely become properties of some others and so on). Moreover, in the shift from open to selective coding, patterns are discovered across categories (e.g., recurrent categories of sections of source code may denote a type of software component). The goal of selective coding is to relate categories together until there are no other additional possible relations to be discovered. The process to be followed is reflected in figure.

In summary, GT is not just a "qualitative data analysis method" - GT encompasses all phases of the research from sampling and data collection up to theory building, rather than simply data analysis. With reference to Peter Naur's "Programming as Theory Building" , we conjecture that a software system is a theory about how it is constructed, structured, and operates. GT offers us a method that allows that theory to spontaneously "emerge" from data, using close reading, analysis, and repeated abstraction. A key tenet of GT is that "All is Data" - meaning that GT procedures can be applied to any phenomena under study - typically interviews or interview transcripts, but also recordings, documentation, or in the case of this work, program source code, operations scripts, deployment assets, configuration management, and more. The insight underlying the REM method is that the theory of a software system, i.e., its software architecture, the guiding principles underlying its design, can be discovered or recovered by applying GT as a "recovery" research method.

REM Method Outline

Because GT lends itself well to qualitative-quantitative analyses and theory-building exercises, it can flexibly be applied to most if not all cases of theory-recovery exercises including software architecture recovery. This section maps GT onto REM for software architecture recovery. To devise a method featuring GT for architecture recovery, a necessary first step is to examine the definition of software architecture. Paraphrasing from: "Software architecture is an abstraction of a software system comprising its elements, their externally visible properties, their relations, and the choices that led to the system and its parts".

Software architecture, according to this definition, means:

- The set of architecture elements (i.e., the set of components and connectors that are the essential parts of a software architecture specification).

- Their visible properties (i.e., the important attributes of these elements).

- The set of relations across architecture elements.

- The abstractions realised by these architecture elements.

- The set of choices that led to those elements, relations and properties.

General architecture recovery thus amounts to: Recovery of software architecture for any software scenario, under any circumstance, with the sole assumption that source artefacts for the software to be analysed are available and analysable by means of visual inspection, possibly assisted by reverse-engineering and other tools.

Using these axioms as a basis, REM allows us to recover items 1, 3 and 4 of the above, while partially aiding in the elaboration of items 2 and 5.

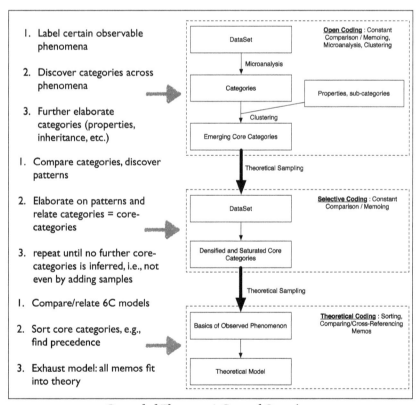

Grounded Theory – A General Overview.

REM recovers architecture elements by systematically coding the entire set of available system artefacts. To bootstrap the coding, an initial set of codes (referred to as GT-codes from now on, to avoid confusion with actual software code) is inferred from whatever architecture knowledge is available. In our case, we used concerns that originally drove the creation of the project under study—the FARC. Notwithstanding, a classical Grounded Theory methodology may also be applied without an initial set of GT-codes. For example, a pilot study on random areas of code or a reduced data sample may be used to generate an initial GT-codes list.

A key principle to drive this direct investigation is to visually inspect and label source elements following the exact order with which the operational system is built and deployed. This principle serves two purposes: (a) the build order is an expression of the dependencies that the software architecture has to uphold - architecture recovery efforts, therefore, need to elicit independent components and middleware (which are black-boxes in the architecture being recovered) before their dependent counterparts; (b) also, the build order allows for traceability of the recovered software architecture to make sure it is, in fact, reliably reflecting reality; this may not include all modules in the source code.

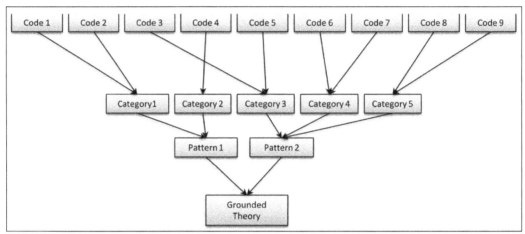

Grounded Theory in Practice, Discovering Patterns.

For example, assume you want to recover a modern cloud application X whose build and deploy script is specified in TOSCA, i.e., the standard "Topology and Orchestration Specification for Cloud Applications". A valuable starting code-list may be inferred from the TOSCA specification itself, while the TOSCA blueprint for application X is most definitely the starting point for an architecture recovery exercise.

REM is arranged into four stages:

- GT-Coding and Micro-Analysis: This stage features the use of GT-codes as part of micro-analysis of source elements. The goal of this stage is to label source elements using GT-codes (e.g., assuming reverse-engineering to UML class or composite structure diagrams is possible, GT-codes can be expressed as stereotypes in a UML architecture recovery profile). Also, following the classical GT process, the stage includes the incremental refinement of the GT-codes profile with insights, relations and memos learned iteratively from stage A). For example, the use of UML can help ensure code coverage (i.e., allowing analysts to know what is being recovered, and where, across the system). Also, along with the use of UML to represent source code artefacts, a UML profile can contain GT-codes in the form of UML stereotypes. Profiles also make it easier to elaborate stereotype relations and characteristics as the GT process unfolds. The stage is iterated upon until no unlabelled source element exists;

- GT-codes Categorisation: this stage features an analysis of codes as part of UML profiles, and potentially partially automated) from stage A) via the constant-comparison principle. The goal is to generate "saturated" categories, i.e., including as many GT-codes as possible;

- Recovery of Architecture Elements: this stage features an analysis to understand structural decomposition relations *across* categories and core- categories generated as part of GT, to identify architectural concepts;

- Theoretical Coding of Relations and High-Level Abstraction: this stage features a step of constant observations and comparisons that produces the software architecture abstractions we seek. For example, UML can be used to instrument an instance of the above GT process that can be partially automated with model-to-model transformation to search recurrent clusters and interfaces to produce a corresponding UML component diagram and/or a composite-structure diagram. By enacting this process we discover any orphan elements or ambiguities.

GT-coding and Micro-analysis

REM begins by elaborating an initial list of GT-codes, using architecture knowledge elicited from existing documents, or by conducting a pilot study. Micro-analysis consists of visually inspecting every source element, analysing and establishing the source element's role as part of the system. The goal of this analysis is to label every artefact (an entire Java class, for example) that reflects a concern or a function. As part of this process, analysts are required to annotate source elements with "memos"—notes about possible structural decomposition properties or other characteristics typical of software architecture (e.g., modularization). In our case-study, for example, the REM GT-coding list started from a list of seven stakeholder concerns that drove the de- sign and implementation of FARC years before (e.g., front-end decoupling, availability, etc.). Using these seven concerns as initial GT-codes we started a micro-analysis of the available software code artefacts (which we call source elements from now on).

In addition, as part of REM GT-codes definition, every GT-code includes a mnemonic aid identifying its meaning.

As previously stated, to aid the application of GT-codes throughout micro- analysis of reverse-engineered diagrams, GT-codes are realised as diagrams themselves. This aids REM in four ways: (a) GT-codes are easily applicable to reverse-engineered source elements in the form of diagram objects; (b) memos are more easily assignable to GT-coded source elements, e.g., as tagged values for defined stereotypes; (c) relations among GT-codes are easily captured in the diagram; (d) the profiles and annotations may be studied for further modernisation.

GT-codes Categorisation and Recovery of Architecture Elements

Categorisation of GT-codes starts immediately after the first pass of micro-analysis coding is complete (i.e., after the phenomena are "labelled"—the topmost step 1 on figure). This pass typically generates hundreds of GT-codes (302 distinct labels, in our case). The REM categorisation step is conducted incrementally on these GT-codes, iteratively moving back and forth between the two artefacts involved, in our case: (a) the UML profiles containing REM GT-codes (to visually spot relations); and (b) the GT-coded source elements (to confirm the relations).

Also, during categorisation, the notion of architecture elements begins to emerge. In essence, the categorisation step uses memos—annotations on the possible structural decomposition and characteristics of the system for the purpose of formulating modularity and decomposition hypotheses for analysed source elements (step 1 of "Selective Coding" in figure). These hypotheses are then confirmed or disproved by again inspecting the related source elements (step 2 of "Selective

Coding" in figure). This approach is consistent with identifying what Baldwin and Clark call design rules, i.e., decisions that decouple architectural elements into related but independent modules. Note that this approach can benefit from automation beyond what REM offers in its purest form, e.g., by using architectural analysis tools such as Titan.

The resulting process of categorisation (step 3 of "Selective Coding" in figure. Concludes when: (a) no additional decomposition and modularity hypotheses can be formulated, and (b) there are no more memos left to aid hypotheses formulation.

The core-categories distilled in the process above match the definition of architecture elements, since they represent the sets of source elements clustered by semantic similarity and matched by design rules. In other words, they are the core parts of the system that cannot be further abstracted.

Theoretical Coding: Recovering Relations and High-level Abstraction

The theoretical coding part of REM features the tool- assisted creation of a structural decomposition of the software architecture. Following the architecture-driven modernisation standard, this view was realised, in our case study, using a UML 2.x component diagram and its creation was aided by model-transformation. For example, in our proof-of-concept application of REM, a series of 4 model transformations were sufficient for this purpose and acted jointly as follows:

- Produce a UML package with one distinct package per core-category elicited during Selective Coding.

- Produce a UML component diagram containing a component for every Core-Category.

- Build relations in the component diagram across components that: (a) reflect Core-Categories with memoed and coded relations to other core-categories that emerged during GT-coding; (b) reflect relations found among code-constructs during reverse-engineering.

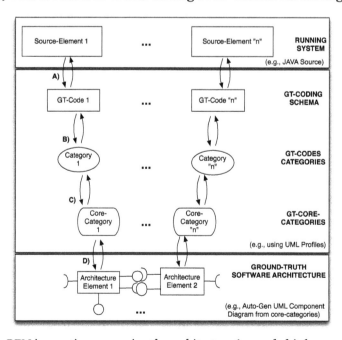

REM in practice, recovering the architecture (grounded-) theory.

- Produce interfaces for components that reflect Core-Categories grounded in source elements that identify system end-points by design (e.g., interfaces have public methods only).

Reapplying REM

In summary, the REM methodology is depicted in figure above. The methodology can be summarised in compacted form as the incremental workflow of the following steps:

- [OPTIONAL] Elaborate initial GT-codes list, e.g., using ancestral architecture knowledge elicited from existing documents or conducting a pilot study:

  ○ Use the GT-codes list to label reverse-engineered source elements, starting from program build artefacts.

  ○ Augment list containing codes with memos, i.e., code-inspection in- sights learned iteratively from step A).

  ○ Repeat until no further source element exists.

- Analyse codes via the constant-comparison principle - the goal is to generate saturated categories encompassing all GT-codes.

- Analyse saturated categories via constant-comparison and pattern- matching principles - the goal is to generate saturated clusters of saturated categories.

Software Architecture Erosion

Software architecture erosion refers to the gap between the planned and actual architecture of a software system as observed in its implementation. Architecture erosion is a common and recurring problem faced by Agile development teams. Unfortunately, the process of solving this problem is usually ad hoc or very manual, without adequate visibility at the architecture level. One effective solution is the reflexion model technique. The technique is a lightweight way of comparing high-level architecture models with the actual source code implementation while also specifying and checking architectural constraints. The diagram below is an example of the reflexion model technique.

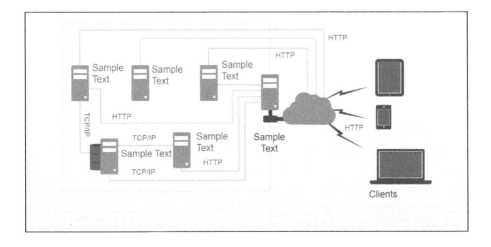

Architecture erosion can result in lower quality, increased complexity, and harder-to-maintain software. As these changes happen, it becomes more and more difficult to understand the originally planned software architecture. This is particularly important in an Agile environment where, according to the Agile Manifesto, working software is valued over comprehensive documentation and responding to change is valued over following a plan. In reality, this means that the architecture is evolving as the software is evolving. Therefore, the software changes need special attention (architectural assessment) from software architects. If this does not happen, the architecture could erode or become overly complex. Uncontrolled growth of a software system can lead to architectural issues that are difficult and expensive to fix.

Avoiding Architecture Erosion

Architecture erosion can be avoided or corrected by continuously monitoring and improving the software. Continuous checking of the implemented architecture against the intended architecture is a good strategy for detecting software erosion. Once architectural issues have been found, refactoring should be used to fix them. In an Agile environment, you should combine development activities with lightweight continuous architectural improvement to avoid or reverse architecture erosion. The process of continuous architectural improvement can be broken down into four steps:

- Architecture Assessment:
  - Identify architecture smells and design problems.
  - Create a list of identified architectural issues.
- Prioritization:
  - Decide the order in which the architectural issues will be tackled starting with strategic design issues or high-importance requirements first.
- Selection:
  - Choose the appropriate refactoring pattern to fix the issue. If none exist, create your own.
- Test:
  - Make sure the behaviors of the system did not change.
  - Update the architecture assessment to make sure you fixed the design problems and did not introduce new issues. A lightweight reflexion technique tool like Lattix Architect can make this process easier.

This is particularly useful in Agile development. In a Scrum environment, architecture refactoring should be integrated into Sprints by adding time for refactoring both code and architecture. During the Sprint, architects need to check their architecture, while testers and product owners should validate the system still meets requirements. Architecture refactoring should be done once during a Sprint as opposed to code refactoring, which should be done daily. If it is done less often, fixing architectural issues involves more time and complexity as more code changes are added on top of design issues. If done more often, the architecture could change needlessly and add to software complexity. Architectural problems not solved in a current Sprint should be saved and maintained in a backlog.

References

- Architectural-description, computer-science, topics: sciencedirect.com, Retrieved 13 March, 2019

- Woods, E.; Hilliard, R. (2005). "Architecture Description Languages in Practice Session Report". 5th Working IEEE/IFIP Conference on Software Architecture (WICSA'05). P. 243. Doi:10.1109/WICSA.2005.15. ISBN 978-0-7695-2548-8

- General-methods-for-software-architecture-recovery-a-potential-approach-and-its-evaluation: researchgate. net, Retrieved 14 April, 2019

- Li, J.; Pilkington, N. T.; Xie, F.; Liu, Q. (2010). "Embedded architecture description language". Journal of Systems and Software. 83 (2): 235. Citeseerx 10.1.1.134.8898. Doi:10.1016/j.jss.2009.09.043

- Architecture-erosion-in-agile-development: dzone.com, Retrieved 15 May, 2019

Software Architecture Description Languages

4

- **Architecture Analysis & Design Language**

- **Dually**

- **EAST-ADL**

- **Darwin**

- **ERIL**

- **Real Time Object Oriented Modeling**

- **Wright**

- **Unified Modeling Language**

The computer language which is used to create a description of a software architecture is known as an architecture description language. Some of the popular languages are DUALLy, EAST-ADL, Darwin, Unified Modeling Language and ERIL. This chapter discusses in detail these architectural description languages to provide a thorough understanding of the subject.

Architecture Description Languages (ADLs) are computer languages describing the software and hardware architecture of a system. The description may cover software features such as processes, threads, data, and subprograms as well as hardware component such as processors, devices, buses, and memory. The connections between the components can be described in logical as well as physical terms.

The difference between an ADL and a programming language or a modelling language is not totally clear. There are some requirements for a language to be classified as an ADL:

- It should be suitable for communicating architecture to all interested parties.

- It should support the tasks of architecture creation, refinement and validation.

- It should provide a basis for further implementation, so it must be able to add information to the ADL specification to enable the final system specification to be derived from the ADL.

- It should provide the ability to represent most of the common architectural styles.

- It should support analytical capabilities or provide quick generating prototype implementations.

Most ADLs have some common features:

- They have a graphical syntax as well a formally defined syntax and semantics.

- They often have features for modeling distributed systems.

- Little support for capturing design information, except through general purpose annotation mechanisms.

- They often have ability to represent hierarchical levels of detail including the creation of substructures by instantiating templates.

ADLs have several advantages as well as disadvantages. One advance is that they are designed to represent architectures in a formal way. Another advantage is that they often are designed to be readable to both human and machines. A disadvantage is that there is not yet an agreement of what the ADLs shall represent, especially when it comes to the behaviour of the system.

A system is constituted by components. These components can be defined on a high or low level. For instance, a GPS receiver can be modelled as a simple device that on request returns the current longitude, latitude, and altitude. On the other hand, it can be modelled as a complex component with every part explicitly described. The designer can start by defining a rough model at a high level and then incrementally refine the model.

Most ADLs support aggregation; that is, one component can encapsulate other components. A common concept among ADLs is the division of a component into interface and implementation. The interface is the connection of the component to other component, such as ports. The implementation takes care of the intern parts of the component. The concept is similar to interfaces and classes in Java.

Languages

There are a lot of languages designed to address the problems of modelling a system. Some of them are described here.

Architecture Analysis and Design Language

The Architecture Analysis & Design Language (AADL) is an architecture description language standardized by SAE. AADL was first developed in the field of avionics, and was known formerly as the Avionics Architecture Description Language.

The Architecture Analysis & Design Language is derived from MetaH, an architecture description language made by the Advanced Technology Center of Honeywell. AADL is used to model the software and hardware architecture of an embedded, real-time system. Due to its emphasis on the embedded domain, AADL contains constructs for modeling both software and hardware components (with the hardware components named "execution platform" components within the standard). This architecture model can then be used either as a design documentation, for analyses (such as schedulability and flow control) or for code generation (of the software portion), like UML.

AADL Eco-system

AADL is defined by a core language that defines a single notation for both system and software aspects. Having a single model ease the analysis tools by having only one single representation of the system. The language specifies system-specific characteristics using properties.

The language can be extended with the following methods:

- User-defined properties: user can extend the set of applicable properties and add their own to specify their own requirements.

- Language annexes: the core language is enhanced by annex languages that enrich the architecture description. For now, the following annexes have been defined:

  - Behavior annex: add components behavior with state machines.

  - Error-model annex: specifies fault and propagation concerns.

  - ARINC653 annex: defines modelling patterns for modelling avionics system.

  - Data-Model annex: describes the modelling of specific data constraint with AADL.

AADL Tools

AADL is supported by a wide range of tools:

- OSATE that includes a modeling platform, a graphical viewer and a constraint query languages.

- Ocarina, an AADL toolchain for generating code from models.

- TASTE toolchain supported by the European Space Agency.

DUALLy

DUALLy is an MDE framework to create interoperability among Architecture Description Languages (ADLs). It is developed at the Computer Science Department of the University of L'Aquila. DUALLy enables the transformation of a model conforming to a specific architecture description language into corresponding models conforming to other architecture description languages.

Interoperability

Supporting ADLs interoperability and change propagation is intrinsically complex. Furthermore, the lack of automation does not allow the easy addition of new description languages, and does not guarantee change propagation to multiple models in a finite number of steps. In general, changes occurring in an architecture model have a strong impact on all the other related architecture models (each of them possibly conforming to different architecture description languages). In order to keep models in a consistent state, changes need to be propagated from the updated model to all the others. When dealing with multiple architecture description languages, propagating changes may be a complex task; such a task is inevitable and requires to be managed by a dedicated approach.

In DUALLy, the interoperability among various architecture description languages is ensured via model transformation techniques. Instead of creating a point-to-point relationship among all languages, DUALLY defines the transformations among architecture description languages by passing through A0, which is a core set of architectural concepts defined as generally as possible (to potentially represent and support any kind of architectural representation) and extensible (in order to add domain specificities). In other words, A0 acts as a bridge among the different architectural languages to be related together. The star architecture of DUALLy enables an agile and easy integration of architecture description languages. The DUALLy transformation system is made of a series of model-to-model transformations that enable information migration among architecture models. These model-to-model transformations are constructed automatically by executing higher-order transformations (i.e., transformations taking other transformations as input or producing other transformations as output).

While DUALLy transforms a model into any other by passing first through an A0 model, model changes are propagated accordingly first to the A0 model and successively forwarded to any other architectural model (it has to be noted that the obtained result is independent from the order followed in the forwarding). Under the assumption that concurrent modifications to different models cannot apply, the DUALLY architecture ensures the convergence of the change propagation process, that is, it ensures by construction that a modification of a model within the network is propagated to all the other models in a finite number of steps.

EAST-ADL

EAST-ADL is an Architecture Description Language (ADL) for automotive embedded systems, developed in several European research projects. It is designed to complement AUTOSAR with descriptions at higher level of abstractions. Aspects covered by EAST-ADL include vehicle features, functions, requirements, variability, software components, hardware components and communication.

EAST-ADL is a domain-specific language using meta-modeling constructs such as classes, attributes, and relationships. It is based on concepts from UML, SysML and AADL, but adapted for automotive needs and compliance with AUTOSAR. There is an EAST-ADL UML2 profile which is used in UML2 tools for user modeling.

The EAST-ADL definition also serves as the specification for implementation in domain-specific tools.

EAST-ADL contains several abstraction levels. The software- and electronics-based functionality of the vehicle are described at different levels of abstraction. The proposed abstraction levels and the contained elements provide a separation of concerns and an implicit style for using the modeling elements. The embedded system is complete on each abstraction level, and parts of the model are linked with various traceability relations. This makes it possible to trace an entity from feature down to components in hardware and software.

EAST-ADL is defined with the development of safety-related embedded control systems as a benchmark. The EAST-ADL scope comprises support for the main phases of software development, from early analysis via functional design to the implementation and back to integration and validation on vehicle level. The main role of EAST-ADL is that of providing an integrated system model. On this basis, several concerns are addressed:

- Documentation, in terms of an integrated system model.

- Communication between engineers, by providing predefined views as well as related information.

- Analysis, through the description of system structure and properties.

Behavioural models for simulation or code generation are supported as references from EAST-ADL functions to external models, such as a subsystem in MATLAB/Simulink.

Organisation of EAST-ADL Meta-model

The EAST-ADL meta-model is organized according to 4 abstraction levels:

- Vehicle level contains modeling elements to represent intended functionality in a solution-independent way.

- Analysis level represents the abstract functional decomposition of the vehicle with the principal internal and external interfaces.

- Design level has the detailed functional definition, a hardware architecture and allocations of functions to hardware.

- Implementation level relies on AUTOSAR elements and does not have EAST-ADL-specific constructs for the core structure.

For all abstraction levels, relevant extension elements for requirements, behavior, variability and dependability are associated to the core structure.

Relation between EAST-ADL and AUTOSAR

Instead of providing modeling entities for the lowest abstraction level, i.e. implementation level, EAST-ADL uses unmodified AUTOSAR entities for this purpose and provides means to link EAST-ADL elements on higher abstraction levels to AUTOSAR elements. Thus, EAST-ADL and AUTOSAR in concert provide means for efficient development and management of the complexity of automotive embedded systems from early analysis right down to implementation. Concepts from model-based development and component-based development reinforce one another. An early, high-level representation of the system can evolve seamlessly into the detailed specifications of the AUTOSAR language. In addition, the EAST-ADL incorporates the following system development concerns:

- Modeling of requirements and verification/validation information.

- Feature modeling and support for software system product lines.

- Modeling of variability of the system design.

- Structural and behavioral modeling of functions and hardware entities in the context of distributed systems.

- Environment, i.e., plant model and adjacent systems.

- Non-functional operational properties such as a definition of function timing and failure modes, supporting system level analysis.

The EAST-ADL metamodel is specified according to the same rules as the AUTOSAR metamodel, which means that the two sets of elements can co-exist in the same model. The dependency is unidirectional from EAST-ADL to AUTOSAR, such that AUTOSAR is independent of EAST-ADL. However, relevant EAST-ADL elements can reference AUTOSAR elements to provide EAST-ADL support for requirements, variability, safety, etc. to the AUTOSAR domain.

A model may thus be defined where AUTOSAR elements represent the software architecture and EAST-ADL elements extend the AUTOSAR model with orthogonal aspects and represents abstract system information through e.g. function and feature models. Such model can be defined in UML, by applying both an EAST-ADL profile and an AUTOSAR profile, or in a domain specific tool based on a merged AUTOSAR and EAST-ADL metamodel.

Modeling Tools and File Format

EAST-ADL tool support is still limited, although a UML profile is available and domain specific tools such as MentorGraphics VSA, MetaCase MetaEdit+ and Systemite SystemWeaver have been tailored for EAST-ADL in the context of research projects and with customers. Papyrus UML, extended within the ATESST project as a concept demonstrator has EAST-ADL support, and MagicDraw, can also provide EAST-ADL palettes, diagrams, etc. In the case of UML, developers also need to have knowledge of UML (classes, stereotypes, arrow types.) for modeling with EAST-ADL. Many automotive engineers, in particular mechanical engineers, hardware developers, process experts) do not have this knowledge and prefer other approaches. EATOP is an upcoming initiative to make an Eclipse-based implementation of the EAST-ADL meta-model.

An XML-based exchange format, EAXML, allows tools to exchange EAST-ADL models. The EAXML schema is autogenerated from the EAST-ADL metamodel according to the same principles as the AUTOSAR ARXML schema. Currently, the exchange format is supported by the EAST-ADL prototype of Mentor Graphics VSA, MetaEdit+ and SystemWeaver. For UML tooling, it is possible to exchange models using XMI, subject to the XMI compatibility between tools.

Darwin

Darwin is an architecture description language (ADL). It can be used in a software engineering context to describe the organisation of a piece of software in terms of components, their interfaces and the bindings between components.

Darwin encourages a component- or object-based approach to program structuring in which the unit of structure (the component) hides its behaviour behind a well-defined interface. Programs are constructed by creating instances of component types and binding their interfaces together. Darwin considers such compositions also to be types and hence encourages hierarchical composition. The general form of a Darwin program is therefore the tree in which the root and all intermediate nodes are composite components; the leaves are primitive components encapsulating behavioural as opposed to structural aspects.

ERIL

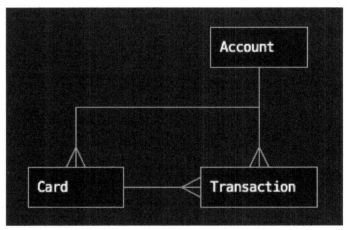

An example ERIL diagram with 3 classes and 3 one-to-many relationships.

ERIL (Entity-Relationship and Inheritance Language) is a visual language for representing the data structure of a computer system. As its name suggests, ERIL is based on entity-relationship diagrams and class diagrams. ERIL combines the relational and object-oriented approaches to data modeling.

ERIL can be seen as a set of guidelines aimed at improving the readability of structure diagrams. These guidelines were borrowed from DRAKON, a variant of flowcharts created within the Russian space program. ERIL itself was developed by Stepan Mitkin.

The ERIL guidelines for drawing diagrams:

- Lines must be straight, either strictly vertical or horizontal.

- Vertical lines mean ownership (composition).

- Horizontal lines mean peer relationships (aggregation).

- Line intersections are not allowed.

- It is not recommended to fit the whole data model on a single diagram. Draw many simple diagrams instead.

- The same class (table) can appear several times on the same diagram.

- Use the following standard symbols to indicate the type of the relationship:
  - One-to-one: a simple line.
  - One-to-many, two-way: a line with a "paw".
  - One-to-many, one-way: an arrow.
  - Many-to-many: a line with two "paws".
- Do not lump together inheritance and data relationships.

Indexes

A class (table) in ERIL can have several indexes. Each index in ERIL can include one or more fields, similar to indexes in relational databases. ERIL indexes are logical. They can optionally be implemented by real data structures.

Links

Links between classes (tables) in ERIL are implemented by the so-called "link" fields. Link fields can be of different types according to the link type:

- Reference;
- Collection of references.

Example: there is a one-to-many link between Documents and Lines. One Document can have many Lines. Then the Document.Lines field is a collection of references to the lines that belong to the document. Line.Document is a reference to the document that contains the line.

Link fields are also logical. They may or may not be implemented physically in the system.

Usage

ERIL is supposed to model any kind of data regardless of the storage. The same ERIL diagram can represent data stored in a relational database, in a NoSQL database, XML file or in the memory.

ERIL diagrams serve two purposes. The primary purpose is to explain the data structure of an existing or future system or component. The secondary purpose is to automatically generate source code from the model. Code that can be generated includes specialized collection classes, hash and comparison functions, data retrieval and modification procedures, SQL data-definition code, etc. Code generated from ERIL diagrams can ensure referential and uniqueness data integrity. Serialization code of different kinds can also be automatically generated. In some ways ERIL can be compared to object-relational mapping frameworks.

Real Time Object Oriented Modeling

ROOM was developed in the early 1990s for modeling Real-time systems. The initial focus was on telecommunications, even though ROOM can be applied to any event-driven real-time system.

ROOM was supported by ObjecTime Developer (commercial) and is now implemented by the official Eclipse project eTrice.

When UML2 was defined (version 2 of UML with real time extensions), many elements of ROOM were taken over.

Concepts and Key Notions of ROOM

ROOM is a modeling language for the definition of software systems. It allows the complete code generation for the whole system from the model. ROOM comes with a textual as well as with a graphical notation. Typically the generated code is accompanied with manually written code, e.g. for graphical user interfaces (GUI). The code is compiled and linked against a runtime library which provides base classes and basic services (e.g. messaging).

ROOM describes a software system along three dimensions: structure, behavior and inheritance.

Structure

The structural view in ROOM is composed of actors or capsules. Actors can communicate with each other using ports. Those ports are connected by bindings. Actors do exchange messages asynchronously via ports and bindings. To each port a unique protocol is assigned. A protocol in ROOM defines a set of outgoing and a set of incoming messages. Ports can be connected with a binding if they belong to the same protocol and are conjugate to each other. That means that one port is sending the outgoing messages of the protocol and receiving the incoming ones. This port is called the regular port. Its peer port, the conjugated port, receives the outgoing messages and sends the incoming ones of the protocol. In other words, a port is the combination of a required and a provided interface in a role (since one and the same protocol can be used by several ports of an actor).

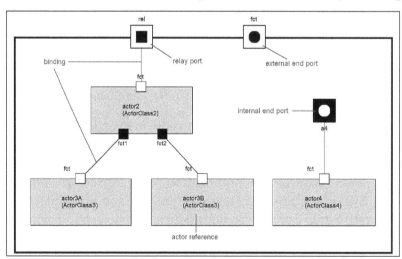

Example of a structure diagram.

An actor can contain other actors (as a composition). In ROOM these are called *actor references* or *actor refs* for short. This allows to create structural hierarchies of arbitrary depth.

The actor's ports can be part of its interface (visible from the exterior) or part of its structure (used by itself) or both. Ports that are part of the interface only are called relay ports. They are directly connected to a port of a sub actor (they are delegating to the sub actor). Ports that are part of the structure only are called internal end ports. Ports that belong to both, structure and interface, are called external end ports.

Behavior

Each actor in ROOM has a behavior which is defined by means of a hierarchical finite-state machine, or just state machine for short. A state machine is a directed graph consisting of nodes called states and edges called transitions. State transitions are triggered by incoming messages from an internal or external end port. In this context the messages sometimes are also called events or signals. If a transition specifies a certain trigger then it is said to fire if the state machine is in the source state of the transition and a message of the type specified by the trigger arrives. Afterwards the state is changed to the target state of the transition.

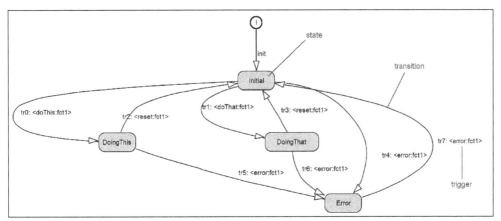

ROOM behavior diagramm (state machine as a state chart).

During the state change certain pieces of code are executed. The programmer (or modeler) can attach them to the states and transitions. In ROOM this code is written in the so called *detail level language*, usually the target language of the code generation. A state can have *entry code* and *exit code*. During a state change first the exit code of the source state is executed. Then the *action code* of the firing transition is executed and finally the entry code of the target state. A typical part of those codes is the sending of messages through ports of the actor. State machines in ROOM also have a graphical notation similar to the UML state charts. A state machine can also have a hierarchy in the sense that states can have sub state machines. Similar to the structure this can be extended to arbitrary depth.

An important concept in the context of state machines is the execution model of *run-to-completion*. That means that an actor is processing a message completely before it accepts the next message. Since the run-to-completion semantics is guaranteed by the execution environment, the programmer/modeler doesn't have to deal with classical thread synchronization. And this despite the fact that typical ROOM systems are highly concurrent because of the asynchronous communication. And maybe its worth to stress that the asynchronous nature of ROOM systems is not by accident but reflects the inherent asynchronicity of e.g. the machine being controlled by the software. Definitely this requires another mind set than the one that is needed for functional programming of synchronous systems. But after a short while of getting accustomed it will be evident that asynchronously communicating state machines are perfectly suited for control software.

Inheritance

Like other object oriented programming languages ROOM uses the concept of classes. Actors are classes which can be instantiated as objects several times in the system. Of course each instance of an actor class is in its own state and can communicate with other instances of the same (and other) classes.

Similar to other modern programming languages ROOM allows inheritance of actor classes. It is a single inheritance as an actor class can be derived from another actor class (its *base class*). It inherits all features of the base class like ports and actor refs, but also the state machine. The derived actor class can add further states and transitions to the inherited one.

Layering

A last powerful concept of ROOM is layering. This notion refers to the vertical layers of a software system consisting of services and their clients. ROOM introduces the notions of service access point (SAP) for the client side and service provision point (SPP) for the server side. From the point of view of an actor implementation the SAPs and SPPs work like ports. Like ports they are associated with a protocol. But other than ports they don't have to (and even cannot) be bound explicitly. Rather, an actor is bound to a concrete service by a layer connection and this binding of a service is propagated recursively to all sub actors of this actor. This concept is very similar to dependency injection.

Wright

In software architecture, Wright is an architecture description language developed at Carnegie Mellon University. Wright formalizes a software architecture in terms of concepts such as components, connectors, roles, and ports. The dynamic behavior of different ports of an individual component is described using the Communicating Sequential Processes (CSP) process algebra. The roles that different components interacting through a connector can take are also described using CSP. Due to the formal nature of the behavior descriptions, automatic checks of port/role compatibility, and overall system consistency can be performed.

Wright was principally developed by Robert Allen and David Garlan.

Unified Modeling Language

The Unified Modeling Language (UML) is a general-purpose, developmental, modeling language in the field of software engineering that is intended to provide a standard way to visualize the design of a system.

The creation of UML was originally motivated by the desire to standardize the disparate notational systems and approaches to software design. It was developed by Grady Booch, Ivar Jacobson and James Rumbaugh at Rational Software in 1994–1995, with further development led by them through 1996.

In 1997, UML was adopted as a standard by the Object Management Group (OMG), and has been managed by this organization ever since. In 2005, UML was also published by the International Organization for Standardization (ISO) as an approved ISO standard. Since then the standard has been periodically revised to cover the latest revision of UML.

Generations

Before UML 1.0

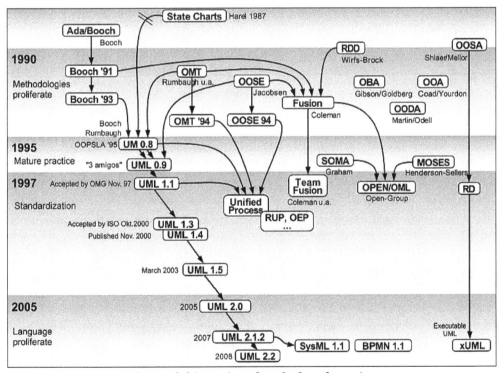

History of object-oriented methods and notation.

UML has been evolving since the second half of the 1990s and has its roots in the object-oriented programming methods developed in the late 1980s and early 1990s. The timeline shows the highlights of the history of object-oriented modeling methods and notation.

It is originally based on the notations of the Booch method, the object-modeling technique (OMT) and object-oriented software engineering (OOSE), which it has integrated into a single language.

Rational Software Corporation hired James Rumbaugh from General Electric in 1994 and after that the company became the source for two of the most popular object-oriented modeling approaches of the day: Rumbaugh's object-modeling technique (OMT) and Grady Booch's method. They were soon assisted in their efforts by Ivar Jacobson, the creator of the object-oriented software engineering (OOSE) method, who joined them at Rational in 1995.

UML 1.x

Under the technical leadership of those three (Rumbaugh, Jacobson and Booch), a consortium called the UML Partners was organized in 1996 to complete the Unified Modeling Language (UML) specification, and propose it to the Object Management Group (OMG) for standardisation. The partnership also contained additional interested parties (for example HP, DEC, IBM and Microsoft). The UML Partners' UML 1.0 draft was proposed to the OMG in January 1997 by the consortium. During the same month the UML Partners formed a group, designed to define the exact meaning of language constructs, chaired by Cris Kobryn and administered by Ed Eykholt, to finalize the specification and integrate it with other standardization efforts. The result of this work, UML 1.1, was submitted to the OMG in August 1997 and adopted by the OMG in November 1997.

After the first release a task force was formed to improve the language, which released several minor revisions, 1.3, 1.4, and 1.5.

The standards it produced (as well as the original standard) have been noted as being ambiguous and inconsistent.

Cardinality Notation

As with database Chen, Bachman, and ISO ER diagrams, class models are specified to use "look-across" cardinalities, even though several authors (Merise, Elmasri & Navathe amongst others) prefer same-side or "look-here" for roles and both minimum and maximum cardinalities. Recent researchers (Feinerer, Dullea et al.) have shown that the "look-across" technique used by UML and ER diagrams is less effective and less coherent when applied to n-ary relationships of order strictly greater than 2.

Feinerer says: "Problems arise if we operate under the look-across semantics as used for UML associations. Hartmann investigates this situation and shows how and why different transformations fail.", and: "As we will see on the next few pages, the look-across interpretation introduces several difficulties which prevent the extension of simple mechanisms from binary to n-ary associations."

UML 2

UML 2.0 major revision replaced version 1.5 in 2005, which was developed with an enlarged consortium to improve the language further to reflect new experience on usage of its features.

Although UML 2.1 was never released as a formal specification, versions 2.1.1 and 2.1.2 appeared in 2007, followed by UML 2.2 in February 2009. UML 2.3 was formally released in May 2010. UML 2.4.1 was formally released in August 2011. UML 2.5 was released in October 2012 as an "In progress" version and was officially released in June 2015. Formal version 2.5.1 was adopted in December 2017.

There are four parts to the UML 2.x specification:

- The Superstructure that defines the notation and semantics for diagrams and their model elements.

- The Infrastructure that defines the core metamodel on which the Superstructure is based.

- The Object Constraint Language (OCL) for defining rules for model elements.

- The UML Diagram Interchange that defines how UML 2 diagram layouts are exchanged.

The current versions of these standards are:

- UML Superstructure version 2.4.1.

- UML Infrastructure version 2.4.1.

- OCL version 2.3.1.

- UML Diagram Interchange version 1.0.

It continues to be updated and improved by the revision task force, who resolve any issues with the language.

Design

UML offers a way to visualize a system's architectural blueprints in a diagram, including elements such as:

- Any activities (jobs).

- Individual components of the system:

  ◦ And how they can interact with other software components.

- How the system will run.

- How entities interact with others (components and interfaces).

- External user interface.

Although originally intended for object-oriented design documentation, UML has been extended to a larger set of design documentation, and been found useful in many contexts.

Software Development Methods

UML is not a development method by itself; however, it was designed to be compatible with the leading object-oriented software development methods of its time, for example OMT, Booch method, Objectory and especially RUP that it was originally intended to be used with when work began at Rational Software.

Modeling

It is important to distinguish between the UML model and the set of diagrams of a system. A diagram is a partial graphic representation of a system's model. The set of diagrams need not completely cover the model and deleting a diagram does not change the model. The model may also contain documentation that drives the model elements and diagrams (such as written use cases).

UML diagrams represent two different views of a system model:

- Static (or structural) view: emphasizes the static structure of the system using objects, attributes, operations and relationships. It includes class diagrams and composite structure diagrams.

- Dynamic (or behavioral) view: emphasizes the dynamic behavior of the system by showing collaborations among objects and changes to the internal states of objects. This view includes sequence diagrams, activity diagrams and state machine diagrams.

UML models can be exchanged among UML tools by using the XML Metadata Interchange (XMI) format.

In UML, one of the key tools for behavior modelling is the use-case model, caused by OOSE. Use cases are a way of specifying required usages of a system. Typically, they are used to capture the requirements of a system, that is, what a system is supposed to do.

Diagrams

UML 2 has many types of diagrams, which are divided into two categories. Some types represent *structural* information, and the rest represent general types of *behavior*, including a few that represent different aspects of *interactions*. These diagrams can be categorized hierarchically as shown in the following class diagram:

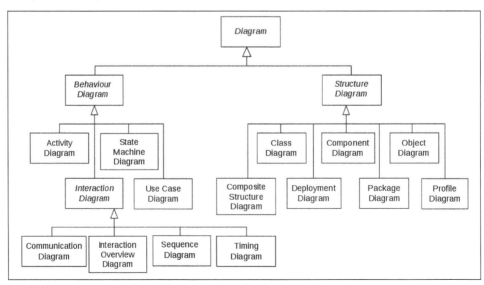

These diagrams may all contain comments or
notes explaining usage, constraint, or intent.

Structure Diagrams

Structure diagrams emphasize the things that must be present in the system being modeled. Since structure diagrams represent the structure, they are used extensively in documenting the software architecture of software systems. For example, the component diagram describes how a software system is split up into components and shows the dependencies among these components.

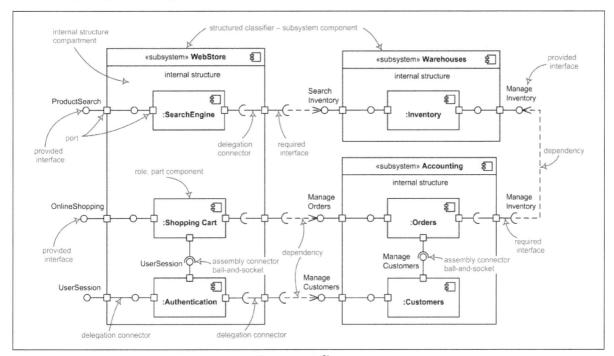

Component diagram.

BankAccount
owner : String balance : Dollars = 0
deposit (amount : Dollars) withdrawal (amount : Dollars)

Class diagram.

Behavior Diagrams

Behavior diagrams emphasize what must happen in the system being modeled. Since behavior diagrams illustrate the behavior of a system, they are used extensively to describe the functionality of software systems. As an example, the activity diagram describes the business and operational step-by-step activities of the components in a system.

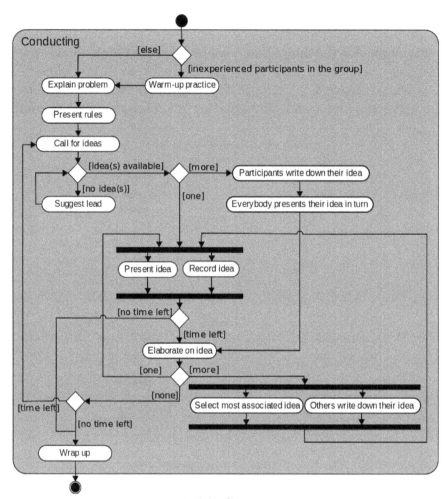

Activity diagram.

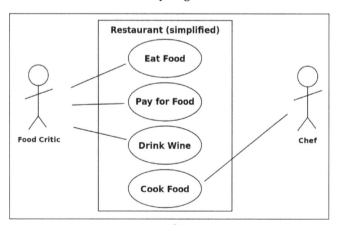

Use case diagram.

Interaction Diagrams

Interaction diagrams, a subset of behavior diagrams, emphasize the flow of control and data among the things in the system being modeled. For example, the sequence diagram shows how objects communicate with each other regarding a sequence of messages.

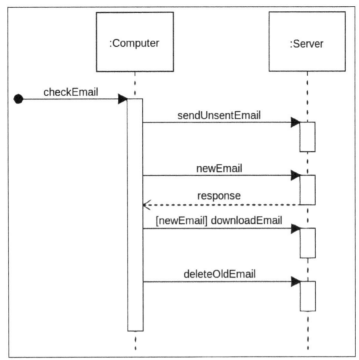

Sequence diagram.

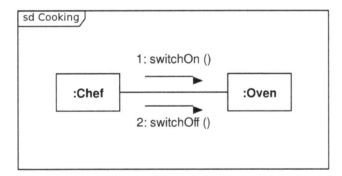

Communication diagram.

Metamodeling

The Object Management Group (OMG) has developed a metamodeling architecture to define the UML, called the Meta-Object Facility. MOF is designed as a four-layered architecture, as shown in the image at right. It provides a meta-meta model at the top, called the M3 layer. This M3-model is the language used by Meta-Object Facility to build metamodels, called M2-models.

The most prominent example of a Layer 2 Meta-Object Facility model is the UML metamodel, which describes the UML itself. These M2-models describe elements of the M1-layer, and thus M1-models. These would be, for example, models written in UML. The last layer is the M0-layer or data layer. It is used to describe runtime instances of the system.

The meta-model can be extended using a mechanism called stereotyping. This has been criticised as being insufficient/untenable by Brian Henderson-Sellers and Cesar Gonzalez-Perez in "Uses and Abuses of the Stereotype Mechanism in UML 1.x and 2.0".

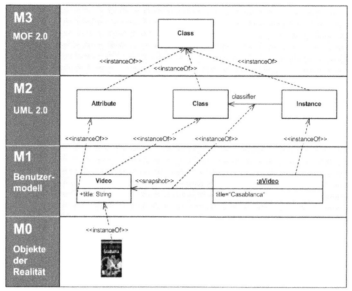

Illustration of the Meta-Object Facility.

Adoption

UML has been marketed for many contexts.

It has been treated, at times, as a design silver bullet, which leads to problems. UML misuse includes overuse (designing every part of the system with it, which is unnecessary) and assuming that novices can design with it.

It is considered a large language, with many constructs. Some people (including Jacobson) feel that UML's size hinders learning (and therefore, using) it.

Structural UML Diagrams

Class Diagram

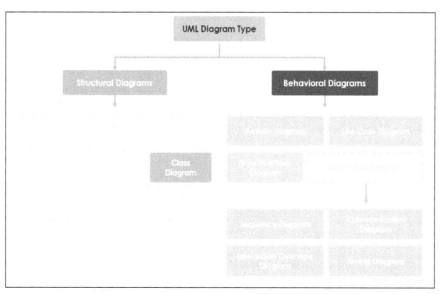

In software engineering, a class diagram in the Unified Modeling Language (UML) is a type of static structure diagram that describes the structure of a system by showing the system's classes, their attributes, operations (or methods), and the relationships among objects.

Purpose of Class Diagrams

- Shows static structure of classifiers in a system.

- Diagram provides a basic notation for other structure diagrams prescribed by UML.

- Helpful for developers and other team members too.

- Business Analysts can use class diagrams to model systems from a business perspective.

A UML class diagram is made up of:

- A set of classes.

- A set of relationships between classes.

Class

A description of a group of objects all with similar roles in the system, which consists of:

- Structural features (attributes) define what objects of the class "know":

  ◦ Represent the state of an object of the class.

  ◦ Are descriptions of the structural or static features of a class.

- Behavioral features (operations) define what objects of the class "can do":

  ◦ Define the way in which objects may interact.

  ◦ Operations are descriptions of behavioral or dynamic features of a class.

Class Notation

A class notation consists of three parts:

- Class Name:

  ◦ The name of the class appears in the first partition.

- Class Attributes:

  ◦ Attributes are shown in the second partition.

  ◦ The attribute type is shown after the colon.

  ◦ Attributes map onto member variables (data members) in code.

- Class Operations (Methods):

  ◦ Operations are shown in the third partition. They are services the class provides.

- ◦ The return type of a method is shown after the colon at the end of the method signature.
- ◦ The return type of method parameters is shown after the colon following the parameter name.
- ◦ Operations map onto class methods in code.

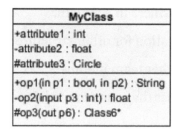

The graphical representation of the class - MyClass as shown above:

- MyClass has 3 attributes and 3 operations.
- Parameter p3 of op2 is of type int.
- op2 returns a float.
- op3 returns a pointer (denoted by a *) to Class6.

Class Relationships

A class may be involved in one or more relationships with other classes. A relationship can be one of the following types: (Refer to the figure on the right for the graphical representation of relationships).

Relationship Type	Graphical Representation
Inheritance (or Generalization): • Represents an "is-a" relationship. • An abstract class name is shown in italics. • SubClass1 and SubClass2 are specializations of Super Class. • A solid line with a hollow arrowhead that point from the child to the parent class.	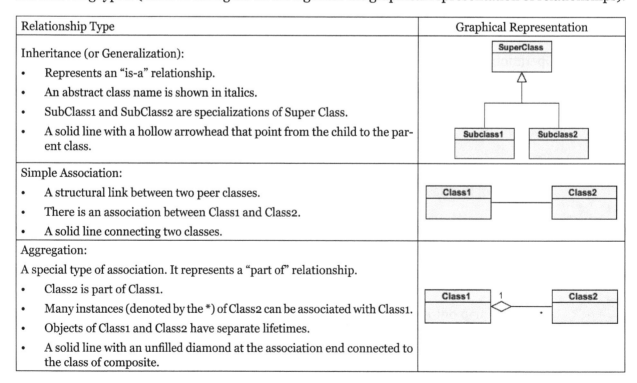
Simple Association: • A structural link between two peer classes. • There is an association between Class1 and Class2. • A solid line connecting two classes.	
Aggregation: A special type of association. It represents a "part of" relationship. • Class2 is part of Class1. • Many instances (denoted by the *) of Class2 can be associated with Class1. • Objects of Class1 and Class2 have separate lifetimes. • A solid line with an unfilled diamond at the association end connected to the class of composite.	

Composition: A special type of aggregation where parts are destroyed when the whole is destroyed. • Objects of Class2 live and die with Class1. • Class2 cannot stand by itself. • A solid line with a filled diamond at the association connected to the class of composite.	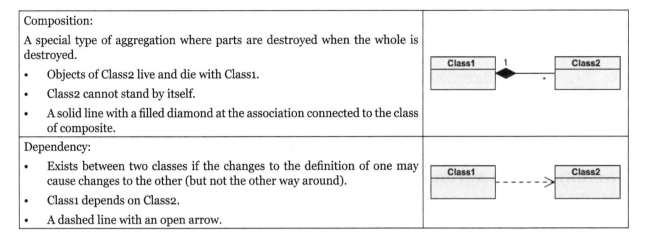
Dependency: • Exists between two classes if the changes to the definition of one may cause changes to the other (but not the other way around). • Class1 depends on Class2. • A dashed line with an open arrow.	

Relationship Names

- Names of relationships are written in the middle of the association line.

- Good relation names make sense when you read them out loud:

  - "Every spreadsheet contains some number of cells".

  - "an expression evaluates to a value".

- They often have a small arrowhead to show the direction in which direction to read the relationship, e.g., expressions evaluate to values, but values do not evaluate to expressions.

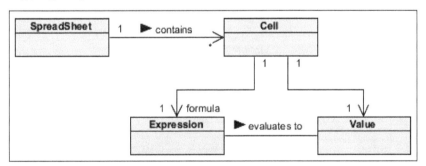

Relationship Roles

- A role is a directional purpose of an association.

- Roles are written at the ends of an association line and describe the purpose played by that class in the relationship:

  - E.g., A cell is related to an expression. The nature of the relationship is that the expression is the formula of the cell.

Navigability

The arrows indicate whether, given one instance participating in a relationship, it is possible to determine the instances of the other class that are related to it.

The diagram above suggests that,

- Given a spreadsheet, we can locate all of the cells that it contains, but that:

    ○ we cannot determine from a cell in what spreadsheet it is contained.

- Given a cell, we can obtain the related expression and value, but:

    ○ given a value (or expression) we cannot find the cell of which those are attributes.

Visibility of Class Attributes and Operations

In object-oriented design, there is a notation of visibility for attributes and operations. UML identifies four types of visibility: public, protected, private, and package.

The +, -, # and ~ symbols before an attribute and operation name in a class denote the visibility of the attribute and operation.

- + denotes public attributes or operations.

- - denotes private attributes or operations.

- # denotes protected attributes or operations.

- ~ denotes package attributes or operations.

Class visibility example:

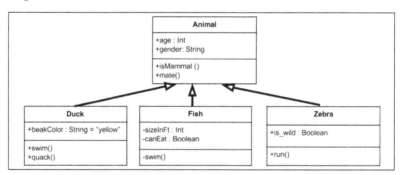

In the example above:

- Attribute1 and op1 of MyClassName are public.

- Attribute3 and op3 are protected.

- Attribute2 and op2 are private.

Access for each of these visibility types is shown below for members of different classes.

Access Right	public (+)	private (-)	protected (#)	Package (~)
Members of the same class	yes	yes	yes	yes
Members of derived classes	yes	no	yes	yes
Members of any other class	yes	no	no	in same package

Multiplicity

How many objects of each class take part in the relationships and multiplicity can be expressed as:

- Exactly one - 1
- Zero or one - 0..1
- Many - 0..* or *
- One or more - 1..*
- Exact Number - e.g. 3..4 or 6
- Or a complex relationship - e.g. 0..1, 3..4, 6.* would mean any number of objects other than 2 or 5

Multiplicity Example

- Requirement: A Student can take many Courses and many Students can be enrolled in one Course.

- In the example below, the class diagram (on the left), describes the statement of the requirement above for the static model while the object diagram (on the right) shows the snapshot (an instance of the class diagram) of the course enrollment for the courses Software Engineering and Database Management respectively).

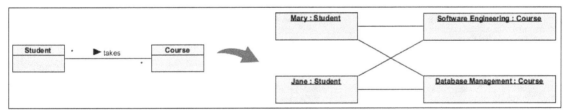

Aggregation Example - Computer and parts

- An aggregation is a special case of association denoting a "consists-of" hierarchy.
- The aggregate is the parent class, the components are the children classes.

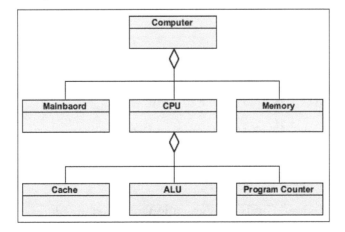

Inheritance Example - Cell Taxonomy

- Inheritance is another special case of an association denoting a "kind-of" hierarchy.

- Inheritance simplifies the analysis model by introducing a taxonomy.

- The child classes inherit the attributes and operations of the parent class.

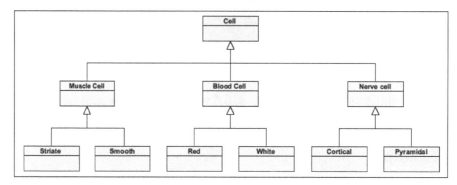

Class Diagram - Diagram Tool Example

A class diagram may also have notes attached to classes or relationships. Notes are shown in grey.

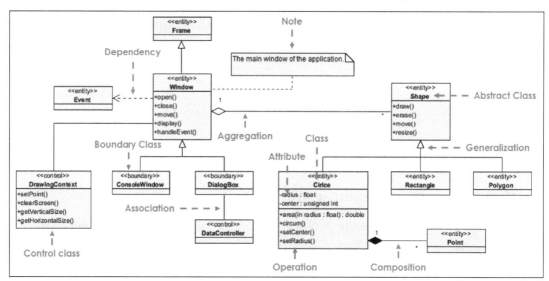

In the example above:

We can interpret the meaning of the above class diagram by reading through the points as following:

- Shape is an abstract class. It is shown in Italics.

- Shape is a superclass. Circle, Rectangle and Polygon are derived from Shape. In other words, a Circle is-a Shape. This is a generalization / inheritance relationship.

- There is an association between DialogBox and DataController.

- Shape is part-of Window. This is an aggregation relationship. Shape can exist without Window.

- Point is part-of Circle. This is a composition relationship. Point cannot exist without a Circle.

- Window is dependent on Event. However, Event is not dependent on Window.

- The attributes of Circle are radius and center. This is an entity class.

- The method names of Circle are area(), circum(), setCenter() and setRadius().

- The parameter radius in Circle is an in parameter of type float.

- The method area() of class Circle returns a value of type double.

- The attributes and method names of Rectangle are hidden. Some other classes in the diagram also have their attributes and method names hidden.

Dealing with Complex System - Multiple or Single Class Diagram

Inevitably, if you are modeling a large system or a large business area, there will be numerous entities you must consider. Should we use multiple or a single class diagram for modeling the problem The answer is:

- Instead of modeling every entity and its relationships on a single class diagram, it is better to use multiple class diagrams.

- Dividing a system into multiple class diagrams makes the system easier to understand, especially if each diagram is a graphical representation of a specific part of the system.

Perspectives of Class Diagram in Software Development Lifecycle

We can use class diagrams in different development phases of a software development lifecycle and typically by modeling class diagrams in three different perspectives (levels of detail) progressively as we move forward:

Conceptual perspective: The diagrams are interpreted as describing things in the real world. Thus, if you take the conceptual perspective you draw a diagram that represents the concepts in the domain under study. These concepts will naturally relate to the classes that implement them. The conceptual perspective is considered language-independent.

Specification perspective: The diagrams are interpreted as describing software abstractions or components with specifications and interfaces but with no commitment to a particular implementation. Thus, if you take the specification perspective we are looking at the interfaces of the software, not the implementation.

Implementation perspective: The diagrams are interpreted as describing software implementations in a particular technology and language.

Component Diagram

Component diagrams are different in terms of nature and behavior. Component diagrams are used to model the physical aspects of a system. Now the question is, what are these physical aspects? Physical aspects are the elements such as executables, libraries, files, documents, etc. which reside in a node.

Component diagrams are used to visualize the organization and relationships among components in a system. These diagrams are also used to make executable systems.

Purpose of Component Diagrams

Component diagram is a special kind of diagram in UML. It does not describe the functionality of the system but it describes the components used to make those functionalities.

Thus from that point of view, component diagrams are used to visualize the physical components in a system. These components are libraries, packages, files, etc.

Component diagrams can also be described as a static implementation view of a system. Static implementation represents the organization of the components at a particular moment.

A single component diagram cannot represent the entire system but a collection of diagrams is used to represent the whole.

The purpose of the component diagram can be summarized as:

- Visualize the components of a system.

- Construct executables by using forward and reverse engineering.

- Describe the organization and relationships of the components.

Methods to Draw a Component Diagram

Component diagrams are used to describe the physical artifacts of a system. This artifact includes files, executables, libraries, etc.

The purpose of this diagram is different. Component diagrams are used during the implementation phase of an application. However, it is prepared well in advance to visualize the implementation details.

Initially, the system is designed using different UML diagrams and then when the artifacts are ready, component diagrams are used to get an idea of the implementation.

This diagram is very important as without it the application cannot be implemented efficiently. A well-prepared component diagram is also important for other aspects such as application performance, maintenance, etc.

Before drawing a component diagram, the following artifacts are to be identified clearly:

- Files used in the system.

- Libraries and other artifacts relevant to the application.

- Relationships among the artifacts.

After identifying the artifacts, the following points need to be kept in mind.

- Use a meaningful name to identify the component for which the diagram is to be drawn.

- Prepare a mental layout before producing the using tools.

- Use notes for clarifying important points.

Following is a component diagram for order management system. Here, the artifacts are files. The diagram shows the files in the application and their relationships. In actual, the component diagram also contains dlls, libraries, folders, etc.

In the following diagram, four files are identified and their relationships are produced.

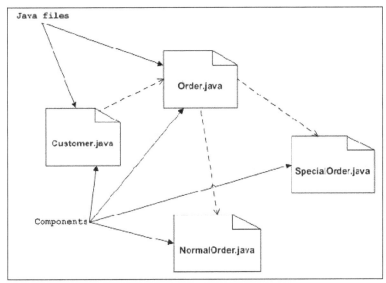

Component diagram of an order management system.

Usage of Component Diagrams

component diagrams are used to visualize the static implementation view of a system. Component diagrams are special type of UML diagrams used for different purposes.

These diagrams show the physical components of a system. To clarify it, we can say that component diagrams describe the organization of the components in a system.

Organization can be further described as the location of the components in a system. These components are organized in a special way to meet the system requirements.

those components are libraries, files, executables, etc. Before implementing the application, these components are to be organized. This component organization is also designed separately as a part of project execution.

Component diagrams are very important from implementation perspective. Thus, the implementation team of an application should have a proper knowledge of the component details.

Component diagrams can be used to:

- Model the components of a system.

- Model the database schema.

- Model the executables of an application.

- Model the system's source code.

Composite Structure Diagram

Composite Structure Diagram is one of the new artifacts added to UML 2.0. A composite structure diagram is a UML structural diagram that contains classes, interfaces, packages, and their relationships, and that provides a logical view of all, or part of a software system. It shows the internal structure (including parts and connectors) of a structured classifier or collaboration.

A composite structure diagram performs a similar role to a class diagram, but allows you to go into further detail in describing the internal structure of multiple classes and showing the interactions between them. You can graphically represent inner classes and parts and show associations both between and within classes.

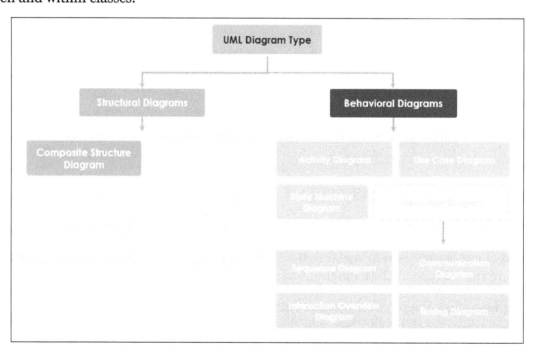

Purpose of Composite Structure Diagram

- Composite Structure Diagrams allow the users to "Peek Inside" an object to see exactly what it is composed of.

- The internal actions of a class, including the relationships of nested classes, can be detailed.

- Objects are shown to be defined as a composition of other classified objects.

Composite Structure Diagram at a Glance

- Composite Structure Diagrams show the internal parts of a class.

- Parts are named: partName:partType[multiplicity].

- Aggregated classes are parts of a class but parts are not necessarily classes, a part is any element that is used to make up the containing class.

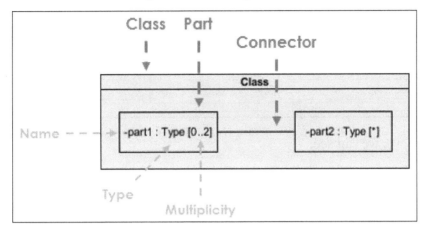

Deriving Composite Structure Diagram from Class Diagram

Online Store

Suppose we are modeling a system for an online store. The client has told us that customers may join a membership program which will provide them with special offers and discounted shipping, so we have extended the customer object to provide a member and standard option.

Let's modeling the online store using a class diagram:

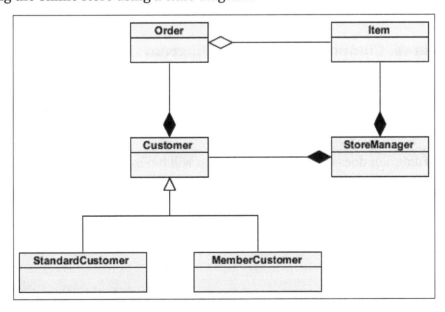

We have a class for Item which may be aggregated by the Order class, which is composed by the Customer class which itself is composed by the StoreManager class. We have a lot of objects that end up within other objects.

Everything looks like it ends up inside StoreManager, so we can create a composite structure diagram to really see what it's made of.

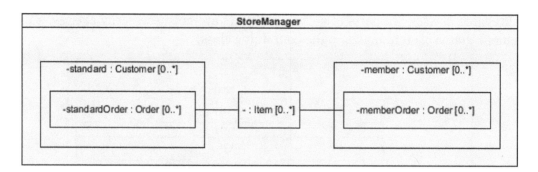

In the example above, we can see:

- StoreManager from its own perspective, instead of the system as a whole.

- StoreManager directly contains two types of objects (Customer and Item) as is indicated by the two composition arrows on the class diagram.

- The composite structure diagram here shows more explicitly is the inclusion of the sub-types of Customer.

- Notice that the type of both of these parts is Customer, as the store sees both as Customer objects.

- We also see a connector which shows the relation between Item and Order.

- Order is not directly contained within the StoreManager class but we can show relations to parts nested within the objects it aggregates.

Class Diagram vs. Composite Structure Diagram

Are two diagram below expressing the same meaning?

In a class diagram the reference between Description and Pricing is ambiguous, strictly speaking, they are not exactly the same.

- The class diagram does show that Description will have a reference to a Pricing object.

- But it does not specify whether the reference between the two objects is contained inside the item explicitly.

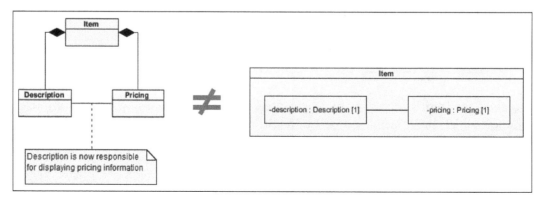

If we use a Composite Structure Diagram, the meaning of the containment of the association relationship is unambiguous.

- The reference between the Description and Pricing objects is contained to objects that are composed by Item.

- The specific implementations of an object's activity can be clearly modeled.

References to External Parts

We have seen examples of how Composite Structure diagrams are great at describing aggregation, but your models will also need to contain references to objects outside of the class you are modeling.

But what about the referencing an external object with Composite Structure Diagram like the example below?

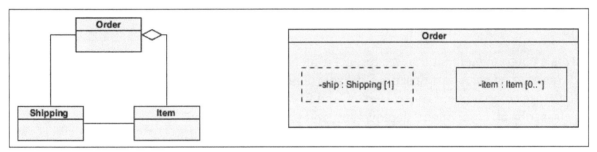

- References to external objects are shown as a part with a dashed rectangle.

- Even though they reference object is outside of the class, the reference itself is within the modeled class and is an important step in showing its implementation.

Basic Concepts of Composite Structure Diagram

The key composite structure entities identified in the UML 2.0 specification are structured classifiers, parts, ports, connectors, and collaborations.

Collaboration

A collaboration describes a structure of collaborating parts (roles). A collaboration is attached to an operation or a classifier through a Collaboration Use. You use a collaboration when you want to define only the roles and connections that are required to accomplish a specific goal of the collaboration.

For example, the goal of a collaboration can be to define the roles or the components of a classifier. By isolating the primary roles, a collaboration simplifes the structure and clarifies behavior in a model.

Example:

In this example the Wheels and the Engine are the Parts of the Collaboration and the FrontAxle and the RearAxle are the Connectors. The Car is the Composite Structure that shows the parts and the connections between the parts.

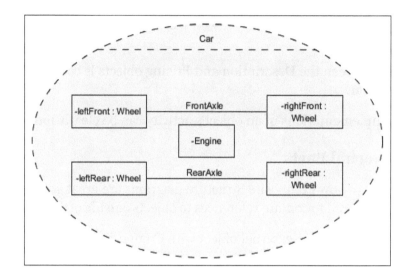

Parts

A part is a diagram element that represents a set of one or more instances that a containing structured classifier owns. A part describes the role of an instance in a classifier. You can create parts in the structure compartment of a classifier, and in several UML diagrams such as composite structure, class, object, component, deployment, and package diagrams.

Port

A port defines the interaction point between a classifier instance and its environment or between the behavior of the classifier and its internal parts.

Interface

Composite Structure diagram supports the ball-and-socket notation for the provided and required interfaces. Interfaces can be shown or hidden in the diagram as needed.

Connector

A line that represents a relationship in a model. When you model the internal structure of a classifier, you can use a connector to indicate a link between two or more instances of a part or a port. The connector defines the relationship between the objects or instances that are bound to roles in the same structured classifier and it identifies the communication between those roles. The product automatically specifies the kind of connector to create.

Composite Structure Diagram Example - Computer System

Let's develop the composite structure diagram for a computer system which include the following a list of the components:

- Power Supply Unit (PSU).

- Hard Disk Drive (HDD).

- DVD-RW.

- Optical Drive (DVD-RW).

- Memory Module (MM).

We will assume for the moment that the mainboard is of the type that has a sound card and display adapter built in:

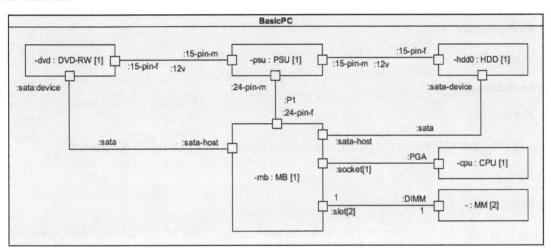

Deployment Diagram

Deployment diagrams are used to visualize the topology of the physical components of a system, where the software components are deployed. Deployment diagrams are used to describe the static deployment view of a system. Deployment diagrams consist of nodes and their relationships.

Purpose of Deployment Diagrams

The term Deployment itself describes the purpose of the diagram. Deployment diagrams are used for describing the hardware components, where software components are deployed. Component diagrams and deployment diagrams are closely related.

Component diagrams are used to describe the components and deployment diagrams shows how they are deployed in hardware.

UML is mainly designed to focus on the software artifacts of a system. However, these two diagrams are special diagrams used to focus on software and hardware components.

Most of the UML diagrams are used to handle logical components but deployment diagrams are made to focus on the hardware topology of a system. Deployment diagrams are used by the system engineers.

The purpose of deployment diagrams can be described as:

- Visualize the hardware topology of a system.

- Describe the hardware components used to deploy software components.

- Describe the runtime processing nodes.

Methods to Draw a Deployment Diagram

Deployment diagram represents the deployment view of a system. It is related to the component diagram because the components are deployed using the deployment diagrams. A deployment diagram consists of nodes. Nodes are nothing but physical hardware used to deploy the application.

Deployment diagrams are useful for system engineers. An efficient deployment diagram is very important as it controls the following parameters:

- Performance
- Scalability
- Maintainability
- Portability

Before drawing a deployment diagram, the following artifacts should be identified:

- Nodes
- Relationships among nodes

Following is a sample deployment diagram to provide an idea of the deployment view of order management system. Here, we have shown nodes as:

- Monitor
- Modem
- Caching server
- Server

The application is assumed to be a web-based application, which is deployed in a clustered environment using server 1, server 2, and server 3. The user connects to the application using the Internet. The control flows from the caching server to the clustered environment.

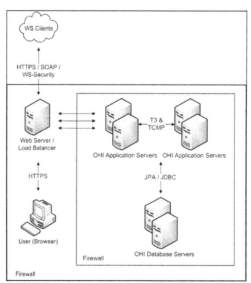

Usage of Deployment Diagrams

Deployment diagrams are mainly used by system engineers. These diagrams are used to describe the physical components (hardware), their distribution, and association.

Deployment diagrams can be visualized as the hardware components/nodes on which the software components reside.

Software applications are developed to model complex business processes. Efficient software applications are not sufficient to meet the business requirements. Business requirements can be described as the need to support the increasing number of users, quick response time, etc.

To meet these types of requirements, hardware components should be designed efficiently and in a cost-effective way.

Now-a-days software applications are very complex in nature. Software applications can be stand-alone, web-based, distributed, mainframe-based and many more. Hence, it is very important to design the hardware components efficiently.

Deployment diagrams can be used:

- To model the hardware topology of a system.
- To model the embedded system.
- To model the hardware details for a client/server system.
- To model the hardware details of a distributed application.
- For Forward and Reverse engineering.

Object Diagram

An Object Diagram can be referred to as a screenshot of the instances in a system and the relationship that exists between them. Since object diagrams depict behaviour when objects have been instantiated, we are able to study the behavior of the system at a particular instant. Object diagrams are vital to portray and understand functional requirements of a system. In other words, "An object diagram in the Unified Modeling Language (UML), is a diagram that shows a complete or partial view of the structure of a modeled system at a specific time."

Difference between an Object and a Class Diagram

An object diagram is similar to a class diagram except it shows the instances of classes in the system. We depict actual classifiers and their relationships making the use of class diagrams. On the other hand, an Object Diagram represents specific instances of classes and relationships between them at a point of time.

What is a Classifier?

In UML a classifier refers to a group of elements that have some common features like methods, attributes and operations. A classifier can be thought of as an abstract metaclass which draws a boundary for a group of instances having common static and dynamic features. For example, we refer a class, an object, a component, or a deployment node as classifiers in UML since they define a common set of properties.

An Object Diagram is a structural diagram which uses notation similar to that of class diagrams. We are able to design object diagrams by instantiating classifiers.

Object Diagrams use real world examples to depict the nature and structure of the system at a particular point in time. Since we are able to use data available within objects, Object diagrams provide a clearer view of the relationships that exist between objects.

A class and its corresponding object.

Notations used in Object Diagrams

- Objects or Instance specifications – When we instantiate a classifier in a system, the object we create represents an entity which exists in the system.We can represent the changes in object over time by creating multiple instance specifications. We use a rectangle to represent an object in an Object Diagram. An object is generally linked to other objects in an object diagram.

Notation for an Object.

For example – In the figure below, two objects of class Student are linked to an object of class College.

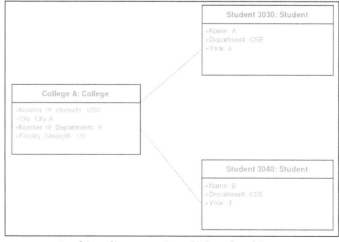

An object diagram using a link and 3 objects.

- Links – We use a link to represent a relationship between two objects.

Notation for a link.

We represent the number of participants on the link for each end of the link. We use the term association for a relationship between two classifiers. The term link is used to specify a relationship between two instance specifications or objects. We use a solid line to represent a link between two objects.

NOTATION	MEANING
0..1	Zero or one
1	One only
0..*	Zero or more
*	Zero or more
1..*	One or more
7	Seven only
0..2	Zero or two
4..7	Four to seven

- Dependency Relationships – We use a dependency relationship to show when one element depends on another element.

Notation for dependency relationship.

- Class diagrams, component diagrams, deployment and object diagrams use dependency relationships. A dependency is used to depict the relationship between dependent and independent entities in the system. Any change in the definition or structure of one element may cause changes to the other. This is a unidirectional kind of relationship between two objects. Dependency relationships are of various types specified with keywords (sometimes within angular brackets").

Abstraction, Binding, Realization, Substitution and Usage are the types of dependency relationships used in UML.

For example – In the figure below, an object of Player class is dependent (or uses) an object of Bat class.

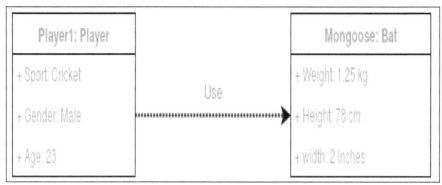

An object diagram using a dependency relationship.

- Association – Association is a reference relationship between two objects (or classes).

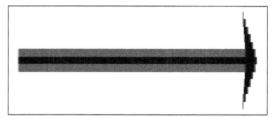

Notation for association.

Whenever an object uses another it is called an association. We use association when one object references members of the other object. Association can be uni-directional or bi-directional. We use an arrow to represent association.

For example – The object of Order class is associated with an object of Customer class.

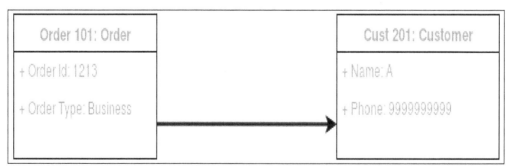

An object diagram using association.

- Aggregation – Aggregation represents a "has a" relationship.

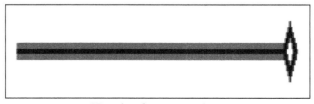

Notation for aggregation.

Aggregation is a specific form of association.on relationship; aggregation is more specific than ordinary association. It is an association that represents a part-whole or part-of relationship. It is a kind of parent -child relationship however it isn't inheritance. Aggregation occurs when the lifecycle of the contained objects does not strongly depend on the lifecycle of container objects.

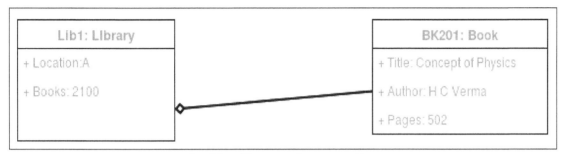

An object diagram using aggregation.

For example – A library has an aggregation relationship with books. Library has books or books are a part of library. The existence of books is independent of the existence of the library.While implementing, there isn't a lot of difference between aggregation and association. We use a hollow diamond on the containing object with a line which joins it to the contained object.

- Composition – Composition is a type of association where the child cannot exist independent of the other.

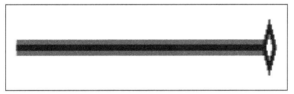

Notation for composition.

- Composition is also a special type of association. It is also a kind of parent child relationship but it is not inheritance. Consider the example of a boy Matt: Matt is composed of legs and arms. Here Matt has a composition relationship with his legs and arms. Here legs and arms cant exist without the existence of their parent object. So whenever independent existence of the child is not possible we use a composition relationship. We use a filled diamond on the containing object with a line which joins it to the contained object.

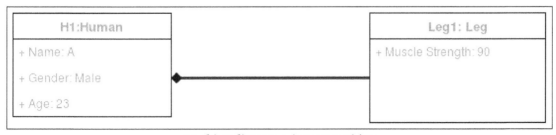

An object diagram using composition.

For Example – In the figure below, consider the object Bank1. Here an account cannot exist without the existence of a bank.

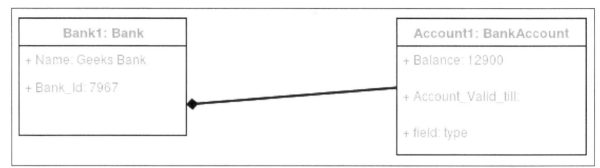

A bank is composed of accounts.

Difference between Association and Dependency

Association and dependency are often confused in their usage. A source of confusion was the use of transient links in UML 1. Meta-models are now handled differently in UML 2 and the issue has been resolved.

There are a large number of dependencies in a system. We only represent the ones which are essential to convey for understanding the system. We need to understand that every association implies a dependency itself. We , however, prefer not to draw it separately. An association implies a dependency similar to a way in which generalization does.

Methods to Draw an Object Diagram

- Draw all the necessary class diagrams for the system.
- Identify the crucial points in time where a system snapshot is needed.
- Identify the objects which cover crucial functionality of the system.
- Identify the relationship between objects drawn.

Uses of an Object Diagram

- Model the static design (similar to class diagrams) or structure of a system using prototypical instances and real data.
- Helps us to understand the functionalities that the system should deliver to the users.
- Understand relationships between objects.
- Visualise, document, construct and design a static frame showing instances of objects and their relationships in the dynamic story of life of a system.
- Verify the class diagrams for completeness and accuracy by using Object Diagrams as specific test cases.
- Discover facts and dependencies between specific instances and depicting specific examples of classifiers.

Package Diagram

Package diagram, a kind of structural diagram, shows the arrangement and organization of model elements in middle to large scale project. Package diagram can show both structure and dependencies between sub-systems or modules, showing different views of a system, for example, as multi-layered (aka multi-tiered) application - multi-layered application model.

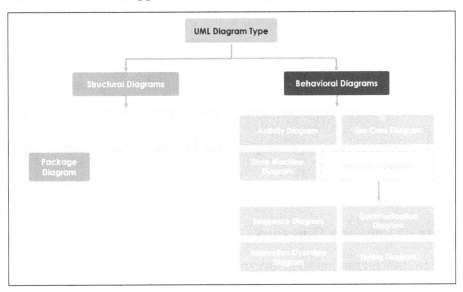

Purpose of Package Diagrams

Package diagrams are used to structure high level system elements. Packages are used for organizing large system which contains diagrams, documents and other key deliverables:

- Package Diagram can be used to simplify complex class diagrams, it can group classes into packages.

- A package is a collection of logically related UML elements.

- Packages are depicted as file folders and can be used on any of the UML diagrams.

Package Diagram at a Glance

Package diagram is used to simplify complex class diagrams, you can group classes into packages. A package is a collection of logically related UML elements.

The diagram below is a business model in which the classes are grouped into packages:

- Packages appear as rectangles with small tabs at the top.

- The package name is on the tab or inside the rectangle.

- The dotted arrows are dependencies.

- One package depends on another if changes in the other could possibly force changes in the first.

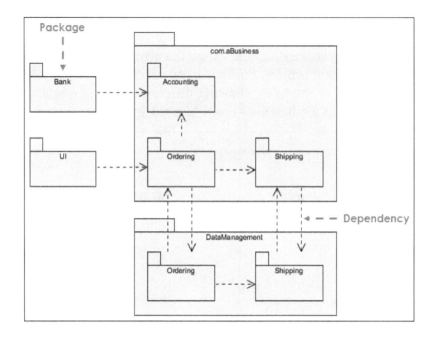

Basic Concepts of Package Diagram

Package diagram follows hierarchal structure of nested packages. Atomic module for nested package are usually class diagrams. There are few constraints while using package diagrams, they are as follows:

- Package name should not be the same for a system, however classes inside different packages could have the same name.

- Packages can include whole diagrams, name of components alone or no components at all.

- Fully qualified name of a package has the following syntax.

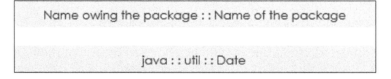

Packages can be represented by the notations with some examples shown below:

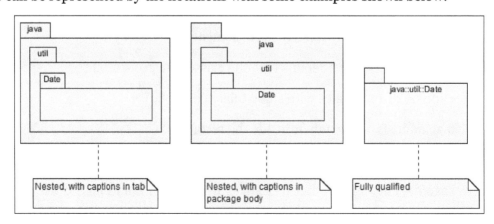

Package Diagram - Dependency Notation

There are two sub-types involved in dependency. They are <<import>> & <<access>>. Though there are two stereotypes users can use their own stereotype to represent the type of dependency between two packages.

Package Diagram Example - Import

<<import>> - one package imports the functionality of other package.

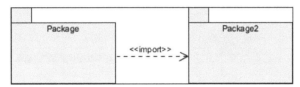

Package Diagram Example - Access

<<access>> - one package requires help from functions of other package.

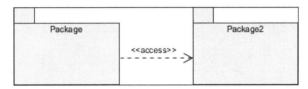

Modeling Complex Grouping

A package diagram is often used to describe the hierarchical relationships (groupings) between packages and other packages or objects. A package represents a namespace.

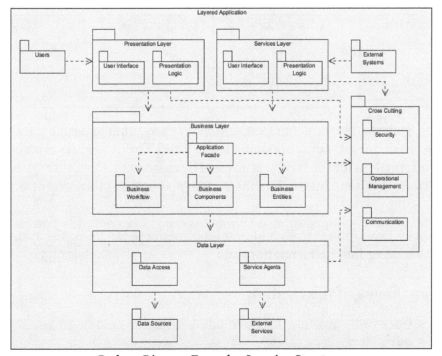

Package Diagram Example - Layering Structure.

Package Diagram Example - Order Subsystem

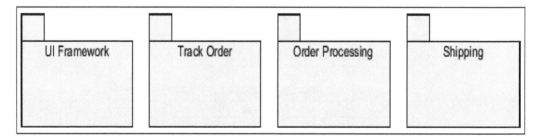

Package Diagram Example - Order Processing System

Order Processing System - The Problem Description: We are going to design package diagram for "Track Order" scenario for an online shopping store. Track Order module is responsible for providing tracking information for the products ordered by customers. Customer types in the tracking serial number, Track Order modules refers the system and updates the current shipping status to the customer.

Based on the project Description we should first identify the packages in the system and then related them together according to the relationship:

Identify the Packages of the System

- There is a track order module, it has to talk with other module to know about the order details, let us call it "Order Details".

- Next after fetching Order Details it has to know about shipping details, let us call that as "Shipping".

Identify the Dependencies in the System

- Track order should get order details from "Order Details" and "Order Details" has to know the tracking info given by the customer. Two modules are accessing each other which suffices <<access>> dual dependency.

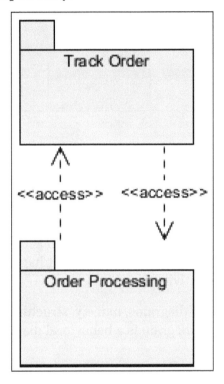

- To know shipping information, "Shipping" can import "Track Order" to make the navigation easier.

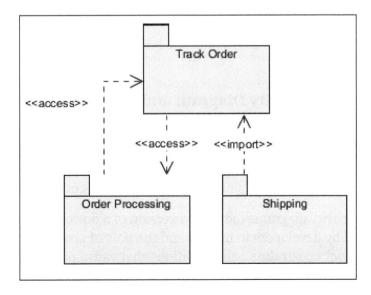

- Finally, Track Order dependency to UI Framework is also mapped which completes our Package Diagram for Order Processing subsystem.

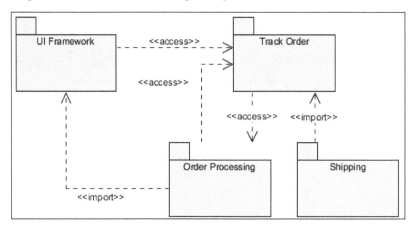

Behavioral UML Diagrams

Activity Diagram

We use Activity Diagrams to illustrate the flow of control in a system and refer to the steps involved in the execution of a use case. We model sequential and concurrent activities using activity diagrams. So, we basically depict workflows visually using an activity diagram. An activity diagram focuses on condition of flow and the sequence in which it happens. We describe or depict what causes a particular event using an activity diagram.

UML models basically three types of diagrams, namely, structure diagrams, interaction diagrams, and behavior diagrams. An activity diagram is a behavioral diagram i.e. it depicts the behavior of a system.

An activity diagram portrays the control flow from a start point to a finish point showing the various decision paths that exist while the activity is being executed. We can depict both sequential processing and concurrent processing of activities using an activity diagram. They are used in business and process modelling where their primary use is to depict the dynamic aspects of a system.

An activity diagram is very similar to a flowchart. So let us understand if an activity diagrams or a flowcharts are any different.

Difference between an Activity Diagram and a Flowchart

Flowcharts were typically invented earlier than activity diagrams. Non programmers use Flow charts to model workflows. For example: A manufacturer uses a flow chart to explain and illustrate how a particular product is manufactured. We can call a flowchart a primitive version of an activity diagram. Business processes where decision making is involved is expressed using a flow chart.

So, programmers use activity diagrams (advanced version of a flowchart) to depict workflows. An activity diagram is used by developers to understand the flow of programs on a high level. It also enables them to figure out constraints and conditions that cause particular events. A flow chart converges into being an activity diagram if complex decisions are being made.

Brevity is the soul of wit. We need to convey a lot of information with clarity and make sure it is short. So an activity diagram helps people on both sides i.e. Businessmen and Developers to interact and understand systems.

Difference between a use Case Diagram and an Activity Diagram

An activity diagram is used to model the workflow depicting conditions, constraints, sequential and concurrent activities. On the other hand, the purpose of a Use Case is to just depict the functionality i.e. what the system does and not how it is done. So in simple terms, an activity diagram shows 'How' while a Use case shows 'What' for a particular system.

The levels of abstraction also vary for both of them. An activity diagram can be used to illustrate a business process (high level implementation) to a stand alone algorithm (ground level implementation). However, Use cases have a low level of abstraction. They are used to show a high level of implementation only.

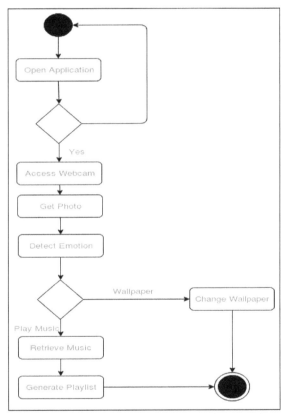

An activity diagram for an emotion based music player.

The above figure depicts an activity diagram for an emotion based music player which can also be used to change the wallpaper.

The various components used in the diagram and the standard notations are explained below.

Activity Diagram Notations

- Initial State – The starting state before an activity takes place is depicted using the initial state.

Notation for initial state or start state.

A process can have only one initial state unless we are depicting nested activities. We use a black filled circle to depict the initial state of a system. For objects, this is the state when they are instantiated. The Initial State from the UML Activity Diagram marks the entry point and the initial Activity State.

For example – Here the initial state is the state of the system before the application is opened.

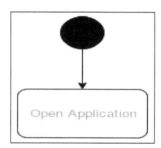

Initial state symbol being used.

- Action or Activity State – An activity represents execution of an action on objects or by objects. We represent an activity using a rectangle with rounded corners. Basically any action or event that takes place is represented using an activity.

Notation for an activity state.

For example – Consider the previous example of opening an application opening the application is an activity state in the activity diagram.

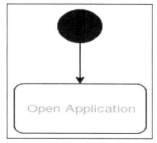

Activity state symbol being used.

- Action Flow or Control flows – Action flows or Control flows are also referred to as paths and edges. They are used to show the transition from one activity state to another.

Notation for control Flow.

An activity state can have multiple incoming and outgoing action flows. We use a line with an arrow head to depict a Control Flow. If there is a constraint to be adhered to while making the transition it is mentioned on the arrow.

- Consider the example – Here both the states transit into one final state using action flow symbols i.e. arrows.

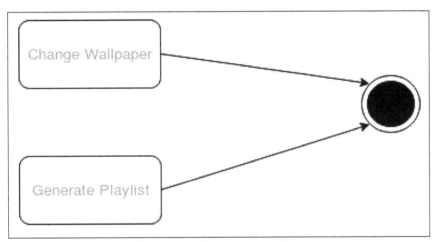

Using action flows for transitions.

- Decision node and Branching – When we need to make a decision before deciding the flow of control, we use the decision node.

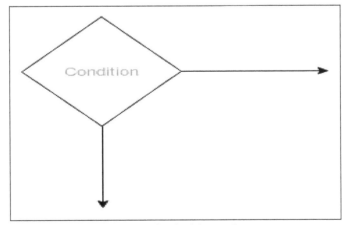

Notation for decision node.

The outgoing arrows from the decision node can be labelled with conditions or guard expressions. It always includes two or more output arrows.

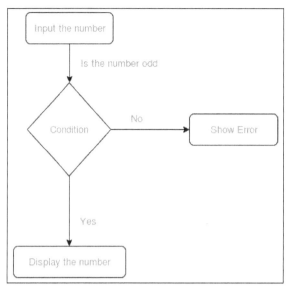

An activity diagram using decision node.

- Guards – A Guard refers to a statement written next to a decision node on an arrow sometimes within square brackets.

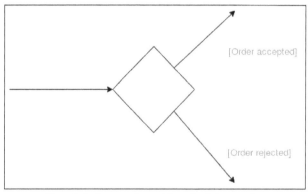

Guards being used next to a decision node.

The statement must be true for the control to shift along a particular direction. Guards help us know the constraints and conditions which determine the flow of a process.

- Fork – Fork nodes are used to support concurrent activities.

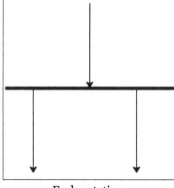

Fork notation.

When we use a fork node when both the activities get executed concurrently i.e. no decision is made before splitting the activity into two parts. Both parts need to be executed in case of a fork statement.

We use a rounded solid rectangular bar to represent a Fork notation with incoming arrow from the parent activity state and outgoing arrows towards the newly created activities.

For example: In the example below, the activity of making coffee can be split into two concurrent activities and hence we use the fork notation.

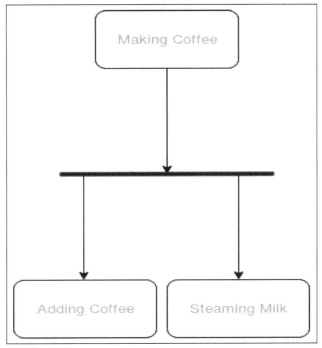

A diagram using fork.

• Join – Join nodes are used to support concurrent activities converging into one. For join notations we have two or more incoming edges and one outgoing edge.

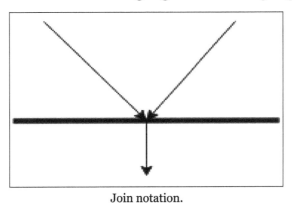

Join notation.

For example – When both activities i.e. steaming the milk and adding coffee get completed, we converge them into one final activity.

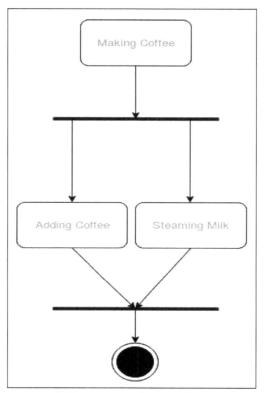

A diagram using join notation.

- Merge or Merge Event – Scenarios arise when activities which are not being executed concurrently have to be merged. We use the merge notation for such scenarios. We can merge two or more activities into one if the control proceeds onto the next activity irrespective of the path chosen.

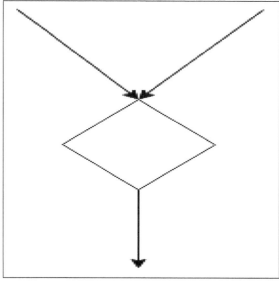

Merge notation.

For example – In the diagram below: we can't have both sides executing concurrently, but they finally merge into one. A number can't be both odd and even at the same time.

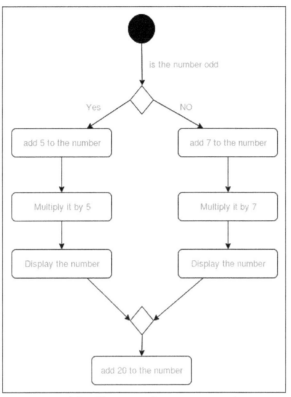

An activity diagram using merge notation.

- Swimlanes – We use swimlanes for grouping related activities in one column. Swimlanes group related activities into one column or one row. Swimlanes can be vertical and horizontal. Swimlanes are used to add modularity to the activity diagram. It is not mandatory to use swimlanes. They usually give more clarity to the activity diagram. It's similar to creating a function in a program. It's not mandatory to do so, but, it is a recommended practice.

Swimlanes notation.

We use a rectangular column to represent a swimlane as shown in the figure above.

For example – Here different set of activities are executed based on if the number is odd or even. These activities are grouped into a swimlane.

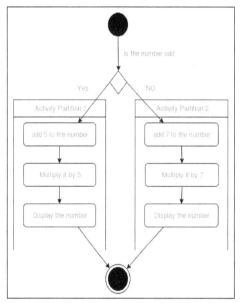

An activity diagram making use of swimlanes.

- Time Event

Time event notation.

We can have a scenario where an event takes some time to complete. We use an hourglass to represent a time event.

For example – Let us assume that the processing of an image takes takes a lot of time. Then it can be represented as shown below.

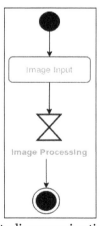

An activity diagram using time event.

- Final State or End State – The state which the system reaches when a particular process or activity ends is known as a Final State or End State. We use a filled circle within a circle notation to represent the final state in a state machine diagram. A system or a process can have multiple final states.

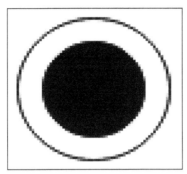

Notation for final state.

How to Draw an Activity Diagram

- Identify the initial state and the final states.

- Identify the intermediate activities needed to reach the final state from he initial state.

- Identify the conditions or constraints which cause the system to change control flow.

- Draw the diagram with appropriate notations.

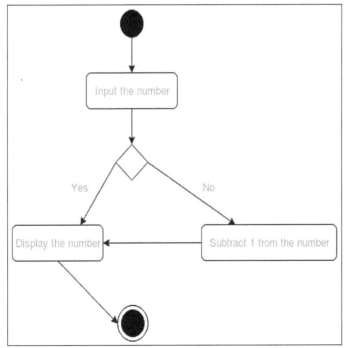

An activity diagram.

The above diagram prints the number if it is odd otherwise it subtracts one from the number and displays it.

Uses of an Activity Diagram

- Dynamic modelling of the system or a process.

- Illustrate the various steps involved in a UML use case.

- Model software elements like methods,operations and functions.

- We can use Activity diagrams to depict concurrent activities easily.

- Show the constraints, conditions and logic behind algorithms.

Communication Diagram

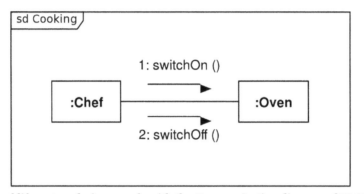

Real life system design sample with the Communication diagram of UML.

A communication diagram in the Unified Modeling Language (UML) 2.0, is a simplified version of the UML 1.x collaboration diagram.

UML has four types of interaction diagrams:

- Sequence diagram

- Communication diagram

- Interaction overview diagram

- Timing diagram

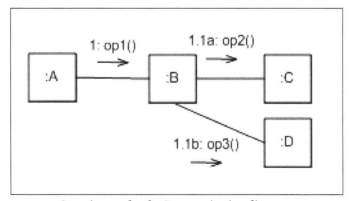

Generic sample of a Communication diagram.

A Communication diagram models the interactions between objects or parts in terms of sequenced messages. Communication diagrams represent a combination of information taken from Class, Sequence, and Use Case Diagrams describing both the static structure and dynamic behavior of a system.

However, communication diagrams use the free-form arrangement of objects and links as used in Object diagrams. In order to maintain the ordering of messages in such a free-form diagram, messages are labeled with a chronological number and placed near the link the message is sent over. Reading a communication diagram involves starting at message 1.0, and following the messages from object to object.

Communication diagrams show a lot of the same information as sequence diagrams, but because of how the information is presented, some of it is easier to find in one diagram than the other. Communication diagrams show which elements each one interacts with better, but sequence diagrams show the order in which the interactions take place more clearly.

Interaction Diagram

From the term Interaction, it is clear that the diagram is used to describe some type of interactions among the different elements in the model. This interaction is a part of dynamic behavior of the system.

This interactive behavior is represented in UML by two diagrams known as Sequence diagram and Collaboration diagram. The basic purpose of both the diagrams are similar.

Sequence diagram emphasizes on time sequence of messages and collaboration diagram emphasizes on the structural organization of the objects that send and receive messages.

Purpose of Interaction Diagrams

The purpose of interaction diagrams is to visualize the interactive behavior of the system. Visualizing the interaction is a difficult task. Hence, the solution is to use different types of models to capture the different aspects of the interaction.

Sequence and collaboration diagrams are used to capture the dynamic nature but from a different angle.

The purpose of interaction diagram is:

- To capture the dynamic behaviour of a system.

- To describe the message flow in the system.

- To describe the structural organization of the objects.

- To describe the interaction among objects.

Methods to Draw an Interaction Diagram

The purpose of interaction diagrams is to capture the dynamic aspect of a system. So to capture the dynamic aspect, we need to understand what a dynamic aspect is and how it is visualized. Dynamic aspect can be defined as the snapshot of the running system at a particular moment.

We have two types of interaction diagrams in UML. One is the sequence diagram and the other is the collaboration diagram. The sequence diagram captures the time sequence of the message flow from one object to another and the collaboration diagram describes the organization of objects in a system taking part in the message flow.

Following things are to be identified clearly before drawing the interaction diagram:

- Objects taking part in the interaction.

- Message flows among the objects.

- The sequence in which the messages are flowing.

- Object organization.

Following are two interaction diagrams modeling the order management system. The first diagram is a sequence diagram and the second is a collaboration diagram.

The Sequence Diagram

The sequence diagram has four objects (Customer, Order, SpecialOrder and NormalOrder).

The following diagram shows the message sequence for *SpecialOrder* object and the same can be used in case of *NormalOrder* object. It is important to understand the time sequence of message flows. The message flow is nothing but a method call of an object.

The first call is sendOrder () which is a method of Order object. The next call is confirm () which is a method of SpecialOrder object and the last call is Dispatch () which is a method of SpecialOrder object. The following diagram mainly describes the method calls from one object to another, and this is also the actual scenario when the system is running.

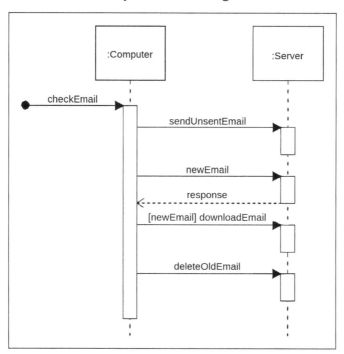

The Collaboration Diagram

The second interaction diagram is the collaboration diagram. It shows the object organization as seen in the following diagram. In the collaboration diagram, the method call sequence is indicated by some numbering technique. The number indicates how the methods are called one after another. We have taken the same order management system to describe the collaboration diagram.

Method calls are similar to that of a sequence diagram. However, difference being the sequence diagram does not describe the object organization, whereas the collaboration diagram shows the object organization.

To choose between these two diagrams, emphasis is placed on the type of requirement. If the time sequence is important, then the sequence diagram is used. If organization is required, then collaboration diagram is used.

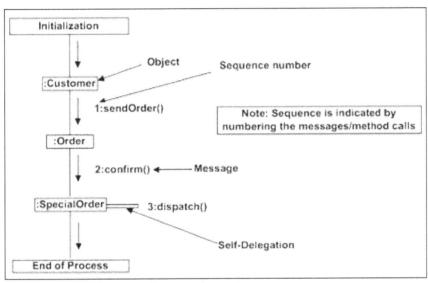

Collaboration diagram of an order nanagement system.

Usage of use Interaction Diagram

Interaction diagrams are used to describe the dynamic nature of a system. Now, we will look into the practical scenarios where these diagrams are used. To understand the practical application, we need to understand the basic nature of sequence and collaboration diagram.

The main purpose of both the diagrams are similar as they are used to capture the dynamic behavior of a system. However, the specific purpose is more important to clarify and understand.

Sequence diagrams are used to capture the order of messages flowing from one object to another. Collaboration diagrams are used to describe the structural organization of the objects taking part in the interaction. A single diagram is not sufficient to describe the dynamic aspect of an entire system, so a set of diagrams are used to capture it as a whole.

Interaction diagrams are used when we want to understand the message flow and the structural organization. Message flow means the sequence of control flow from one object to another. Structural organization means the visual organization of the elements in a system.

Interaction diagrams can be used:

- To model the flow of control by time sequence.

- To model the flow of control by structural organizations.

- For forward engineering.

- For reverse engineering.

UML Statechart

UML state machine, also known as UML statechart, is a significantly enhanced realization of the mathematical concept of a finite automaton in computer science applications as expressed in the Unified Modeling Language (UML) notation.

The concepts behind it are about organizing the way a device, computer program, or other (often technical) process works such that an entity or each of its sub-entities is always in exactly one of a number of possible states and where there are well-defined conditional transitions between these states.

UML state machine is an object-based variant of Harel statechart, adapted and extended by UML. The goal of UML state machines is to overcome the main limitations of traditional finite-state machines while retaining their main benefits. UML statecharts introduce the new concepts of hierarchically nested states and orthogonal regions, while extending the notion of actions. UML state machines have the characteristics of both Mealy machines and Moore machines. They support actions that depend on both the state of the system and the triggering event, as in Mealy machines, as well as entry and exit actions, which are associated with states rather than transitions, as in Moore machines.

The term "UML state machine" can refer to two kinds of state machines: *behavioral state machines* and *protocol state machines*. Behavioral state machines can be used to model the behavior of individual entities (e.g., class instances). Protocol state machines are used to express usage protocols and can be used to specify the legal usage scenarios of classifiers, interfaces, and ports.

Basic State Machine Concepts

Many software systems are event-driven, which means that they continuously wait for the occurrence of some external or internal event such as a mouse click, a button press, a time tick, or an arrival of a data packet. After recognizing the event, such systems react by performing the appropriate computation that may include manipulating the hardware or generating "soft" events that trigger other internal software components. (That's why event-driven systems are alternatively called reactive systems.) Once the event handling is complete, the system goes back to waiting for the next event.

The response to an event generally depends on both the type of the event and on the internal state of the system and can include a change of state leading to a state transition. The pattern of events, states, and state transitions among those states can be abstracted and represented as a finite-state machine (FSM).

The concept of a FSM is important in event-driven programming because it makes the event handling explicitly dependent on both the event-type and on the state of the system. When used correctly, a state machine can drastically cut down the number of execution paths through the code, simplify the conditions tested at each branching point, and simplify the switching between different modes of execution. Conversely, using event-driven programming without an underlying FSM model can lead programmers to produce error prone, difficult to extend and excessively complex application code.

Basic UML State Diagrams

UML preserves the general form of the traditional state diagrams. The UML state diagrams are directed graphs in which nodes denote states and connectors denote state transitions. For example, figure below shows a UML state diagram corresponding to the computer keyboard state machine. In UML, states are represented as rounded rectangles labeled with state names. The transitions, represented as arrows, are labeled with the triggering events followed optionally by the list of executed actions. The initial transition originates from the solid circle and specifies the default state when the system first begins. Every state diagram should have such a transition, which should not be labeled, since it is not triggered by an event. The initial transition can have associated actions.

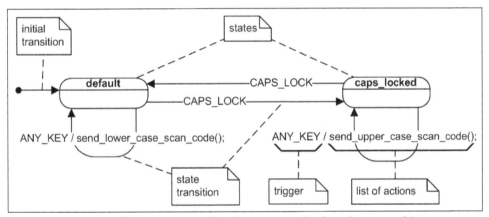

UML state diagram representing the computer keyboard state machine.

Events

An event is something that happens that affects the system. Strictly speaking, in the UML specification, the term event refers to the type of occurrence rather than to any concrete instance of that occurrence. For example, Keystroke is an event for the keyboard, but each press of a key is not an event but a concrete instance of the Keystroke event. Another event of interest for the keyboard might be Power-on, but turning the power on tomorrow at 10:05:36 will be just an instance of the Power-on event.

An event can have associated parameters, allowing the event instance to convey not only the occurrence of some interesting incident but also quantitative information regarding that occurrence. For example, the Keystroke event generated by pressing a key on a computer keyboard has associated parameters that convey the character scan code as well as the status of the Shift, Ctrl, and Alt keys.

An event instance outlives the instantaneous occurrence that generated it and might convey this occurrence to one or more state machines. Once generated, the event instance goes through a processing life cycle that can consist of up to three stages. First, the event instance is received when it is accepted and waiting for processing (e.g., it is placed on the event queue). Later, the event instance is dispatched to the state machine, at which point it becomes the current event. Finally, it is consumed when the state machine finishes processing the event instance. A consumed event instance is no longer available for processing.

States

Each state machine has a state, which governs reaction of the state machine to events. For example, when you strike a key on a keyboard, the character code generated will be either an uppercase or a lowercase character, depending on whether the Caps Lock is active. Therefore, the keyboard's behavior can be divided into two states: the "default" state and the "caps_locked" state. (Most keyboards include an LED that indicates that the keyboard is in the "caps_locked" state.) The behavior of a keyboard depends only on certain aspects of its history, namely whether the Caps Lock key has been pressed, but not, for example, on how many and exactly which other keys have been pressed previously. A state can abstract away all possible (but irrelevant) event sequences and capture only the relevant ones.

In the context of software state machines (and especially classical FSMs), the term state is often understood as a single state variable that can assume only a limited number of a priori determined values (e.g., two values in case of the keyboard, or more generally - some kind of variable with an enum type in many programming languages). The idea of state variable (and classical FSM model) is that the value of the state variable fully defines the current state of the system at any given time. The concept of the state reduces the problem of identifying the execution context in the code to testing just the state variable instead of many variables, thus eliminating a lot of conditional logic.

Extended States

In practice, however, interpreting the whole state of the state machine as a single state variable quickly becomes impractical for all state machines beyond very simple ones. Indeed, even if we have a single 32-bit integer in our machine state, it could contribute to over 4 billion different states - and will lead to a premature state explosion. This interpretation is not practical, so in UML state machines the whole state of the state machine is commonly split into (a) enumeratable state variable and (b) all the other variables which are named extended state. Another way to see it is to interpret enumeratable state variable as a qualitative aspect and extended state as quantitative aspects of the whole state. In this interpretation, a change of variable does not always imply a change of the qualitative aspects of the system behavior and therefore does not lead to a change of state.

State machines supplemented with extended state variables are called extended state machines and UML state machines belong to this category. Extended state machines can apply the underlying formalism to much more complex problems than is practical without including extended state variables. For example, if we have to implement some kind of limit in our FSM (say, limiting number of keystrokes on keyboard to 1000), without extended state we'd need to create and process 1000 states - which is not practical; however, with an extended state machine we can introduce a key_count variable, which is initialized to 1000 and decremented by every keystroke without changing state variable.

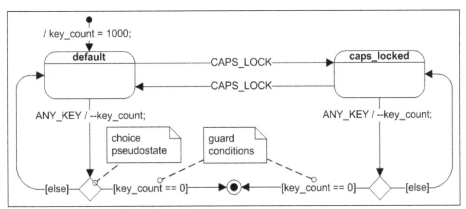

Extended state machine of "cheap keyboard" with extended
state variable key_count and various guard conditions.

The state diagram is an example of an extended state machine, in which the complete condition of the system (called the extended state) is the combination of a qualitative aspect—the state variable—and the quantitative aspects—the extended state variables.

The obvious advantage of extended state machines is flexibility. For example, changing the limit governed by key_count from 1000 to 10000 keystrokes, would not complicate the extended state machine at all. The only modification required would be changing the initialization value of the key_count extended state variable during initialization.

This flexibility of extended state machines comes with a price, however, because of the complex coupling between the "qualitative" and the "quantitative" aspects of the extended state. The coupling occurs through the guard conditions attached to transitions.

Guard Conditions

Guard conditions (or simply guards) are Boolean expressions evaluated dynamically based on the value of extended state variables and event parameters. Guard conditions affect the behavior of a state machine by enabling actions or transitions only when they evaluate to TRUE and disabling them when they evaluate to FALSE. In the UML notation, guard conditions are shown in square brackets (e.g., [key_count == 0]).

The need for guards is the immediate consequence of adding memory extended state variables to the state machine formalism. Used sparingly, extended state variables and guards make up a powerful mechanism that can simplify designs. On the other hand, it is possible to abuse extended states and guards quite easily.

Actions and Transitions

When an event instance is dispatched, the state machine responds by performing actions, such as changing a variable, performing I/O, invoking a function, generating another event instance, or changing to another state. Any parameter values associated with the current event are available to all actions directly caused by that event.

Switching from one state to another is called state transition, and the event that causes it is called the triggering event, or simply the trigger. In the keyboard example, if the keyboard is in the "default" state when the CapsLock key is pressed, the keyboard will enter the "caps_locked" state. However, if the keyboard is already in the "caps_locked" state, pressing CapsLock will cause a different transition—from the "caps_locked" to the "default" state. In both cases, pressing CapsLock is the triggering event.

In extended state machines, a transition can have a guard, which means that the transition can "fire" only if the guard evaluates to TRUE. A state can have many transitions in response to the same trigger, as long as they have nonoverlapping guards; however, this situation could create problems in the sequence of evaluation of the guards when the common trigger occurs. The UML specification intentionally does not stipulate any particular order; rather, UML puts the burden on the designer to devise guards in such a way that the order of their evaluation does not matter. Practically, this means that guard expressions should have no side effects, at least none that would alter evaluation of other guards having the same trigger.

Run-to-completion Execution Model

All state machine formalisms, including UML state machines, universally assume that a state machine completes processing of each event before it can start processing the next event. This model of execution is called run to completion, or RTC.

In the RTC model, the system processes events in discrete, indivisible RTC steps. New incoming events cannot interrupt the processing of the current event and must be stored (typically in an event queue) until the state machine becomes idle again. These semantics completely avoid any internal concurrency issues within a single state machine. The RTC model also gets around the conceptual problem of processing actions associated with transitions, where the state machine is not in a well-defined state (is between two states) for the duration of the action. During event processing, the system is unresponsive (unobservable), so the ill-defined state during that time has no practical significance.

However, that RTC does not mean that a state machine has to monopolize the CPU until the RTC step is complete. The preemption restriction only applies to the task context of the state machine that is already busy processing events. In a multitasking environment, other tasks (not related to the task context of the busy state machine) can be running, possibly preempting the currently executing state machine. As long as other state machines do not share variables or other resources with each other, there are no concurrency hazards.

The key advantage of RTC processing is simplicity. Its biggest disadvantage is that the responsiveness of a state machine is determined by its longest RTC step. Achieving short RTC steps can often significantly complicate real-time designs.

UML Extensions to the Traditional FSM Formalism

Though the traditional FSMs are an excellent tool for tackling smaller problems, it's also generally known that they tend to become unmanageable, even for moderately involved systems. Due to the phenomenon known as state and transition explosion, the complexity of a traditional FSM tends to grow much faster than the complexity of the system it describes. This happens because the traditional state machine formalism inflicts repetitions. For example, if you try to represent the behavior of a simple pocket calculator with a traditional FSM, you'll immediately notice that many events (e.g., the Clear or Off button presses) are handled identically in many states. A conventional FSM shown in the figure below, has no means of capturing such a commonality and requires repeating the same actions and transitions in many states. What's missing in the traditional state machines is the mechanism for factoring out the common behavior in order to share it across many states.

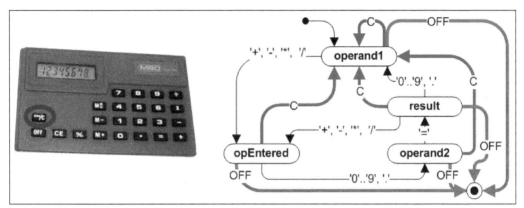

A pocket calculator (left) and the traditional state machine with multiple transitions Clear and Off (right).

UML state machines address exactly this shortcoming of the conventional FSMs. They provide a number of features for eliminating the repetitions so that the complexity of a UML state machine no longer explodes but tends to faithfully represent the complexity of the reactive system it describes. Obviously, these features are very interesting to software developers, because only they make the whole state machine approach truly applicable to real-life problems.

Hierarchically Nested States

The most important innovation of UML state machines over the traditional FSMs is the introduction of hierarchically nested states (that is why statecharts are also called hierarchical state machines, or HSMs). The semantics associated with state nesting are as follows: If a system is in the nested state, for example "result" (called the substate), it also (implicitly) is in the surrounding state "on" (called the superstate). This state machine will attempt to handle any event in the context of the substate, which conceptually is at the lower level of the hierarchy. However, if the substate "result" does not prescribe how to handle the event, the event is not quietly discarded as in a traditional "flat" state machine; rather, it is automatically handled at the higher level context of the superstate "on". This is what is meant by the system being in state "result" as well as "on". Of course, state nesting is not limited to one level only, and the simple rule of event processing applies recursively to any level of nesting.

States that contain other states are called composite states; conversely, states without internal structure are called simple states. A nested state is called a direct substate when it is not contained by any other state; otherwise, it is referred to as a transitively nested substate.

Because the internal structure of a composite state can be arbitrarily complex, any hierarchical state machine can be viewed as an internal structure of some (higher-level) composite state. It is conceptually convenient to define one composite state as the ultimate root of state machine hierarchy. In the UML specification, every state machine has a top state (the abstract root of every state machine hierarchy), which contains all the other elements of the entire state machine. The graphical rendering of this all-enclosing top state is optional.

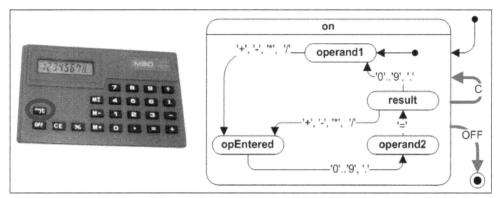

A pocket calculator (left) and the UML state machine with state nesting (right).

As you can see, the semantics of hierarchical state decomposition are designed to facilitate reusing of behavior. The substates (nested states) need only define the differences from the superstates (containing states). A substate can easily inherit the common behavior from its superstate(s) by simply ignoring commonly handled events, which are then automatically handled by higher-level states. In other words, hierarchical state nesting enables programming by difference.

The aspect of state hierarchy emphasized most often is abstraction—an old and powerful technique for coping with complexity. Instead of addressing all aspects of a complex system at the same time, it is often possible to ignore (abstract away) some parts of the system. Hierarchical states are an ideal mechanism for hiding internal details because the designer can easily zoom out or zoom in to hide or show nested states.

However, composite states don't simply hide complexity; they also actively reduce it through the powerful mechanism of hierarchical event processing. Without such reuse, even a moderate increase in system complexity could lead to an explosive increase in the number of states and transitions. For example, the hierarchical state machine representing the pocket calculator avoids repeating the transitions Clear and Off in virtually every state. Avoiding repetition allows the growth of HSMs to remain proportionate to growth in system complexity. As the modeled system grows, the opportunity for reuse also increases and thus potentially counteracts the disproportionate increase in numbers of states and transitions typical of traditional FSMs.

Orthogonal Regions

Analysis by hierarchical state decomposition can include the application of the operation 'exclusive-OR' to any given state. For example, if a system is in the "on" superstate, it may be the case that it is also in either "operand1" substate OR the "operand2" substate OR the "opEntered" substate OR the "result" substate. This would lead to description of the "on" superstate as an 'OR-state'.

UML statecharts also introduce the complementary AND-decomposition. Such decomposition means that a composite state can contain two or more orthogonal regions (orthogonal means compatible and independent in this context) and that being in such a composite state entails being in all its orthogonal regions simultaneously.

Orthogonal regions address the frequent problem of a combinatorial increase in the number of states when the behavior of a system is fragmented into independent, concurrently active parts. For example, apart from the main keypad, a computer keyboard has an independent numeric keypad. the two states of the main keypad already identified: "default" and "caps_locked". The numeric keypad also can be in two states—"numbers" and "arrows"—depending on whether Num Lock is active. The complete state space of the keyboard in the standard decomposition is therefore the Cartesian product of the two components (main keypad and numeric keypad) and consists of four states: "default–numbers," "default–arrows," "caps_locked–numbers," and "caps_locked–arrows." However, this would be an unnatural representation because the behavior of the numeric keypad does not depend on the state of the main keypad and vice versa. The use of orthogonal regions allows the mixing of independent behaviors as a Cartesian product to be avoided and, instead, for them to remain separate.

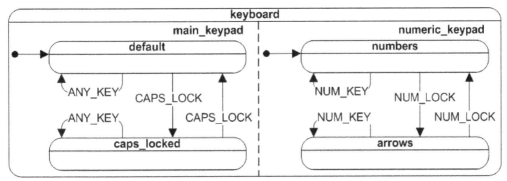

Two orthogonal regions (main keypad and numeric keypad) of a computer keyboard.

Note that if the orthogonal regions are fully independent of each other, their combined complexity is simply additive, which means that the number of independent states needed to model the system is simply the sum $k + l + m + ...$, where $k, l, m, ...$ denote numbers of OR-states in each orthogonal region. However, the general case of mutual dependency, on the other hand, results in multiplicative complexity, so in general, the number of states needed is the product $k \times l \times m \times ....$

In most real-life situations, orthogonal regions would be only approximately orthogonal (i.e. not truly independent). Therefore, UML statecharts provide a number of ways for orthogonal regions to communicate and synchronize their behaviors. Among these rich sets of (sometimes complex) mechanisms, perhaps the most important feature is that orthogonal regions can coordinate their behaviors by sending event instances to each other.

Even though orthogonal regions imply independence of execution (allowing more or less concurrency), the UML specification does not require that a separate thread of execution be assigned to each orthogonal region (although this can be done if desired). In fact, most commonly, orthogonal regions execute within the same thread. The UML specification requires only that the designer does not rely on any particular order for event instances to be dispatched to the relevant orthogonal regions.

Entry and Exit Actions

Every state in a UML statechart can have optional entry actions, which are executed upon entry to a state, as well as optional exit actions, which are executed upon exit from a state. Entry and exit actions are associated with states, not transitions. Regardless of how a state is entered or exited, all its entry and exit actions will be executed. Because of this characteristic, statecharts behave like Moore machines. The UML notation for state entry and exit actions is to place the reserved word "entry" (or "exit") in the state right below the name compartment, followed by the forward slash and the list of arbitrary actions.

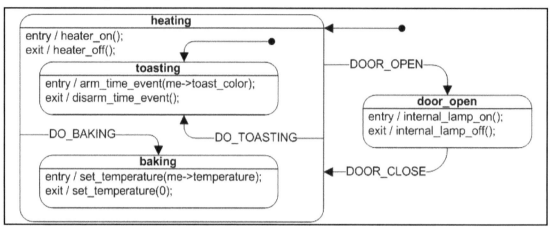

Toaster oven state machine with entry and exit actions.

The value of entry and exit actions is that they provide means for guaranteed initialization and cleanup, very much like class constructors and destructors in Object-oriented programming. For example, consider the "door_open" state which corresponds to the toaster oven behavior while the door is open. This state has a very important safety-critical requirement: Always disable the heater when the door is open. Additionally, while the door is open, the internal lamp illuminating the oven should light up.

Of course, such behavior could be modeled by adding appropriate actions (disabling the heater and turning on the light) to every transition path leading to the "door_open" state (the user may open the door at any time during "baking" or "toasting" or when the oven is not used at all). It should not be forgotten to extinguish the internal lamp with every transition leaving the "door_open" state. However, such a solution would cause the repetition of actions in many transitions. More importantly, such an approach leaves the design error-prone during subsequent amendments to behavior (e.g., the next programmer working on a new feature, such as top-browning, might simply forget to disable the heater on transition to "door_open").

Entry and exit actions allow implementation of desired behavior in a safer, simpler, and more intuitive way. it could be specified that the exit action from "heating" disables the heater, the entry action to "door_open" lights up the oven lamp, and the exit action from "door_open" extinguishes the lamp. The use of entry and exit actions is preferable to placing an action on a transition because it avoids repetitive coding and improves function by eliminating a safety hazard; (heater on while door open). The semantics of exit actions guarantees that, regardless of the transition path, the heater will be disabled when the toaster is not in the "heating" state.

Because entry actions are executed automatically whenever an associated state is entered, they often determine the conditions of operation or the identity of the state, very much as a class constructor determines the identity of the object being constructed. For example, the identity of the "heating" state is determined by the fact that the heater is turned on. This condition must be established before entering any substate of "heating" because entry actions to a substate of "heating," like "toasting," rely on proper initialization of the "heating" superstate and perform only the differences from this initialization. Consequently, the order of execution of entry actions must always proceed from the outermost state to the innermost state (top-down).

Not surprisingly, this order is analogous to the order in which class constructors are invoked. Construction of a class always starts at the very root of the class hierarchy and follows through all inheritance levels down to the class being instantiated. The execution of exit actions, which corresponds to destructor invocation, proceeds in the exact reverse order (bottom-up).

Internal Transitions

Very commonly, an event causes only some internal actions to execute but does not lead to a change of state (state transition). In this case, all actions executed comprise the internal transition. For example, when one types on a keyboard, it responds by generating different character codes. However, unless the Caps Lock key is pressed, the state of the keyboard does not change (no state transition occurs). In UML, this situation should be modeled with internal transitions, The UML notation for internal transitions follows the general syntax used for exit (or entry) actions, except instead of the word entry (or exit) the internal transition is labeled with the triggering event.

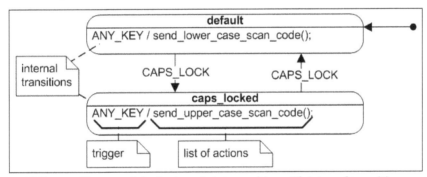

UML state diagram of the keyboard state machine with internal transitions.

In the absence of entry and exit actions, internal transitions would be identical to self-transitions (transitions in which the target state is the same as the source state). In fact, in a classical Mealy machine, actions are associated exclusively with state transitions, so the only way to execute actions without changing state is through a self-transition. However, in the presence of entry and exit actions, as in UML statecharts, a self-transition involves the execution of exit and entry actions and therefore it is distinctively different from an internal transition.

In contrast to a self-transition, no entry or exit actions are ever executed as a result of an internal transition, even if the internal transition is inherited from a higher level of the hierarchy than the currently active state. Internal transitions inherited from superstates at any level of nesting act as if they were defined directly in the currently active state.

Transition Execution Sequence

State nesting combined with entry and exit actions significantly complicates the state transition semantics in HSMs compared to the traditional FSMs. When dealing with hierarchically nested states and orthogonal regions, the simple term *current state* can be quite confusing. In an HSM, more than one state can be active at once. If the state machine is in a leaf state that is contained in a composite state (which is possibly contained in a higher-level composite state, and so on), all the composite states that either directly or transitively contain the leaf state are also active. Furthermore, because some of the composite states in this hierarchy might have orthogonal regions, the current active state is actually represented by a tree of states starting with the single top state at the root down to individual simple states at the leaves. The UML specification refers to such a state tree as state configuration.

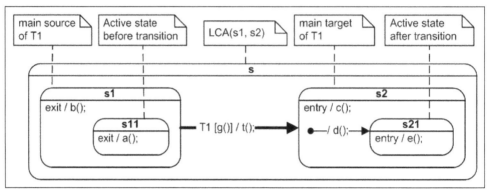

State roles in a state transition.

In UML, a state transition can directly connect any two states. These two states, which may be composite, are designated as the main source and the main target of a transition. The figure shows a simple transition example and explains the state roles in that transition. The UML specification prescribes that taking a state transition involves executing the following actions in the following sequence:

- Evaluate the guard condition associated with the transition and perform the following steps only if the guard evaluates to TRUE.

- Exit the source state configuration.

- Execute the actions associated with the transition.

- Enter the target state configuration.

The transition sequence is easy to interpret in the simple case of both the main source and the main target nesting at the same level. For example, transition T1 causes the evaluation of the guard g(); followed by the sequence of actions: a(); b(); t(); c(); d(); and e(); assuming that the guard g() evaluates to TRUE.

However, in the general case of source and target states nested at different levels of the state hierarchy, it might not be immediately obvious how many levels of nesting need to be exited. The UML specification prescribes that a transition involves exiting all nested states from the current active state (which might be a direct or transitive substate of the main source state) up to, but not including, the least common ancestor (LCA) state of the main source and main target states. As the name indicates, the LCA is the lowest composite state that is simultaneously a superstate (ancestor) of both the source and the target states. , the order of execution of exit actions is always from the most deeply nested state (the current active state) up the hierarchy to the LCA but without exiting the LCA. For instance, the LCA(s1,s2) of states "s1" and "s2" is state "s."

Entering the target state configuration commences from the level where the exit actions left off (i.e., from inside the LCA). Entry actions must be executed starting from the highest-level state down the state hierarchy to the main target state. If the main target state is composite, the UML semantics prescribes to "drill" into its submachine recursively using the local initial transitions. The target state configuration is completely entered only after encountering a leaf state that has no initial transitions.

Local versus External Transitions

Before UML 2, the only transition semantics in use was the external transition, in which the main source of the transition is always exited and the main target of the transition is always entered. UML 2 preserved the "external transition" semantics for backward compatibility, but introduced also a new kind of transition called local transition. For many transition topologies, external and local transitions are actually identical. However, a local transition doesn't cause exit from and re-entry to the main source state if the main target state is a substate of the main source. In addition, a local state transition doesn't cause exit from and reentry to the main target state if the main target is a superstate of the main source state.

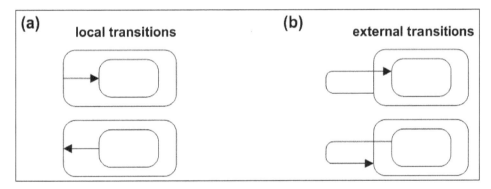

The figure contrasts local (a) and external (b) transitions. In the top row, you see the case of the main source containing the main target. The local transition does not cause exit from the source, while the external transition causes exit and reentry to the source. In the bottom row of the figure, you can see the case of the main target containing the main source. The local transition does not cause entry to the target, whereas the external transition causes exit and reentry to the target.

Event Deferral

Sometimes an event arrives at a particularly inconvenient time, when a state machine is in a state that cannot handle the event. In many cases, the nature of the event is such that it can be postponed (within limits) until the system enters another state, in which it is better prepared to handle the original event.

UML state machines provide a special mechanism for deferring events in states. In every state, you can include a clause [event list]/defer. If an event in the current state's deferred event list occurs, the event will be saved (deferred) for future processing until a state is entered that does not list the event in its deferred event list. Upon entry to such a state, the UML state machine will automatically recall any saved event(s) that are no longer deferred and will then either consume or discard these events. It is possible for a superstate to have a transition defined on an event that is deferred by a substate. Consistent with other areas in the specification of UML state machines, the substate takes precedence over the superstate, the event will be deferred and the transition for the superstate will not be executed. In the case of orthogonal regions where one orthogonal region defers an event and another consumes the event, the consumer takes precedence and the event is consumed and not deferred.

The Limitations of UML State Machines

Harel statecharts, which are the precursors of UML state machines, have been invented as "a visual formalism for complex systems", so from their inception, they have been inseparably associated with graphical representation in the form of state diagrams. However, it is important to understand that the concept of UML state machine transcends any particular notation, graphical or textual. The UML specification makes this distinction apparent by clearly separating state machine semantics from the notation.

However, the notation of UML statecharts is not purely visual. Any nontrivial state machine requires a large amount of textual information (e.g., the specification of actions and guards). The exact syntax of action and guard expressions isn't defined in the UML specification, so many people use either structured English or, more formally, expressions in an implementation language such as C, C++, or Java. In practice, this means that UML statechart notation depends heavily on the specific programming language.

Nevertheless, most of the statecharts semantics are heavily biased toward graphical notation. For example, state diagrams poorly represent the sequence of processing, be it order of evaluation of guards or order of dispatching events to orthogonal regions. The UML specification sidesteps these problems by putting the burden on the designer not to rely on any particular sequencing. However, it is the case that when UML state machines are actually implemented, there is inevitably full control over order of execution, giving rise to criticism that the UML semantics may be unnecessarily restrictive. Similarly, statechart diagrams require a lot of plumbing gear (pseudostates, like joins, forks, junctions, choicepoints, etc.) to represent the flow of control graphically. In other words, these elements of the graphical notation do not add much value in representing flow of control as compared to plain structured code.

The UML notation and semantics are really geared toward computerized UML tools. A UML state machine, as represented in a tool, is not just the state diagram, but rather a mixture of graphical and textual representation that precisely captures both the state topology and the actions. The users of the tool can get several complementary views of the same state machine, both visual and textual, whereas the generated code is just one of the many available views.

Use Case Diagram

A use case diagram at its simplest is a representation of a user's interaction with the system that shows the relationship between the user and the different use cases in which the user is involved. A use case diagram can identify the different types of users of a system and the different use cases and will often be accompanied by other types of diagrams as well. The use cases are represented by either circles or ellipses.

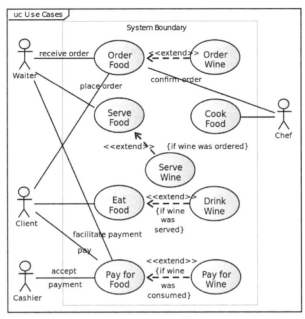

A UML use case diagram for the interaction of a
client (the actor) within a restaurant (the system).

Application

While a use case itself might drill into a lot of detail about every possibility, a use-case diagram can help provide a higher-level view of the system. It has been said before that "Use case diagrams are the blueprints for your system". They provide the simplified and graphical representation of what the system must actually do.

Due to their simplistic nature, use case diagrams can be a good communication tool for stakeholders. The drawings attempt to mimic the real world and provide a view for the stakeholder to understand how the system is going to be designed. Siau and Lee conducted research to determine if there was a valid situation for use case diagrams at all or if they were unnecessary. What was found was that the use case diagrams conveyed the intent of the system in a more simplified manner to stakeholders and that they were "interpreted more completely than class diagrams".

The purpose of the use case diagrams is simply to provide the high level view of the system and convey the requirements in laypeople's terms for the stakeholders. Additional diagrams and documentation can be used to provide a complete functional and technical view of the system.

Sequence Diagram

A sequence diagram is the most commonly used interaction diagram:

Interaction Diagram: An interaction diagram is used to show the interactive behavior of a system. Since visualizing the interactions in a system can be a cumbersome task, we use different types of interaction diagrams to capture various features and aspects of interaction in a system.

Sequence Diagrams: A sequence diagram simply depicts interaction between objects in a sequential order i.e. the order in which these interactions take place. We can also use the terms event diagrams or event scenarios to refer to a sequence diagram. Sequence diagrams describe how and in what order the objects in a system function. These diagrams are widely used by businessmen and software developers to document and understand requirements for new and existing systems.

Sequence Diagram Notations

Actors: An actor in a UML diagram represents a type of role where it interacts with the system and its objects. It is important to note here that an actor is always outside the scope of the system we aim to model using the UML diagram.

Notation symbol for actor.

We use actors to depict various roles including human users and other external subjects. We represent an actor in a UML diagram using a stick person notation. We can have multiple actors in a sequence diagram.

For example: Here the user in seat reservation system is shown as an actor where it exists outside the system and is not a part of the system.

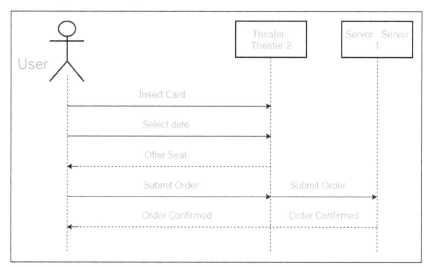

An actor interacting with a seat reservation system.

Lifelines: A lifeline is a named element which depicts an individual participant in a sequence diagram. So basically each instance in a sequence diagram is represented by a lifeline. Lifeline elements are located at the top in a sequence diagram. The standard in UML for naming a lifeline follows the following format – Instance Name : Class Name.

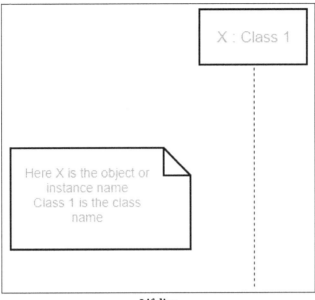

Lifeline

We display a lifeline in a rectangle called head with its name and type. The head is located on top of a vertical dashed line (referred to as the stem) as shown above. If we want to model an unnamed instance, we follow the same pattern except now the portion of lifeline's name is left blank.

Difference between a lifeline and an actor – A lifeline always portrays an object internal to the system whereas actors are used to depict objects external to the system. The following is an example of a sequence diagram:

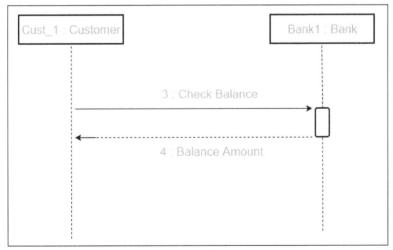

A sequence diagram.

Messages: Communication between objects is depicted using messages. The messages appear in a sequential order on the lifeline. We represent messages using arrows. Lifelines and messages form the core of a sequence diagram.

Messages can be broadly classified into the following categories:

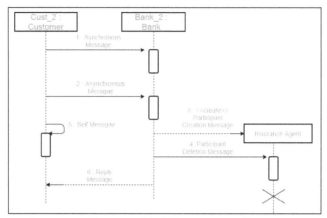

A sequence diagram with different types of messages.

Synchronous messages: A synchronous message waits for a reply before the interaction can move forward. The sender waits until the receiver has completed the processing of the message. The caller continues only when it knows that the receiver has processed the previous message i.e. it receives a reply message. A large number of calls in object oriented programming are synchronous. We use a solid arrow head to represent a synchronous message.

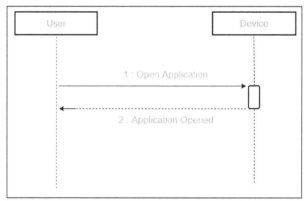

A sequence diagram using a synchronous message.

Asynchronous Messages: An asynchronous message does not wait for a reply from the receiver. The interaction moves forward irrespective of the receiver processing the previous message or not. We use a lined arrow head to represent an asynchronous message.

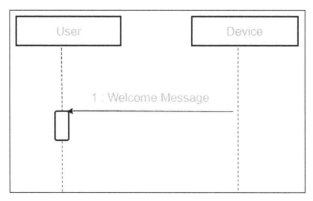

Create message: We use a Create message to instantiate a new object in the sequence diagram. There are situations when a particular message call requires the creation of an object. It is represented with a dotted arrow and create word labelled on it to specify that it is the create Message symbol.

For example: The creation of a new order on a e-commerce website would require a new object of Order class to be created.

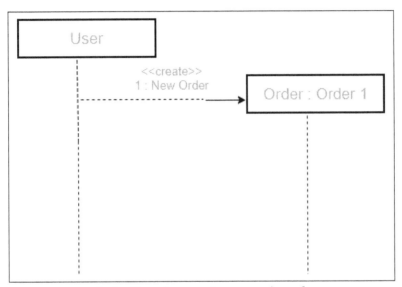

A situation where create message is used.

Delete Message: We use a Delete Message to delete an object. When an object is deallocated memory or is destroyed within the system we use the Delete Message symbol. It destroys the occurrence of the object in the system.It is represented by an arrow terminating with a x.

For example: In the scenario below when the order is received by the user, the object of order class can be destroyed.

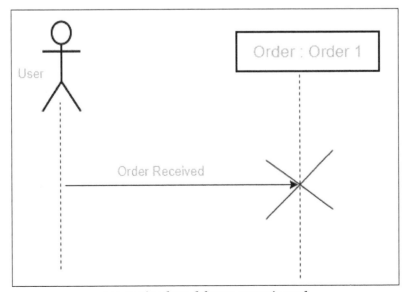

A scenario where delete message is used.

Self Message: Certain scenarios might arise where the object needs to send a message to itself. Such messages are called Self Messages and are represented with a U shaped arrow.

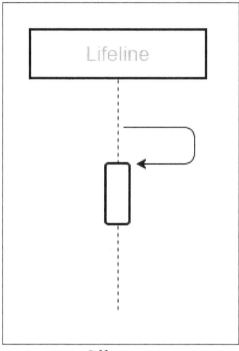

Self message.

For example: Consider a scenario where the device wants to access its webcam. Such a scenario is represented using a self message.

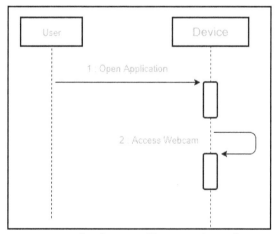

A scenario where a self message is used.

Reply Message: Reply messages are used to show the message being sent from the receiver to the sender. We represent a return/reply message using an open arrowhead with a dotted line. The interaction moves forward only when a reply message is sent by the receiver.

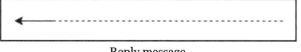

Reply message.

For example: Consider the scenario where the device requests a photo from the user. Here the message which shows the photo being sent is a reply message.

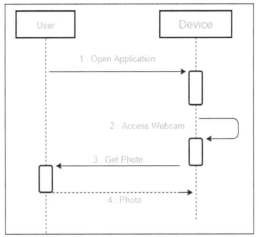

A scenario where a reply message is used.

Found Message: A Found message is used to represent a scenario where an unknown source sends the message. It is represented using an arrow directed towards a lifeline from an end point. For example: Consider the scenario of a hardware failure.

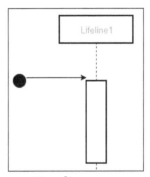

Found message.

It can be due to multiple reasons and we are not certain as to what caused the hardware failure.

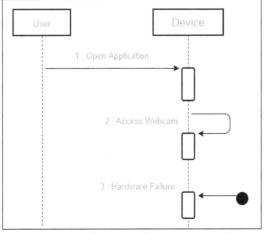

A scenario where found message is used.

Lost Message: A Lost message is used to represent a scenario where the recipient is not known to the system. It is represented using an arrow directed towards an end point from a lifeline. For example: Consider a scenario where a warning is generated.

Lost message.

The warning might be generated for the user or other software/object that the lifeline is interracting with. Since the destination is not known before hand, we use the Lost Message symbol.

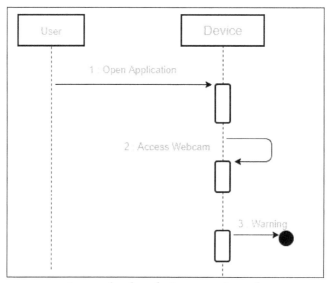

A scenario where lost message is used.

Guards: To model conditions we use guards in UML. They are used when we need to restrict the flow of messages on the pretext of a condition being met. Guards play an important role in letting software developers know the constraints attached to a system or a particular process.

For example: In order to be able to withdraw cash, having a balance greater than zero is a condition that must be met as shown below.

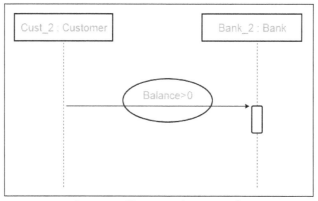

Sequence diagram using a guard.

A sequence diagram for an emotion based music player:

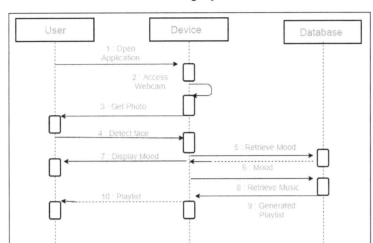

A sequence diagram for an emotion based music player.

The above sequence diagram depicts the sequence diagram for an emotion based music player:

- Firstly the application is opened by the user.

- The device then gets access to the web cam.

- The webcam captures the image of the user.

- The device uses algorithms to detect the face and predict the mood.

- It then requests database for dictionary of possible moods.

- The mood is retrieved from the database.

- The mood is displayed to the user.

- The music is requested from the database.

- The playlist is generated and finally shown to the user.

Uses of sequence diagrams:

- Used to model and visualise the logic behind a sophisticated function, operation or procedure.

- They are also used to show details of UML use case diagrams.

- Used to understand the detailed functionality of current or future systems.

- Visualise how messages and tasks move between objects or components in a system.

References

- What-is-class-diagram, uml-unified-modeling-language, guide: visual-paradigm.com, Retrieved 16 June, 2019

- "ISO/IEC 19505-1:2012 - Information technology - Object Management Group Unified Modeling Language (OMG UML) - Part 1: Infrastructure". Iso.org. 20 April 2012. Retrieved 10 April 2014

- Uml-component-diagram, uml: tutorialspoint.com, Retrieved 17 July, 2019

- Jon Holt Institution of Electrical Engineers (2004). UML for Systems Engineering: Watching the Wheels IET, 2004, ISBN 0-86341-354-4. P.5

- What-is-composite-structure-diagram, uml-unified-modeling-language, guide: visual-paradigm.com, Retrieved 18 August, 2019

- Gemino, A., Parker, D.(2009) "Use case diagrams in support of use case modeling: Deriving understanding from the picture", Journal of Database Management, 20(1), 1-24

- Uml-deployment-diagram, uml: tutorialspoint.com, Retrieved 19 January, 2019

- Unified-modeling-language-uml-object-diagrams: geeksforgeeks.org, Retrieved 20 February, 2019

- What-is-package-diagram, uml-unified-modeling-language, guide: visual-paradigm.com, Retrieved 21 March, 2019

Software Development Processes 5

The splitting of software development work into separate phases for the purpose of improving the planning and management is known as software development process. Some of the techniques used in this field are software prototyping and continuous integration. This chapter closely examines these practices related to software development process to provide an extensive understanding of the subject.

Reading: Software Development Process

In software engineering, a software development methodology (also known as a system development methodology, software development life cycle, software development process, software process) is a division of software development work into distinct phases (or stages) containing activities with the intent of better planning and management. It is often considered a subset of the systems development life cycle. The methodology may include the pre-definition of specific deliverables and artifacts that are created and completed by a project team to develop or maintain an application.

Common methodologies include waterfall, prototyping, iterative and incremental development, spiral development, rapid application development, extreme programming and various types of agile methodology. Some people consider a life-cycle "model" a more general term for a category of methodologies and a software development "process" a more specific term to refer to a specific process chosen by a specific organization. For example, there are many specific software development processes that fit the spiral life-cycle model.

In Practice

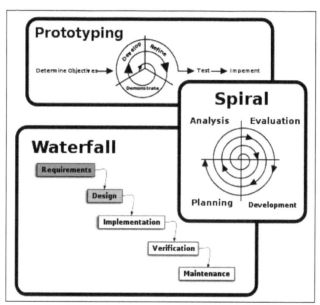

The three basic approaches applied to software
development methodology frameworks.

A variety of such frameworks have evolved over the years, each with its own recognized strengths and weaknesses. One software development methodology framework is not necessarily suitable for use by all projects. Each of the available methodology frameworks are best suited to specific kinds of projects, based on various technical, organizational, project and team considerations.

Software development organizations implement process methodologies to ease the process of development. Sometimes, contractors may require methodologies employed, an example is the U.S. defense industry, which requires a rating based on process models to obtain contracts. The international standard for describing the method of selecting, implementing and monitoring the life cycle for software is ISO/IEC 12207.

A decades-long goal has been to find repeatable, predictable processes that improve productivity and quality. Some try to systematize or formalize the seemingly unruly task of designing software. Others apply project management techniques to designing software. Without effective project management, software projects can easily be delivered late or over budget. With large numbers of software projects not meeting their expectations in terms of functionality, cost, or delivery schedule, it is effective project management that appears to be lacking.

Organizations may create a Software Engineering Process Group (SEPG), which is the focal point for process improvement. Composed of line practitioners who have varied skills, the group is at the center of the collaborative effort of everyone in the organization who is involved with software engineering process improvement.

A particular development team may also agree to programming environment details, such as which integrated development environment is used, and one or more dominant programming paradigms, programming style rules, or choice of specific software libraries or software frameworks. These details are generally not dictated by the choice of model or general methodology.

The software development methodology (also known as SDM) framework didn't emerge until the 1960s. According to Elliott (2004) the systems development life cycle (SDLC) can be considered to be the oldest formalized methodology framework for building information systems. The main idea of the SDLC has been "to pursue the development of information systems in a very deliberate, structured and methodical way, requiring each stage of the life cycle from inception of the idea to delivery of the final system, to be carried out rigidly and sequentially" within the context of the framework being applied. The main target of this methodology framework in the 1960s was "to develop large scale functional business systems in an age of large scale business conglomerates. Information systems activities revolved around heavy data processing and number crunching routines."

Methodologies, processes, and frameworks range from specific proscriptive steps that can be used directly by an organization in day-to-day work, to flexible frameworks that an organization uses to generate a custom set of steps tailored to the needs of a specific project or group. In some cases a "sponsor" or "maintenance" organization distributes an official set of documents that describe the process. Specific examples include:

1970s

- Structured programming since 1969.
- Cap Gemini SDM, originally from PANDATA. SDM stands for System Development Methodology.

1980s

- Structured systems analysis and design method (SSADM) from 1980 onwards.
- Information Requirement Analysis/Soft systems methodology.

1990s

- Object-oriented programming (OOP) developed in the early 1960s, and became a dominant programming approach during the mid-1990s.
- Rapid application development (RAD), since 1991.
- Dynamic systems development method (DSDM), since 1994.

- Scrum, since 1995.

- Team software process, since 1998.

- Rational Unified Process (RUP), maintained by IBM since 1998.

- Extreme programming, since 1999.

2000s

- Agile Unified Process (AUP) maintained since 2005 by Scott Ambler.

Approaches

Several software development approaches have been used since the origin of information technology, in two main categories. Typically an approach or a combination of approaches is chosen by management or a development team.

"Traditional" methodologies such as waterfall that have distinct phases are sometimes known as software development life cycle (SDLC) methodologies, though this term could also be used more generally to refer to any methodology. A "life cycle" approach with distinct phases is in contrast to Agile approaches which define a process of iteration, but where design, construction, and deployment of different pieces can occur simultaneously.

Waterfall Development

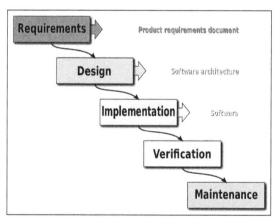

The activities of the software development process represented in the waterfall model. There are several other models to represent this process.

The waterfall model is a sequential development approach, in which development is seen as flowing steadily downwards (like a waterfall) through several phases, typically:

- Requirements analysis resulting in a software requirements specification.

- Software design.

- Implementation.

- Testing.

- Integration, if there are multiple subsystems.

- Deployment (or Installation).

- Maintenance.

The basic principles are:

- Project is divided into sequential phases, with some overlap and splashback acceptable between phases.

- Emphasis is on planning, time schedules, target dates, budgets and implementation of an entire system at one time.

- Tight control is maintained over the life of the project via extensive written documentation, formal reviews, and approval/signoff by the user and information technology management occurring at the end of most phases before beginning the next phase.

The waterfall model is a traditional engineering approach applied to software engineering. A strict waterfall approach discourages revisiting and revising any prior phase once it is complete. This "inflexibility" in a pure waterfall model has been a source of criticism by supporters of other more "flexible" models. It has been widely blamed for several large-scale government projects running over budget, over time and sometimes failing to deliver on requirements due to the Big Design Up Front approach. Except when contractually required, the waterfall model has been largely superseded by more flexible and versatile methodologies developed specifically for software development.

The waterfall model is also commonly taught with the mnemonic A Dance in the Dark Every Monday, representing Analysis, Design, Implementation, Testing, Documentation and Execution, and Maintenance.

Prototyping

Software prototyping, is the development approach of activities during software development, the creation of prototypes, i.e., incomplete versions of the software program being developed.

The basic principles are:

- Not a standalone, complete development methodology, but rather an approach to handle selected parts of a larger, more traditional development methodology (i.e. incremental, spiral, or rapid application development (RAD)).

- Attempts to reduce inherent project risk by breaking a project into smaller segments and providing more ease-of-change during the development process.

- User is involved throughout the development process, which increases the likelihood of user acceptance of the final implementation.

- Small-scale mock-ups of the system are developed following an iterative modification process until the prototype evolves to meet the users' requirements.

- While most prototypes are developed with the expectation that they will be discarded, it is possible in some cases to evolve from prototype to working system.

- A basic understanding of the fundamental business problem is necessary to avoid solving the wrong problems.

Incremental Development

Various methods are acceptable for combining linear and iterative systems development methodologies, with the primary objective of each being to reduce inherent project risk by breaking a project into smaller segments and providing more ease-of-change during the development process.

The basic principles are:

- A series of mini-Waterfalls are performed, where all phases of the Waterfall are completed for a small part of a system, before proceeding to the next increment, or

- Overall requirements are defined before proceeding to evolutionary, mini-Waterfall development of individual increments of a system, or

- The initial software concept, requirements analysis, and design of architecture and system core are defined via Waterfall, followed by iterative Prototyping, which culminates in installing the final prototype, a working system.

Iterative and Incremental Development

Iterative development prescribes the construction of initially small but ever-larger portions of a software project to help all those involved to uncover important issues early before problems or faulty assumptions can lead to disaster.

Spiral Development

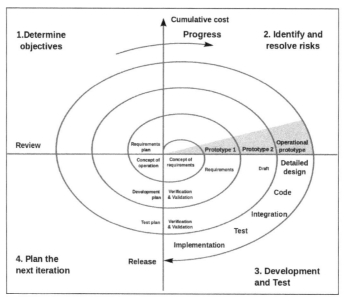

Spiral model.

In 1988, Barry Boehm published a formal software system development "spiral model," which combines some key aspect of the waterfall model and rapid prototyping methodologies, in an effort to combine advantages of top-down and bottom-up concepts. It provided emphasis in a key area many felt had been neglected by other methodologies: deliberate iterative risk analysis, particularly suited to large-scale complex systems.

The basic principles are:

- Focus is on risk assessment and on minimizing project risk by breaking a project into smaller segments and providing more ease-of-change during the development process, as well as providing the opportunity to evaluate risks and weigh consideration of project continuation throughout the life cycle.

- "Each cycle involves a progression through the same sequence of steps, for each part of the product and for each of its levels of elaboration, from an overall concept-of-operation document down to the coding of each individual program."

- Each trip around the spiral traverses four basic quadrants: (1) determine objectives, alternatives, and constraints of the iteration; (2) evaluate alternatives; Identify and resolve risks; (3) develop and verify deliverables from the iteration; and (4) plan the next iteration.

- Begin each cycle with an identification of stakeholders and their "win conditions", and end each cycle with review and commitment.

Rapid Application Development

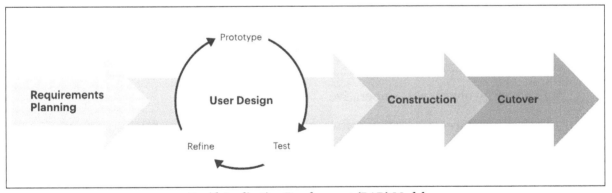

Rapid Application Development (RAD) Model.

Rapid application development (RAD) is a software development methodology, which favors iterative development and the rapid construction of prototypes instead of large amounts of up-front planning. The "planning" of software developed using RAD is interleaved with writing the software itself. The lack of extensive pre-planning generally allows software to be written much faster, and makes it easier to change requirements.

The rapid development process starts with the development of preliminary data models and business process models using structured techniques. In the next stage, requirements are verified using prototyping, eventually to refine the data and process models. These stages are repeated iteratively; further development results in "a combined business requirements and technical design statement to be used for constructing new systems".

The term was first used to describe a software development process introduced by James Martin in 1991. According to Whitten, it is a merger of various structured techniques, especially data-driven Information Engineering, with prototyping techniques to accelerate software systems development.

The basic principles of rapid application development are:

- Key objective is for fast development and delivery of a high quality system at a relatively low investment cost.

- Attempts to reduce inherent project risk by breaking a project into smaller segments and providing more ease-of-change during the development process.

- Aims to produce high quality systems quickly, primarily via iterative Prototyping (at any stage of development), active user involvement, and computerized development tools. These tools may include Graphical User Interface (GUI) builders, Computer Aided Software Engineering (CASE) tools, Database Management Systems (DBMS), fourth-generation programming languages, code generators, and object-oriented techniques.

- Key emphasis is on fulfilling the business need, while technological or engineering excellence is of lesser importance.

- Project control involves prioritizing development and defining delivery deadlines or "timeboxes." If the project starts to slip, emphasis is on reducing requirements to fit the timebox, not in increasing the deadline.

- Generally includes joint application design (JAD), where users are intensely involved in system design, via consensus building in either structured workshops, or electronically facilitated interaction.

- Active user involvement is imperative.

- Iteratively produces production software, as opposed to a throwaway prototype.

- Produces documentation necessary to facilitate future development and maintenance.

- Standard systems analysis and design methods can be fitted into this framework.

Agile Development

"Agile software development" refers to a group of software development methodologies based on iterative development, where requirements and solutions evolve via collaboration between self-organizing cross-functional teams. The term was coined in the year 2001 when the Agile Manifesto was formulated.

Agile software development uses iterative development as a basis but advocates a lighter and more people-centric viewpoint than traditional approaches. Agile processes fundamentally incorporate iteration and the continuous feedback that it provides to successively refine and deliver a software system.

There are many agile methodologies, including:

- Dynamic systems development method (DSDM)

- Kanban

- Scrum

Code and Fix

"Code and fix" development is not so much a deliberate strategy as a result of schedule pressure on software developers. Without much of a design in the way, programmers immediately begin producing code. At some point, testing begins (often late in the development cycle), and the unavoidable bugsmust then be fixed before the product can be shipped. Programming without a planned-out design is also known as cowboy coding.

Other

Other high-level software project methodologies include:

- Chaos model—The main rule is always resolve the most important issue first.

- Incremental funding methodology—an iterative approach.

- Structured systems analysis and design method—a specific version of waterfall.

- Slow programming, as part of the larger Slow Movement, emphasizes careful and gradual work without (or minimal) time pressures. Slow programming aims to avoid bugs and overly quick release schedules.

- V-Model (software development)—an extension of the waterfall model.

- Unified Process (UP) is an iterative software development methodology framework, based on Unified Modeling Language (UML). UP organizes the development of software into four phases, each consisting of one or more executable iterations of the software at that stage of development: inception, elaboration, construction, and guidelines. Many tools and products exist to facilitate UP implementation. One of the more popular versions of UP is theRational Unified Process (RUP).

Process Meta-models

Some "process models" are abstract descriptions for evaluating, comparing, and improving the specific process adopted by an organization.

- ISO/IEC 12207 is the international standard describing the method to select, implement, and monitor the life cycle for software.

- The Capability Maturity Model Integration (CMMI) is one of the leading models and based on best practice. Independent assessments grade organizations on how well they follow their defined processes, not on the quality of those processes or the software produced. CMMI has replaced CMM.

- ISO 9000 describes standards for a formally organized process to manufacture a product and the methods of managing and monitoring progress. Although the standard was originally created for the manufacturing sector, ISO 9000 standards have been applied to software development as well. Like CMMI, certification with ISO 9000 does not guarantee the quality of the end result, only that formalized business processes have been followed.

- ISO/IEC 15504 Information technology — Process assessment also known as Software Process Improvement Capability Determination (SPICE), is a "framework for the assessment of software processes". This standard is aimed at setting out a clear model for process comparison. SPICE is used much like CMMI. It models processes to manage, control, guide and monitor software development. This model is then used to measure what a development organization or project team actually does during software development. This information is analyzed to identify weaknesses and drive improvement. It also identifies strengths that can be continued or integrated into common practice for that organization or team.

- Soft systems methodology – a general method for improving management processes

- Method engineering – a general method for improving information system processes

Formal Methods

Formal methods are mathematical approaches to solving software (and hardware) problems at the requirements, specification, and design levels. Formal methods are most likely to be applied to safety-critical or security-critical software and systems, such as avionics software. Software safety assurance standards, such as DO-178B, DO-178C, and Common Criteria demand formal methods at the highest levels of categorization.

For sequential software, examples of formal methods include the B-Method, the specification languages used in automated theorem proving, RAISE, and the Z notation.

Formalization of software development is creeping in, in other places, with the application of Object Constraint Language (and specializations such as Java Modeling Language) and especially with model-driven architecture allowing execution of designs, if not specifications.

For concurrent software and systems, Petri nets, process algebra, and finite state machines allow executable software specification and can be used to build up and validate application behavior.

Another emerging trend in software development is to write a specification in some form of logic—usually a variation of first-order logic (FOL)—and then to directly execute the logic as though it were a program. The OWL language, based on Description Logic (DL), is an example. There is also work on mapping some version of English (or another natural language) automatically to and from logic, and executing the logic directly. Examples are Attempto Controlled English, and Internet Business Logic, which do not seek to control the vocabulary or syntax. A feature of systems that support bidirectional English-logic mapping and direct execution of the logic is that they can be made to explain their results, in English, at the business or scientific level.

System Development Life Cycle

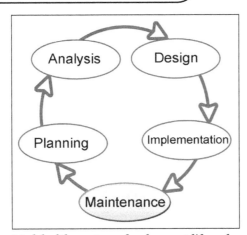

Model of the systems development life cycle,
highlighting the maintenance phase.

The systems development life cycle (SDLC), also referred to as the application development life-cycle, is a process for planning, creating, testing, and deploying an information system. The systems development lifecycle concept applies to a range of hardware and software configurations, as a system can be composed of hardware only, software only, or a combination of both. There are usually six stages in this cycle: analysis, design, development and testing, implementation, documentation, and evaluation.

A systems development life cycle is composed of a number of clearly defined and distinct work phases which are used by systems engineers and systems developers to plan for, design, build, test, and deliver information systems. Like anything that is manufactured on an assembly line, an SDLC aims to produce high-quality systems that meet or exceed customer expectations, based on customer requirements, by delivering systems which move through each clearly defined phase, within scheduled time frames and cost estimates. Computer systems are complex and often (especially with the recent rise of service-oriented architecture) link multiple traditional systems potentially supplied by different software vendors. To manage this level of complexity, a number of SDLC models or methodologies have been created, such as waterfall, spiral, Agile software development, rapid prototyping, incremental, and synchronize and stabilize.

SDLC can be described along a spectrum of agile to iterative to sequential methodologies. Agile methodologies, such as XP and Scrum, focus on lightweight processes which allow for rapid changes (without necessarily following the pattern of SDLC approach) along the development cycle. Iterative methodologies, such as Rational Unified Process and dynamic systems development method, focus on limited project scope and expanding or improving products by multiple iterations. Sequential or big-design-up-front (BDUF) models, such as waterfall, focus on complete and correct planning to guide large projects and risks to successful and predictable results. Other models, such as anamorphic development, tend to focus on a form of development that is guided by project scope and adaptive iterations of feature development.

In project management a project can be defined both with a project life cycle (PLC) and an SDLC, during which slightly different activities occur. According to Taylor (2004), "the project life cycle encompasses all the activities of the project, while the systems development life cycle focuses on realizing the product requirements".

SDLC is used during the development of an IT project, it describes the different stages involved in the project from the drawing board, through the completion of the project.

The SDLC is not a methodology per se, but rather a description of the phases in the life cycle of a software application. These phases (broadly speaking) are, investigation, analysis, design, build, test, implement, and maintenance and support. All software development methodologies (such as the more commonly known waterfall and scrum methodologies) follow the SDLC phases but the method of doing that varies vastly between methodologies. In the Scrum methodology, for example, one could say a single user story goes through all the phases of the SDLC within a single two-week sprint. Contrast this to the waterfall methodology, as another example, where every business requirement (recorded in the analysis phase of the SDLC in a document called the Business Requirements Specification) is translated into feature/functional descriptions (recorded in the design phase in a document called the Functional Specification) which are then all built in one go as a collection of solution features typically over a period of three to nine months, or more. These methodologies are obviously quite different approaches, yet they both contain the SDLC phases in which a requirement is born, then travels through the life cycle phases ending in the final phase of maintenance and support, after-which (typically) the whole life cycle starts again for a subsequent version of the software application.

The product life cycle describes the process for building information systems in a very deliberate, structured and methodical way, reiterating each stage of the product's life. The systems development life cycle, according to Elliott & Strachan & Radford (2004), "originated in the 1960s, to develop large scale functional business systems in an age of large scale business conglomerates. Information systems activities revolved around heavy data processing and number crunching routines".

Several systems development frameworks have been partly based on SDLC, such as the structured systems analysis and design method (SSADM) produced for the UK government Office of Government Commerce in the 1980s. Ever since, according to Elliott (2004), "the traditional life cycle approaches to systems development have been increasingly replaced with alternative approaches and frameworks, which attempted to overcome some of the inherent deficiencies of the traditional SDLC".

Phases

The system development life cycle framework provides a sequence of activities for system designers and developers to follow. It consists of a set of steps or phases in which each phase of the SDLC uses the results of the previous one.

The SDLC adheres to important phases that are essential for developers—such as planning, analysis, design, and implementation—and are explained in the section below. This includes evaluation of the currently used system, information gathering, feasibility studies, and request approval. A number of SDLC models have been created, including waterfall, fountain, spiral, build and fix, rapid prototyping, incremental, synchronize, and stabilize. The oldest of these, and the best known, is the waterfall model, a sequence of stages in which the output of each stage becomes the input for the next. These stages can be characterized and divided up in different ways, including the following:

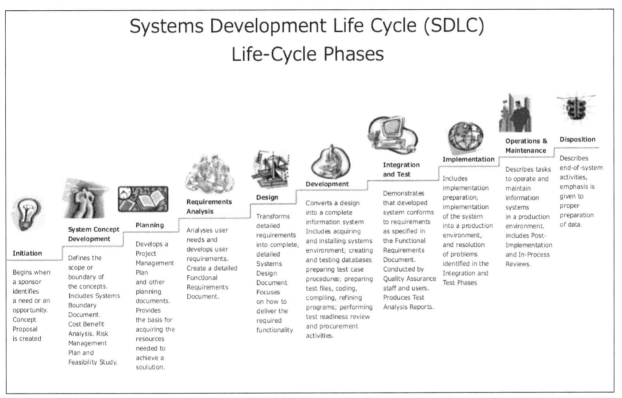

A ten-phase version of the systems development life cycle.

Preliminary analysis: Begin with a preliminary analysis, propose alternative solutions, describe costs and benefits, and submit a preliminary plan with recommendations.

- Conduct the preliminary analysis: Discover the organization's objectives and the nature and scope of the problem under study. Even if a problem refers only to a small segment of the organization itself, find out what the objectives of the organization itself are. Then see how the problem being studied fits in with them.

- Propose alternative solutions: After digging into the organization's objectives and specific problems, several solutions may have been discovered. However, alternate proposals may still come from interviewing employees, clients, suppliers, and/or consultants. Insight may also be gained by researching what competitors are doing.

- Cost benefit analysis: Analyze and describe the costs and benefits of implementing the proposed changes. In the end, the ultimate decision on whether to leave the system as is, improve it, or develop a new system will be guided by this and the rest of the preliminary analysis data.

Systems analysis, requirements definition: Define project goals into defined functions and operations of the intended application. This involves the process of gathering and interpreting facts, diagnosing problems, and recommending improvements to the system. Project goals will be further aided by analysis of end-user information needs and the removal of any inconsistencies and incompleteness in these requirements.

A series of steps followed by the developer include:

- Collection of facts: Obtain end user requirements through documentation, client interviews, observation, and questionnaires.

- Scrutiny of the existing system: Identify pros and cons of the current system in-place, so as to carry forward the pros and avoid the cons in the new system.

- Analysis of the proposed system: Find solutions to the shortcomings described in step two and prepare the specifications using any specific user proposals.

Systems design: At this step desired features and operations are described in detail, including screen layouts, business rules, process diagrams, pseudocode, and other documentation.

- Development: The real code is written here.

- Integration and testing: All the pieces are brought together into a special testing environment, then checked for errors, bugs, and interoperability.

- Acceptance, installation, deployment: This is the final stage of initial development, where the software is put into production and runs actual business.

- Maintenance: During the maintenance stage of the SDLC, the system is assessed/evaluated to ensure it does not become obsolete. This is also where changes are made to initial software.

- Evaluation: Some companies do not view this as an official stage of the SDLC, while others consider it to be an extension of the maintenance stage, and may be referred to in some circles as post-implementation review. This is where the system that was developed, as well as the entire process, is evaluated. Some of the questions that need to be answered include if the newly implemented system meets the initial business requirements and objectives, if the system is reliable and fault-tolerant, and if it functions according to the approved functional requirements. In addition to evaluating the software that was released, it is important to assess the effectiveness of the development process. If there are any aspects of the entire process (or certain stages) that management is not satisfied with, this is the time to improve.

- Disposal: In this phase, plans are developed for discontinuing the use of system information, hardware, and software and making the transition to a new system. The purpose here is to properly move, archive, discard, or destroy information, hardware, and software that is being replaced, in a manner that prevents any possibility of unauthorized disclosure of sensitive data. The disposal activities ensure proper migration to a new system. Particular emphasis is given to proper preservation and archiving of data processed by the previous system. All of this should be done in accordance with the organization's security requirements.

In the following diagram, these stages of the systems development life cycle are divided in ten steps, from definition to creation and modification of IT work products:

Not every project will require that the phases be sequentially executed. However, the phases are interdependent. Depending upon the size and complexity of the project, phases may be combined or may overlap.

System Investigation

First the IT system proposal is investigated. During this step, consider all current priorities that would be affected and how they should be handled. Before any system planning is done, a feasibility study should be conducted to determine if creating a new or improved system is a viable solution. This will help to determine the costs, benefits, resource requirements, and specific user needs required for completion. The development process can only continue once management approves of the recommendations from the feasibility study.

The following represent different components of the feasibility study:

- Operational feasibility.

- Financial feasibility.

- Technical feasibility.

- Human factors feasibility.

- Legal/Political feasibility.

Analysis

The goal of analysis is to determine where the problem is, in an attempt to fix the system. This step involves breaking down the system in different pieces to analyze the situation, analyzing project goals, breaking down what needs to be created, and attempting to engage users so that definite requirements can be defined.

Design

In systems design, the design functions and operations are described in detail, including screen layouts, business rules, process diagrams, and other documentation. The output of this stage will describe the new system as a collection of modules or subsystems.

The design stage takes as its initial input the requirements identified in the approved requirements document. For each requirement, a set of one or more design elements will be produced as a result of interviews, workshops, and/or prototype efforts.

Design elements describe the desired system features in detail, and they generally include functional hierarchy diagrams, screen layout diagrams, tables of business rules, business process diagrams, pseudo-code, and a complete entity-relationship diagram with a full data dictionary. These design elements are intended to describe the system in sufficient detail, such that skilled developers and engineers may develop and deliver the system with minimal additional input design.

Environments

Environments are controlled areas where systems developers can build, distribute, install, configure, test, and execute systems that move through the SDLC. Each environment is aligned with different areas of the SDLC and is intended to have specific purposes. Examples of such environments include the:

- Development environment, where developers can work independently of each other before trying to merge their work with the work of others;

- Common build environment, where merged work can be built, together, as a combined system;

- Systems integration testing environment, where basic testing of a system's integration points to other upstream or downstream systems can be tested;

- User acceptance testing environment, where business stakeholders can test against their original business requirements; and

- Production environment, where systems finally get deployed for final use by their intended end users.

Testing

The code is tested at various levels in software testing. Unit, system, and user acceptance testings are often performed. This is a grey area as many different opinions exist as to what the stages of testing are and how much, if any iteration occurs. Iteration is not generally part of the waterfall model, but the means to rectify defects and validate fixes prior to deployment is incorporated into this phase.

The following are types of testing that may be relevant, depending on the type of system under development:

- Defect testing the failed scenarios, including
- Path testing
- Data set testing
- Unit testing
- System testing
- Integration testing
- Black-box testing
- White-box testing
- Regression testing
- Automation testing
- User acceptance testing
- Software performance testing

Training and Transition

Once a system has been stabilized through adequate testing, the SDLC ensures that proper training on the system is performed or documented before transitioning the system to its support staff and end users. Training usually covers operational training for those people who will be responsible for supporting the system as well as training for those end users who will be using the system after its delivery to a production operating environment.

After training has been successfully completed, systems engineers and developers transition the system to its final production environment, where it is intended to be used by its end users and supported by its support and operations staff.

Operations and Maintenance

The deployment of the system includes changes and enhancements before the decommissioning or sunset of the system. Maintaining the system is an important aspect of SDLC. As key personnel change positions in the organization, new changes will be implemented. There are two approaches to system development: the traditional approach (structured) and object oriented. Information engineering includes the traditional system approach, which is also called the structured analysis and design technique. The object oriented approach views information system as a collection of objects that are integrated with each other to make a full and complete information system.

Evaluation

The final phase of the SDLC is to measure the effectiveness of the system and evaluate potential enhancements.

Systems Analysis and Design

The systems analysis and design (SAD) is the process of developing information systems (IS) that effectively use hardware, software, data, processes, and people to support the company's businesses objectives. System analysis and design can be considered the meta-development activity, which serves to set the stage and bound the problem. SAD can be leveraged to set the correct balance among competing high-level requirements in the functional and non-functional analysis domains. System analysis and design interacts strongly with distributed enterprise architecture, enterprise I.T. Architecture, and business architecture, and relies heavily on concepts such as partitioning, interfaces, personae and roles, and deployment/operational modeling to arrive at a high-level system description. This high level description is then further broken down into the components and modules which can be analyzed, designed, and constructed separately and integrated to accomplish the business goal. SDLC and SAD are cornerstones of full life cycle product and system planning.

Object-Oriented Analysis

Object-oriented analysis (OOA) is the process of analyzing a task (also known as a problem domain), to develop a conceptual model that can then be used to complete the task. A typical OOA model would describe computer software that could be used to satisfy a set of customer-defined requirements. During the analysis phase of problem-solving, a programmer might consider a written requirements statement, a formal vision document, or interviews with stakeholders or other interested parties. The task to be addressed might be divided into several subtasks (or domains), each representing a different business, technological, or other areas of interest. Each subtask would be analyzed separately. Implementation constraints, (e.g., concurrency, distribution, persistence, or how the system is to be built) are not considered during the analysis phase; rather, they are addressed during object-oriented design (OOD).

The conceptual model that results from OOA will typically consist of a set of use cases, one or more UML class diagrams, and a number of interaction diagrams. It may also include some kind of user interface mock-up.

The input for object-oriented design is provided by the output of object-oriented analysis. Realize that an output artifact does not need to be completely developed to serve as input of object-oriented design; analysis and design may occur in parallel, and in practice the results of one activity can feed the other in a short feedback cycle through an iterative process. Both analysis and design can be performed incrementally, and the artifacts can be continuously grown instead of completely developed in one shot.

Some typical (but common to all types of design analysis) input artifacts for object-oriented:

- Conceptual model: Conceptual model is the result of object-oriented analysis, it captures concepts in the problem domain. The conceptual model is explicitly chosen to be independent of implementation details, such as concurrency or data storage.

- Use case: Use case is a description of sequences of events that, taken together, lead to a system doing something useful. Each use case provides one or more scenarios that convey how the system should interact with the users called actors to achieve a specific business goal or function. Use case actors may be end users or other systems. In many circumstances use cases are further elaborated into use case diagrams. Use case diagrams are used to identify the actor (users or other systems) and the processes they perform.

- System Sequence Diagram: System Sequence diagram (SSD) is a picture that shows, for a particular scenario of a use case, the events that external actors generate, their order, and possible inter-system events.

- User interface documentations (if applicable): Document that shows and describes the look and feel of the end product's user interface. It is not mandatory to have this, but it helps to visualize the end-product and therefore helps the designer.

- Relational data model (if applicable): A data model is an abstract model that describes how data is represented and used. If an object database is not used, the relational data model should usually be created before the design, since the strategy chosen for object-relational mapping is an output of the OO design process. However, it is possible to develop the relational data model and the object-oriented design artifacts in parallel, and the growth of an artifact can stimulate the refinement of other artifacts.

Life Cycle

Management and Control

The SDLC phases serve as a programmatic guide to project activity and provide a flexible but consistent way to conduct projects to a depth matching the scope of the project. Each of the SDLC phase objectives are described in this section with key deliverables, a description of recommended tasks, and a summary of related control objectives for effective management. It is critical for the project manager to establish and monitor control objectives during each SDLC phase while executing projects. Control objectives help to provide a clear statement of the desired result or purpose and should be used throughout the entire SDLC process. Control objectives can be grouped into major categories (domains), and relate to the SDLC phases as shown in the figure.

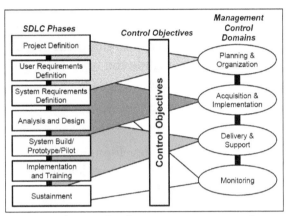

SPIU phases related to management controls.

To manage and control any SDLC initiative, each project will be required to establish some degree of a work breakdown structure (WBS) to capture and schedule the work necessary to complete the project. The WBS and all programmatic material should be kept in the "project description". The WBS format is mostly left to the project manager to establish in a way that best describes the project work.

There are some key areas that must be defined in the WBS as part of the SDLC policy. The following diagram describes three key areas that will be addressed in the WBS in a manner established by the project manager. The diagram shows coverage spans numerous phases of the SDLC but the associated MCD has a subset of primary mappings to the SDLC phases. For example, Analysis and Design is primarily performed as part of the Acquisition and Implementation Domain and System Build and Prototype is primarily performed as part of delivery and support.

Work Breakdown Structured Organization

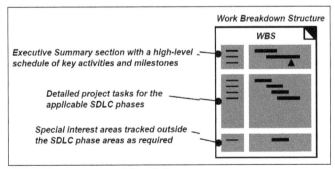

Work breakdown structure.

The upper section of the work breakdown structure (WBS) should identify the major phases and milestones of the project in a summary fashion. In addition, the upper section should provide an overview of the full scope and timeline of the project and will be part of the initial project description effort leading to project approval. The WBS is based on the seven systems development life cycle phases as a guide for WBS task development. The WBS elements should consist of milestones and "tasks" as opposed to "activities" and have a definitive period (usually two weeks or more). Each task must have a measurable output (e.x. document, decision, or analysis). A WBS task may rely on one or more activities (e.g. software engineering, systems engineering) and may require close coordination with other tasks, either internal or external to the project. Any part of the project needing support from contractors should have a statement of work (SOW) written to include the appropriate tasks from the SDLC phases. The development of a SOW does not occur during a specific phase of SDLC but is developed to include the work from the SDLC process that may be conducted by external resources such as contractors.

Baselines

Baselines are an important part of the systems development life cycle. These baselines are established after four of the five phases of the SDLC and are critical to the iterative nature of the model. Each baseline is considered as a milestone in the SDLC.

- Functional baseline: established after the conceptual design phase.

- Allocated baseline: established after the preliminary design phase.

- Product baseline: established after the detail design and development phase.

- Updated product baseline: established after the production construction phase.

Complementary Methodologies

Complementary software development methods to systems development life cycle are:

- Software prototyping.

- Joint applications development (JAD).

- Rapid application development (RAD).

- Extreme programming (XP).

- Open-source development.

- End-user development.

- Object-oriented programming.

Comparison of Methodology Approaches (Post, & Anderson 2006)							
	SDLC	RAD	Open source	Objects	JAD	Prototyping	End User
Control	Formal	MIS	Weak	Standards	Joint	User	User
Time frame	Long	Short	Medium	Any	Medium	Short	Short –
Users	Many	Few	Few	Varies	Few	One or two	One

MIS staff	Many	Few	Hundreds	Split	Few	One or two	None
Transaction/DSS	Transaction	Both	Both	Both	DSS	DSS	DSS
Interface	Minimal	Minimal	Weak	Windows	Crucial	Crucial	Crucial
Documentation and training	Vital	Limited	Internal	In Objects	Limited	Weak	None
Integrity and security	Vital	Vital	Unknown	In Objects	Limited	Weak	Weak
Reusability	Limited	Some	Maybe	Vital	Limited	Weak	None

Strengths and Weaknesses

Few people in the modern computing world would use a strict waterfall model for their SDLC as many modern methodologies have superseded this thinking. Some will argue that the SDLC no longer applies to models like Agile computing, but it is still a term widely in use in technology circles. The SDLC practice has advantages in traditional models of systems development that lends itself more to a structured environment. The disadvantages to using the SDLC methodology is when there is need for iterative development or (i.e. web development or e-commerce) where stakeholders need to review on a regular basis the software being designed.

A comparison of the strengths and weaknesses of SDLC:

Strength and Weaknesses of SDLC	
Strengths	Weaknesses
Control	Increased development time
Monitor large projects	Increased development cost
Detailed steps	Systems must be defined up front
Evaluate costs and completion targets	Rigidity
Documentation	Hard to estimate costs, project overruns
Well defined user input	User input is sometimes limited
Ease of maintenance	Little parallelism
Development and design standards	Automation of documentation and standards is limited
Tolerates changes in MIS of staffing	Does not tolerate changes in requirements
	Projects canned early on the result in little or no value

An alternative to the SDLC is rapid application development, which combines prototyping, joint application development and implementation of CASE tools. The advantages of RAD are speed, reduced development cost, and active user involvement in the development process.

System Lifecycle

The system lifecycle in systems engineering is a view of a system or proposed system that addresses all phases of its existence to include system conception, design and development, production and/or construction, distribution, operation, maintenance and support, retirement, phase-out and disposal.

Conceptual Design

The conceptual design stage is the stage where an identified need is examined, requirements for potential solutions are defined, potential solutions are evaluated and a system specification is developed. The system specification represents the technical requirements that will provide overall guidance for system design. Because this document determines all future development, the stage cannot be completed until a conceptual design review has determined that the system specification properly addresses the motivating need.

Key steps within the conceptual design stage include:

- Need identification.

- Feasibility analysis.

- System requirements analysis.

- System specification.

- Conceptual design review.

Preliminary System Design

During this stage of the system lifecycle, subsystems that perform the desired system functions are designed and specified in compliance with the system specification. Interfaces between subsystems are defined, as well as overall test and evaluation requirements. At the completion of this stage, a development specification is produced that is sufficient to perform detailed design and development.

Key steps within the preliminary design stage include:

- Functional analysis.

- Requirements allocation.

- Detailed trade-off studies.

- Synthesis of system options.

- Preliminary design of engineering models.

- Development specification.

- Preliminary design review.

For example, as the system analyst of Viti Bank, you have been tasked to examine the current information system. Viti Bank is a fast growing bank in Fiji. Customers in remote rural areas are finding difficulty to access the bank services. It takes them days or even weeks to travel to a location to access the bank services. With the vision of meeting the customers needs, the bank has requested your services to examine the current system and to come up with solutions or recommendations of how the current system can be provided to meet its needs.

Detail Design and Development

This stage includes the development of detailed designs that brings initial design work into a completed with form of specifications. This work includes the specification of interfaces between the system and its intended environment and a comprehensive evaluation of the systems logistical, maintenance and support requirements. The detail design and development is responsible for producing the product, process and material specifications and may result in substantial changes to the development specification.

Key steps within the detail design and development stage include:

- Detailed design.

- Detailed synthesis.

- Development of engineering and prototype models.

- Revision of development specification.

- Product, process and material specification.

- Critical design review.

Production and Construction

During the production and/or construction stage the product is built or assembled in accordance with the requirements specified in the product, process and material specifications and is deployed and tested within the operational target environment. System assessments are conducted in order to correct deficiencies and adapt the system for continued improvement.

Key steps within the product construction stage include:

- Production and/or construction of system components.

- Acceptance testing.

- System distribution and operation.

- Operational testing and evaluation.

- System assessment.

Utilization and Support

Once fully deployed, the system is used for its intended operational role and maintained within its operational environment.

Key steps within the utilization and support stage include:

- System operation in the user environment.

- Change management.

- System modifications for improvement.

- System assessment.

Phase-out and Disposal

Effectiveness and efficiency of the system must be continuously evaluated to determine when the product has met its maximum effective lifecycle. Considerations include: Continued existence of operational need, matching between operational requirements and system performance, feasibility of system phase-out versus maintenance, and availability of alternative systems.

Continuous Integration

In software engineering, continuous integration (CI) is the practice of merging all developers' working copies to a shared mainline several times a day. Grady Booch first proposed the term CI in his 1991 method, although he did not advocate integrating several times a day. Extreme programming (XP) adopted the concept of CI and did advocate integrating more than once per day – perhaps as many as tens of times per day.

Rationale

The main aim of CI is to prevent integration problems, referred to as "integration hell" in early descriptions of XP. CI is not universally accepted as an improvement over frequent integration, so it is important to distinguish between the two as there is disagreement about the virtues of each.

In XP, CI was intended to be used in combination with automated unit tests written through the practices of test-driven development. Initially this was conceived of as running and passing all unit tests in the developer's local environment before committing to the mainline. This helps avoid one developer's work-in-progress breaking another developer's copy. Where necessary, partially complete features can be disabled before committing, using feature toggles for instance.

Later elaborations of the concept introduced build servers, which automatically ran the unit tests periodically or even after every commit and reported the results to the developers. The use of build servers (not necessarily running unit tests) had already been practised by some teams outside the XP community. Nowadays, many organisations have adopted CI without adopting all of XP.

In addition to automated unit tests, organisations using CI typically use a build server to implement *continuous* processes of applying quality control in general — small pieces of effort, applied frequently. In addition to running the unit and integration tests, such processes run additional static and dynamic tests, measure and profile performance, extract and format documentation from the source code and facilitate manual QA processes. This continuous application of quality control aims to improve the quality of software, and to reduce the time taken to deliver it, by replacing the traditional practice of applying quality control *after* completing all development. This is very similar to the original idea of integrating more frequently to make integration easier, only applied to QA processes.

In the same vein, the practice of continuous delivery further extends CI by making sure the software checked in on the mainline is always in a state that can be deployed to users and makes the deployment process very rapid.

Workflow

When embarking on a change, a developer takes a copy of the current code base on which to work. As other developers submit changed code to the source code repository, this copy gradually ceases to reflect the repository code. Not only can the existing code base change, but new code can be added as well as new libraries, and other resources that create dependencies, and potential conflicts.

The longer development continues on a branch without merging back to the mainline, the greater the risk of multiple integration conflicts and failures when the developer branch is eventually merged back. When developers submit code to the repository they must first update their code to reflect the changes in the repository since they took their copy. The more changes the repository contains, the more work developers must do before submitting their own changes.

Eventually, the repository may become so different from the developers' baselines that they enter what is sometimes referred to as "merge hell", or "integration hell", where the time it takes to integrate exceeds the time it took to make their original changes.

Continuous integration involves integrating early and often, so as to avoid the pitfalls of "integration hell". The practice aims to reduce rework and thus reduce cost and time.

A complementary practice to CI is that before submitting work, each programmer must do a complete build and run (and pass) all unit tests. Integration tests are usually run automatically on a CI server when it detects a new commit.

Common Practices

Continuous integration – the practice of frequently integrating one's new or changed code with the existing code repository – should occur frequently enough that no intervening window remains between commit and build, and such that no errors can arise without developers noticing them and correcting them immediately. Normal practice is to trigger these builds by every commit to a repository, rather than a periodically scheduled build. The practicalities of doing this in a multi-developer environment of rapid commits are such that it is usual to trigger a short time after each commit, then to start a build when either this timer expires, or after a rather longer interval since the last build. Note that since each new commit resets the timer used for the short time trigger, this is the same technique used in many button debouncing algorithms [ex:]. In this way the commit events are "debounced" to prevent unnecessary builds between a series of rapid-fire commits. Many automated tools offer this scheduling automatically.

Another factor is the need for a version control system that supports atomic commits, i.e. all of a developer's changes may be seen as a single commit operation. There is no point in trying to build from only half of the changed files.

To achieve these objectives, continuous integration relies on the following principles.

Maintain a Code Repository

This practice advocates the use of a revision control system for the project's source code. All artifacts required to build the project should be placed in the repository. In this practice and in the revision control community, the convention is that the system should be buildable from a fresh checkout and not require additional dependencies. Extreme Programming advocate Martin Fowler also mentions that where branching is supported by tools, its use should be minimised. Instead, it is preferred for changes to be integrated rather than for multiple versions of the software to be maintained simultaneously. The mainline (or trunk) should be the place for the working version of the software.

Automate the Build

A single command should have the capability of building the system. Many build tools, such as make, have existed for many years. Other more recent tools are frequently used in continuous integration environments. Automation of the build should include automating the integration, which often includes deployment into a production-like environment. In many cases, the build script not only compiles binaries, but also generates documentation, website pages, statistics and distribution media (such as Debian DEB, Red Hat RPM or Windows MSI files).

Make the Build Self-testing

Once the code is built, all tests should run to confirm that it behaves as the developers expect it to behave.

Everyone Commits to the Baseline Every Day

By committing regularly, every committer can reduce the number of conflicting changes. Checking in a week's worth of work runs the risk of conflicting with other features and can be very difficult to resolve. Early, small conflicts in an area of the system cause team members to communicate about the change they are making. Committing all changes at least once a day (once per feature built) is generally considered part of the definition of Continuous Integration. In addition performing a nightly build is generally recommended. These are lower bounds; the typical frequency is expected to be much higher.

Every Commit (to Baseline) should be Built

The system should build commits to the current working version to verify that they integrate correctly. A common practice is to use Automated Continuous Integration, although this may be done manually. Automated Continuous Integration employs a continuous integration server or daemon to monitor the revision control system for changes, then automatically run the build process.

Keep the Build Fast

The build needs to complete rapidly, so that if there is a problem with integration, it is quickly identified.

Test in a Clone of the Production Environment

Having a test environment can lead to failures in tested systems when they deploy in the production environment because the production environment may differ from the test environment in a significant way. However, building a replica of a production environment is cost prohibitive.

Instead, the test environment, or a separate pre-production environment ("staging") should be built to be a scalable version of the production environment to alleviate costs while maintaining technology stack composition and nuances. Within these test environments, service virtualisation is commonly used to obtain on-demand access to dependencies (e.g., APIs, third-party applications, services, mainframes, etc.) that are beyond the team's control, still evolving, or too complex to configure in a virtual test lab.

Make it Easy to get the Latest Deliverables

Making builds readily available to stakeholders and testers can reduce the amount of rework necessary when rebuilding a feature that doesn't meet requirements. Additionally, early testing reduces the chances that defects survive until deployment. Finding errors earlier can reduce the amount of work necessary to resolve them.

All programmers should start the day by updating the project from the repository. That way, they will all stay up to date.

Everyone can See the Results of the Latest Build

It should be easy to find out whether the build breaks and, if so, who made the relevant change and what that change was.

Automate Deployment

Most CI systems allow the running of scripts after a build finishes. In most situations, it is possible to write a script to deploy the application to a live test server that everyone can look at. A further advance in this way of thinking is continuous deployment, which calls for the software to be deployed directly into production, often with additional automation to prevent defects or regressions.

Costs and Benefits

Continuous integration is intended to produce benefits such as:

- Integration bugs are detected early and are easy to track down due to small change sets. This saves both time and money over the lifespan of a project.

- Avoids last-minute chaos at release dates, when everyone tries to check in their slightly incompatible versions.

- When unit tests fail or a bug emerges, if developers need to revert the codebase to a bug-free state without debugging, only a small number of changes are lost (because integration happens frequently).

- Constant availability of a "current" build for testing, demo, or release purposes.

- Frequent code check-in pushes developers to create modular, less complex code.

With continuous automated testing benefits can include:

- Enforces discipline of frequent automated testing.

- Immediate feedback on system-wide impact of local changes.

- Software metrics generated from automated testing and CI (such as metrics for code coverage, code complexity, and feature completeness) focus developers on developing functional, quality code, and help develop momentum in a team.

Some downsides of continuous integration can include:

- Constructing an automated test suite requires a considerable amount of work, including ongoing effort to cover new features and follow intentional code modifications.

  ◦ Testing is considered a best practice for software development in its own right, regardless of whether or not continuous integration is employed, and automation is an integral part of project methodologies like test-driven development.

  ◦ Continuous integration can be performed without any test suite, but the cost of quality assurance to produce a releasable product can be high if it must be done manually and frequently.

- There is some work involved to set up a build system, and it can become complex, making it difficult to modify flexibly.

  ◦ However, there are a number of continuous integration software projects, both proprietary and open-source, which can be used.

- Continuous Integration is not necessarily valuable if the scope of the project is small or contains untestable legacy code.

- Value added depends on the quality of tests and how testable the code really is.

- Larger teams means that new code is constantly added to the integration queue, so tracking deliveries (while preserving quality) is difficult and builds queueing up can slow down everyone.

- With multiple commits and merges a day, partial code for a feature could easily be pushed and therefore integration tests will fail until the feature is complete.

- Safety and mission-critical development assurance require rigorous documentation and in-process review that are difficult to achieve using Continuous Integration. This type of life cycle often requires additional steps be completed prior to product release when regulatory approval of the product is required.

Software Prototyping

Software prototyping is the activity of creating prototypes of software applications, i.e., incomplete versions of the software program being developed. It is an activity that can occur in software development and is comparable to prototyping as known from other fields, such as mechanical engineering or manufacturing.

A prototype typically simulates only a few aspects of, and may be completely different from, the final product.

Prototyping has several benefits: the software designer and implementer can get valuable feedback from the users early in the project. The client and the contractor can compare if the software made matches the software specification, according to which the software program is built. It also allows the software engineer some insight into the accuracy of initial project estimates and whether the deadlines and milestones proposed can be successfully met. The degree of completeness and the techniques used in prototyping have been in development and debate since its proposal in the early 1970s.

The purpose of a prototype is to allow users of the software to evaluate developers' proposals for the design of the eventual product by actually trying them out, rather than having to interpret and evaluate the design based on descriptions. Software prototyping provides an understanding of the software's functions and potential threats or issues. Prototyping can also be used by end users to describe and prove requirements that have not been considered, and that can be a key factor in the commercial relationship between developers and their clients. Interaction design in particular makes heavy use of prototyping with that goal.

This process is in contrast with the 1960s and 1970s monolithic development cycle of building the entire program first and then working out any inconsistencies between design and implementation, which led to higher software costs and poor estimates of time and cost. The monolithic approach has been dubbed the "Slaying the (software) Dragon" technique, since it assumes that the software designer and developer is a single hero who has to slay the entire dragon alone. Prototyping can also avoid the great expense and difficulty of having to change a finished software product.

An early example of large-scale software prototyping was the implementation of NYU's Ada/ED translator for the Ada programming language. It was implemented in SETL with the intent of producing an executable semantic model for the Ada language, emphasizing clarity of design and user interface over speed and efficiency. The NYU Ada/ED system was the first validated Ada implementation, certified on April 11, 1983.

Outline of the Prototyping Process

The process of prototyping involves the following steps:

- Identify basic requirements: Determine basic requirements including the input and output information desired. Details, such as security, can typically be ignored.

- Develop initial prototype: The initial prototype is developed that includes only user interfaces.

- Review: The customers, including end-users, examine the prototype and provide feedback on potential additions or changes.

- Revise and enhance the prototype: Using the feedback both the specifications and the prototype can be improved. Negotiation about what is within the scope of the contract/product may be necessary. If changes are introduced then a repeat of steps #3 and #4 may be needed.

Dimensions of Prototypes

Horizontal Prototype

A common term for a user interface prototype is the horizontal prototype. It provides a broad view of an entire system or subsystem, focusing on user interaction more than low-level system functionality, such as database access. Horizontal prototypes are useful for:

- Confirmation of user interface requirements and system scope,

- Demonstration version of the system to obtain buy-in from the business,

- Develop preliminary estimates of development time, cost and effort.

Vertical Prototype

A vertical prototype is an enhanced complete elaboration of a single subsystem or function. It is useful for obtaining detailed requirements for a given function, with the following benefits:

- Refinement database design,

- Obtain information on data volumes and system interface needs, for network sizing and performance engineering,

- Clarify complex requirements by drilling down to actual system functionality.

Types of Prototyping

Software prototyping has many variants. However, all of the methods are in some way based on two major forms of prototyping: throwaway prototyping and evolutionary prototyping.

Throwaway Prototyping

Also called close-ended prototyping. Throwaway or rapid prototyping refers to the creation of a model that will eventually be discarded rather than becoming part of the final delivered software. After preliminary requirements gathering is accomplished, a simple working model of the system is constructed to visually show the users what their requirements may look like when they are implemented into a finished system. It is also a rapid prototyping.

Rapid prototyping involves creating a working model of various parts of the system at a very early stage, after a relatively short investigation. The method used in building it is usually quite informal, the most important factor being the speed with which the model is provided. The model then becomes the starting point from which users can re-examine their expectations and clarify their requirements. When this goal has been achieved, the prototype model is 'thrown away', and the system is formally developed based on the identified requirements.

The most obvious reason for using throwaway prototyping is that it can be done quickly. If the users can get quick feedback on their requirements, they may be able to refine them early in the development of the software. Making changes early in the development lifecycle is extremely cost effective since there is nothing at that point to redo. If a project is changed after a considerable amount of work has been done then small changes could require large efforts to implement since software systems have many dependencies. Speed is crucial in implementing a throwaway prototype, since with a limited budget of time and money little can be expended on a prototype that will be discarded.

Another strength of throwaway prototyping is its ability to construct interfaces that the users can test. The user interface is what the user sees as the system, and by seeing it in front of them, it is much easier to grasp how the system will function.

It is asserted that revolutionary rapid prototyping is a more effective manner in which to deal with user requirements-related issues, and therefore a greater enhancement to software productivity overall. Requirements can be identified, simulated, and tested far more quickly and cheaply when issues of evolvability, maintainability, and software structure are ignored. This, in turn, leads to the accurate specification of requirements, and the subsequent construction of a valid and usable system from the user's perspective, via conventional software development models.

Prototypes can be classified according to the fidelity with which they resemble the actual product in terms of appearance, interaction and timing. One method of creating a low fidelity throwaway prototype is paper prototyping. The prototype is implemented using paper and pencil, and thus mimics the function of the actual product, but does not look at all like it. Another method to easily build high fidelity throwaway prototypes is to use a GUI Builder and create a click dummy, a prototype that looks like the goal system, but does not provide any functionality.

The usage of storyboards, animatics or drawings is not exactly the same as throwaway prototyping, but certainly falls within the same family. These are non-functional implementations but show how the system will look.

Summary: In this approach the prototype is constructed with the idea that it will be discarded and the final system will be built from scratch. The steps in this approach are:

- Write preliminary requirements.
- Design the prototype.
- User experiences/uses the prototype, specifies new requirements.
- Repeat if necessary.
- Write the final requirements.

Evolutionary Prototyping

Evolutionary prototyping (also known as breadboard prototyping) is quite different from throwaway prototyping. The main goal when using evolutionary prototyping is to build a very robust prototype in a structured manner and constantly refine it. The reason for this approach is that the evolutionary prototype, when built, forms the heart of the new system, and the improvements and further requirements will then be built.

When developing a system using evolutionary prototyping, the system is continually refined and rebuilt.

"Evolutionary prototyping acknowledges that we do not understand all the requirements and builds only those that are well understood."

This technique allows the development team to add features, or make changes that couldn't be conceived during the requirements and design phase.

For a system to be useful, it must evolve through use in its intended operational environment. A product is never "done;" it is always maturing as the usage environment changes. We often try to define a system using our most familiar frame of reference—where we are now. We make assumptions about the way business will be conducted and the technology base on which the business will be implemented. A plan is enacted to develop the capability, and, sooner or later, something resembling the envisioned system is delivered.

Evolutionary prototypes have an advantage over throwaway prototypes in that they are functional systems. Although they may not have all the features the users have planned, they may be used on an interim basis until the final system is delivered.

"It is not unusual within a prototyping environment for the user to put an initial prototype to practical use while waiting for a more developed version. The user may decide that a 'flawed' system is better than no system at all."

In evolutionary prototyping, developers can focus themselves to develop parts of the system that they understand instead of working on developing a whole system.

To minimize risk, the developer does not implement poorly understood features. The partial system is sent to customer sites. As users work with the system, they detect opportunities for new features and give requests for these features to developers. Developers then take these enhancement requests along with their own and use sound configuration-management practices to change the software-requirements specification, update the design, recode and retest.

Incremental Prototyping

The final product is built as separate prototypes. At the end, the separate prototypes are merged in an overall design. By the help of incremental prototyping the time gap between user and software developer is reduced.

Extreme Prototyping

Extreme prototyping as a development process is used especially for developing web applications. Basically, it breaks down web development into three phases, each one based on the preceding one. The first phase is a static prototype that consists mainly of HTML pages. In the second phase, the screens are programmed and fully functional using a simulated services layer. In the third phase, the services are implemented. The process is called extreme prototyping to draw attention to the second phase of the process, where a fully functional UI is developed with very little regard to the services other than their contract.

Advantages of Prototyping

There are many advantages to using prototyping in software development – some tangible, some abstract.

Reduced time and costs: Prototyping can improve the quality of requirements and specifications provided to developers. Because changes cost exponentially more to implement as they are detected later in development, the early determination of *what the user really wants* can result in faster and less expensive software.

Improved and increased user involvement: Prototyping requires user involvement and allows them to see and interact with a prototype allowing them to provide better and more complete feedback and specifications. The presence of the prototype being examined by the user prevents many misunderstandings and miscommunications that occur when each side believe the other understands what they said. Since users know the problem domain better than anyone on the development team does, increased interaction can result in a final product that has greater tangible and intangible quality. The final product is more likely to satisfy the user's desire for look, feel and performance.

Disadvantages of Prototyping

Using, or perhaps misusing, prototyping can also have disadvantages.

Insufficient analysis: The focus on a limited prototype can distract developers from properly analyzing the complete project. This can lead to overlooking better solutions, preparation of incomplete specifications or the conversion of limited prototypes into poorly engineered final projects that are hard to maintain. Further, since a prototype is limited in functionality it may not scale well if the prototype is used as the basis of a final deliverable, which may not be noticed if developers are too focused on building a prototype as a model.

User confusion of prototype and finished system: Users can begin to think that a prototype, intended to be thrown away, is actually a final system that merely needs to be finished or polished. (They are, for example, often unaware of the effort needed to add error-checking and security features which a prototype may not have.) This can lead them to expect the prototype to accurately model the performance of the final system when this is not the intent of the developers. Users can also become attached to features that were included in a prototype for consideration and then removed from the specification for a final system. If users are able to require all proposed features be included in the final system this can lead to conflict.

Developer misunderstanding of user objectives: Developers may assume that users share their objectives (e.g. to deliver core functionality on time and within budget), without understanding wider commercial issues. For example, user representatives attending Enterprise software (e.g. PeopleSoft) events may have seen demonstrations of "transaction auditing" (where changes are logged and displayed in a difference grid view) without being told that this feature demands additional coding and often requires more hardware to handle extra database accesses. Users might believe they can demand auditing on every field, whereas developers might think this is feature creep because they have made assumptions about the extent of user requirements. If the developer has committed delivery before the user requirements were reviewed, developers are between a rock and a hard place, particularly if user management derives some advantage from their failure to implement requirements.

Developer attachment to prototype: Developers can also become attached to prototypes they have spent a great deal of effort producing; this can lead to problems, such as attempting to convert a limited prototype into a final system when it does not have an appropriate underlying architecture. (This may suggest that throwaway prototyping, rather than evolutionary prototyping, should be used).

Excessive development time of the prototype: A key property to prototyping is the fact that it is supposed to be done quickly. If the developers lose sight of this fact, they very well may try to develop a prototype that is too complex. When the prototype is thrown away the precisely developed requirements that it provides may not yield a sufficient increase in productivity to make up for the time spent developing the prototype. Users can become stuck in debates over details of the prototype, holding up the development team and delaying the final product.

Expense of implementing prototyping: the start up costs for building a development team focused on prototyping may be high. Many companies have development methodologies in place, and changing them can mean retraining, retooling, or both. Many companies tend to just begin prototyping without bothering to retrain their workers as much as they should.

A common problem with adopting prototyping technology is high expectations for productivity with insufficient effort behind the learning curve. In addition to training for the use of a prototyping technique, there is an often overlooked need for developing corporate and project specific underlying structure to support the technology. When this underlying structure is omitted, lower productivity can often result.

Best Projects to use Prototyping

It has been argued that prototyping, in some form or another, should be used all the time. However, prototyping is most beneficial in systems that will have many interactions with the users.

It has been found that prototyping is very effective in the analysis and design of on-line systems, especially for transaction processing, where the use of screen dialogs is much more in evidence. The greater the interaction between the computer and the user, the greater the benefit is that can be obtained from building a quick system and letting the user play with it.

Systems with little user interaction, such as batch processing or systems that mostly do calculations, benefit little from prototyping. Sometimes, the coding needed to perform the system functions may be too intensive and the potential gains that prototyping could provide are too small.

Prototyping is especially good for designing good human-computer interfaces. "One of the most productive uses of rapid prototyping to date has been as a tool for iterative user requirements engineering and human-computer interface design."

Dynamic Systems Development Method

Dynamic Systems Development Method (DSDM) is a framework for delivering business solutions that relies heavily upon prototyping as a core technique, and is itself ISO 9001 approved. It expands upon most understood definitions of a prototype. According to DSDM the prototype may be a diagram, a business process, or even a system placed into production. DSDM prototypes are intended to be incremental, evolving from simple forms into more comprehensive ones.

DSDM prototypes can sometimes be *throwaway* or *evolutionary*. Evolutionary prototypes may be evolved horizontally (breadth then depth) or vertically. Evolutionary prototypes can eventually evolve into final systems.

The four categories of prototypes as recommended by DSDM are:

- Business prototypes – used to design and demonstrates the business processes being automated.

- Usability prototypes – used to define, refine, and demonstrate user interface design usability, accessibility, look and feel.

- Performance and capacity prototypes – used to define, demonstrate, and predict how systems will perform under peak loads as well as to demonstrate and evaluate other non-functional aspects of the system (transaction rates, data storage volume, response time, etc.)

- Capability/technique prototypes – used to develop, demonstrate, and evaluate a design approach or concept.

The DSDM lifecycle of a prototype is to:

- Identify prototype.

- Agree to a plan.

- Create the prototype.

- Review the prototype.

Operational Prototyping

Operational prototyping was proposed by Alan Davis as a way to integrate throwaway and evolutionary prototyping with conventional system development. "It offers the best of both the quick-and-dirty and conventional-development worlds in a sensible manner. Designers develop only well-understood features in building the evolutionary baseline, while using throwaway prototyping to experiment with the poorly understood features."

Davis' belief is that to try to "retrofit quality onto a rapid prototype" is not the correct method when trying to combine the two approaches. His idea is to engage in an evolutionary prototyping methodology and rapidly prototype the features of the system after each evolution.

The specific methodology follows these steps:

- An evolutionary prototype is constructed and made into a baseline using conventional development strategies, specifying and implementing only the requirements that are well understood.

- Copies of the baseline are sent to multiple customer sites along with a trained prototyper.

- At each site, the prototyper watches the user at the system.

- Whenever the user encounters a problem or thinks of a new feature or requirement, the prototyper logs it. This frees the user from having to record the problem, and allows him to continue working.

- After the user session is over, the prototyper constructs a throwaway prototype on top of the baseline system.

- The user now uses the new system and evaluates. If the new changes aren't effective, the prototyper removes them.

- If the user likes the changes, the prototyper writes feature-enhancement requests and forwards them to the development team.

- The development team, with the change requests in hand from all the sites, then produce a new evolutionary prototype using conventional methods.

Obviously, a key to this method is to have well trained prototypers available to go to the user sites. The operational prototyping methodology has many benefits in systems that are complex and have few known requirements in advance.

Evolutionary Systems Development

Evolutionary Systems Development is a class of methodologies that attempt to formally implement evolutionary prototyping.

Systemscraft was designed as a 'prototype' methodology that should be modified and adapted to fit the specific environment in which it was implemented.

Systemscraft was not designed as a rigid 'cookbook' approach to the development process. It is now generally recognised[sic] that a good methodology should be flexible enough to be adjustable to suit all kinds of environment and situation.

The basis of Systemscraft, not unlike evolutionary prototyping, is to create a working system from the initial requirements and build upon it in a series of revisions. Systemscraft places heavy emphasis on traditional analysis being used throughout the development of the system.

Evolutionary Rapid Development

Evolutionary Rapid Development (ERD) was developed by the Software Productivity Consortium, a technology development and integration agent for the Information Technology Office of the Defense Advanced Research Projects Agency (DARPA).

Fundamental to ERD is the concept of composing software systems based on the reuse of components, the use of software templates and on an architectural template. Continuous evolution of system capabilities in rapid response to changing user needs and technology is highlighted by the evolvable architecture, representing a class of solutions. The process focuses on the use of small artisan-based teams integrating software and systems engineering disciplines working multiple, often parallel short-duration timeboxes with frequent customer interaction.

Key to the success of the ERD-based projects is parallel exploratory analysis and development of features, infrastructures, and components with and adoption of leading edge technologies enabling the quick reaction to changes in technologies, the marketplace, or customer requirements.

To elicit customer/user input, frequent scheduled and ad hoc/impromptu meetings with the stakeholders are held. Demonstrations of system capabilities are held to solicit feedback before design/implementation decisions are solidified. Frequent releases (e.g., betas) are made available for use to provide insight into how the system could better support user and customer needs. This assures that the system evolves to satisfy existing user needs.

The design framework for the system is based on using existing published or de facto standards. The system is organized to allow for evolving a set of capabilities that includes considerations for performance, capacities, and functionality. The architecture is defined in terms of abstract interfaces that encapsulate the services and their implementation (e.g., COTS applications). The architecture serves as a template to be used for guiding development of more than a single instance of the system. It allows for multiple application components to be used to implement the services. A core set of functionality not likely to change is also identified and established.

The ERD process is structured to use demonstrated functionality rather than paper products as a way for stakeholders to communicate their needs and expectations. Central to this goal of rapid delivery is the use of the "timebox" method. Timeboxes are fixed periods of time in which specific tasks (e.g., developing a set of functionality) must be performed. Rather than allowing time to expand to satisfy some vague set of goals, the time is fixed (both in terms of calendar weeks and person-hours) and a set of goals is defined that realistically can be achieved within these constraints. To keep development from degenerating into a "random walk," long-range plans are defined to guide the iterations. These plans provide a vision for the overall system and set boundaries (e.g., constraints) for the project. Each iteration within the process is conducted in the context of these long-range plans.

Once an architecture is established, software is integrated and tested on a daily basis. This allows the team to assess progress objectively and identify potential problems quickly. Since small amounts of the system are integrated at one time, diagnosing and removing the defect is rapid. User demonstrations can be held at short notice since the system is generally ready to exercise at all times.

Tools

Efficiently using prototyping requires that an organization have the proper tools and a staff trained to use those tools. Tools used in prototyping can vary from individual tools, such as 4th generation programming languages used for rapid prototyping to complex integrated CASE tools. 4th generation visual programming languages like Visual Basic and ColdFusion are frequently used since they are cheap, well known and relatively easy and fast to use. CASE tools, supporting requirements analysis, like the Requirements Engineering Environment are often developed or selected by the military or large organizations. Object oriented tools are also being developed like LYMB from the GE Research and Development Center. Users may prototype elements of an application themselves in a spreadsheet.

As web-based applications continue to grow in popularity, so too, have the tools for prototyping such applications. Frameworks such as Bootstrap, Foundation, and AngularJS provide the tools necessary to quickly structure a proof of concept. These frameworks typically consist of a set of controls, interactions, and design guidelines that enable developers to quickly prototype web applications.

Screen Generators, Design Tools and Software Factories

Screen generating programs are also commonly used and they enable prototypers to show user's systems that do not function, but show what the screens may look like. Developing Human Computer Interfaces can sometimes be the critical part of the development effort, since to the users the interface essentially is the system.

Software factories can generate code by combining ready-to-use modular components. This makes them ideal for prototyping applications, since this approach can quickly deliver programs with the desired behaviour, with a minimal amount of manual coding.

Application Definition or Simulation Software

A new class of software called Application definition or simulation software enables users to rapidly build lightweight, animated simulations of another computer program, without writing code. Application simulation software allows both technical and non-technical users to experience, test, collaborate and validate the simulated program, and provides reports such as annotations, screenshot and schematics. As a solution specification technique, Application Simulation falls between low-risk, but limited, text or drawing-based mock-ups (or wireframes) sometimes called paper-based prototyping, and time-consuming, high-risk code-based prototypes, allowing software professionals to validate requirements and design choices early on, before development begins. In doing so, the risks and costs associated with software implementations can be dramatically reduced.

To simulate applications one can also use software that simulates real-world software programs for computer-based training, demonstration, and customer support, such as screencasting software as those areas are closely related. There are also more specialised tools.

Requirements Engineering Environment

"The Requirements Engineering Environment (REE), under development at Rome Laboratory since 1985, provides an integrated toolset for rapidly representing, building, and executing models of critical aspects of complex systems."

Requirements Engineering Environment is currently used by the United States Air Force to develop systems. It is:

An integrated set of tools that allows systems analysts to rapidly build functional, user interface, and performance prototype models of system components. These modeling activities are performed to gain a greater understanding of complex systems and lessen the impact that inaccurate requirement specifications have on cost and scheduling during the system development process. Models can be constructed easily, and at varying levels of abstraction or granularity, depending on the specific behavioral aspects of the model being exercised.

REE is composed of three parts. The first, called proto is a CASE tool specifically designed to support rapid prototyping. The second part is called the Rapid Interface Prototyping System or RIP, which is a collection of tools that facilitate the creation of user interfaces. The third part of REE is a user interface to RIP and proto that is graphical and intended to be easy to use.

Rome Laboratory, the developer of REE, intended that to support their internal requirements gathering methodology. Their method has three main parts:

- Elicitation from various sources (users, interfaces to other systems), specification, and consistency checking.

- Analysis that the needs of diverse users taken together do not conflict and are technically and economically feasible.

- Validation that requirements so derived are an accurate reflection of user needs.

In 1996, Rome Labs contracted Software Productivity Solutions (SPS) to further enhance REE to create "a commercial quality REE that supports requirements specification, simulation, user interface prototyping, mapping of requirements to hardware architectures, and code generation". This system is named the Advanced Requirements Engineering Workstation or AREW.

LYMB

LYMB is an object-oriented development environment aimed at developing applications that require combining graphics-based user interfaces, visualization, and rapid prototyping.

Non-relational Environments

Non-relational definition of data (e.g. using Caché or associative models) can help make end-user prototyping more productive by delaying or avoiding the need to normalize data at every iteration of a simulation. This may yield earlier/greater clarity of business requirements, though it does not specifically confirm that requirements are technically and economically feasible in the target production system.

PSDL

PSDL is a prototype description language to describe real-time software. The associated tool set is CAPS (Computer Aided Prototyping System). Prototyping software systems with hard real-time requirements is challenging because timing constraints introduce implementation and hardware dependencies. PSDL addresses these issues by introducing control abstractions that include declarative timing constraints. CAPS uses this information to automatically generate code and associated real-time schedules, monitor timing constraints during prototype execution, and simulate execution in proportional real time relative to a set of parameterized hardware models. It also provides default assumptions that enable execution of incomplete prototype descriptions, integrates prototype construction with a software reuse repository for rapidly realizing efficient implementations, and provides support for rapid evolution of requirements and designs.

Iterative and Incremental Development

Iterative and Incremental development is any combination of both iterative design or iterative method and incremental build model for development.

The basic idea behind this method is to develop a system through repeated cycles (iterative) and in smaller portions at a time (incremental), allowing software developers to take advantage of what was learned during development of earlier parts or versions of the system. Learning comes from both the development and use of the system, where possible key steps in the process start with a simple implementation of a subset of the software requirements and iteratively enhance the evolving versions until the full system is implemented. At each iteration, design modifications are made and new functional capabilities are added.

The procedure itself consists of the initialization step, the iteration step, and the Project Control List. The initialization step creates a base version of the system. The goal for this initial implementation is to create a product to which the user can react. It should offer a sampling of the key aspects of the problem and provide a solution that is simple enough to understand and implement easily. To guide the iteration process, a project control list is created that contains a record of all tasks that need to be performed. It includes items such as new features to be implemented and areas of redesign of the existing solution. The control list is constantly being revised as a result of the analysis phase.

The iteration involves the redesign and implementation of iteration is to be simple, straightforward, and modular, supporting redesign at that stage or as a task added to the project control list. The level of design detail is not dictated by the iterative approach. In a light-weight iterative project the code may represent the major source of documentation of the system; however, in a critical iterative project a formal Software Design Document may be used. The analysis of an iteration is based upon user feedback, and the program analysis facilities available. It involves analysis of the structure, modularity, usability, reliability, efficiency, & achievement of goals. The project control list is modified in light of the analysis results.

Phases

Incremental development slices the system functionality into increments (portions). In each increment, a slice of functionality is delivered through cross-discipline work, from the requirements to the deployment. The Unified Process groups increments/iterations into phases: inception, elaboration, construction, and transition.

- Inception identifies project scope, requirements (functional and non-functional) and risks at a high level but in enough detail that work can be estimated.

- Elaboration delivers a working architecture that mitigates the top risks and fulfills the non-functional requirements.

- Construction incrementally fills-in the architecture with production-ready code produced from analysis, design, implementation, and testing of the functional requirements.

- Transition delivers the system into the production operating environment.

Each of the phases may be divided into 1 or more iterations, which are usually time-boxed rather than feature-boxed. Architects and analysts work one iteration ahead of developers and testers to keep their work-product backlog full.

Usage

Some of those Mercury engineers later formed a new division within IBM, where "another early and striking example of a major IID success [was] the very heart of NASA's space shuttle software—the primary avionics software system, which [they] built from 1977 to 1980. The team applied IID in a series of 17 iterations over 31 months, averaging around eight weeks per iteration. Their motivation for avoiding the waterfall life cycle was that the shuttle program's requirements changed during the software development process."

Some organizations, such as the US Department of Defense, have a preference for iterative methodologies, starting with MIL-STD-498 "clearly encouraging evolutionary acquisition and IID".

The DoD Instruction 5000.2 released in 2000 stated a clear preference for IID:

There are two approaches, evolutionary and single step [waterfall], to full capability. An evolutionary approach is preferred. In this approach, the ultimate capability delivered to the user is divided into two or more blocks, with increasing increments of capability software development shall follow an iterative spiral development process in which continually expanding software versions are based on learning from earlier development. It can also be done in phases.

Recent revisions to DoDI 5000.02 no longer refer to "spiral development," but do advocate the general approach as a baseline for software-intensive development/procurement programs. In addition, the United States Agency for International Development (USAID) also employs an iterative and incremental developmental approach to its programming cycle to design, monitor, evaluate, learn and adapt international development projects with a project management approach that focuses on incorporating collaboration, learning, and adaptation strategies to iterate and adapt programming.

Contrast with Waterfall Development

The main cause due to which most of the software development projects fail is the choice of the model. Hence, it should be made with a great concern.

For example, the Waterfall development paradigm completes the project-wide work-products of each discipline in one step before moving on to the next discipline in the next step. Business value is delivered all at once, and only at the very end of the project, whereas backtracking is possible in an iterative approach. Comparing the two approaches, some patterns begin to emerge:

- User involvement: In the waterfall model, the user is involved in two stages of the model, i.e. requirements and acceptance testing, and possibly creation of user education material. Whereas in the incremental model, the client is involved at each and every stage.

- Variability: The software is delivered to the user only after the build stage of the life cycle is completed, for user acceptance testing. On the other hand, every increment is delivered to the user and after the approval of user, the developer is allowed to move towards the next module.

- Human resources: In the incremental model fewer staff are potentially required as compared to the waterfall model.

- Time limitation: An operational product is delivered after months while in the incremental model the product is given to the user within a few weeks.

- Project size: Waterfall model is unsuitable for small projects while the incremental model is best suitable for small as well as large projects.

Implementation Guidelines

Guidelines that drive software implementation and analysis include:

- Any difficulty in design, coding and testing a modification should signal the need for redesign or re-coding.

- Modifications should fit easily into isolated and easy-to-find modules. If they do not, some redesign is possibly needed.

- Modifications to tables should be especially easy to make. If any table modification is not quickly and easily done, redesign is indicated.

- Modifications should become easier to make as the iterations progress. If they are not, there is a basic problem such as a design flaw or a proliferation of patches.

- Patches should normally be allowed to exist for only one or two iterations. Patches may be necessary to avoid redesigning during an implementation phase.

- The existing implementation should be analyzed frequently to determine how well it measures up to project goals.

- Program analysis facilities should be used whenever available to aid in the analysis of partial implementations.

- User reaction should be solicited and analyzed for indications of deficiencies in the current implementation.

Use in Hardware and Embedded Systems

While the term iterative and incremental development got started in the software industry, many hardware and embedded software development efforts are using iterative and incremental techniques.

Examples of this may be seen in a number of industries. One sector that has recently been substantially affected by this shift of thinking has been the space launch industry, with substantial new competitive forces at work brought about by faster and more extensive technology innovation brought to bear by the formation of private companies pursuing space launch. These companies, such as SpaceX and Rocket Lab, are now both providing commercial orbital launch services in the past decade, something that only six nations had done prior to a decade ago. New innovation in technology development approaches, pricing, and service offerings—including the ability that has existed only since 2016 to fly to space on a previously-flown (reusable) booster stage—further decreasing the price of obtaining access to space.

SpaceX has been explicit about its effort to bring iterative design practices into the space industry, and uses the technique on spacecraft, launch vehicles, electronics and avionics, and operational flight hardware operations.

As the industry has begun to change, other launch competitors are beginning to change their long-term development practices with government agencies as well. For example, the large US launch service provider United Launch Alliance (ULA) began in 2015 a decade-long project to restructure its launch business—reducing two launch vehicles to one—using an iterative and incremental approach to get to a partially-reusable and much lower-cost launch system over the next decade.

Rapid Application Development

Rapid application development (RAD), also called rapid-application building (RAB), is both a general term, used to refer to adaptive software development approaches, as well as the name for Terry Barraclough's approach to rapid development. In general, RAD approaches to software development put less emphasis on planning and more emphasis on an adaptive process. Prototypes are often used in addition to or sometimes even in place of design specifications.

RAD is especially well suited for (although not limited to) developing software that is driven by user interface requirements. Graphical user interface builders are often called rapid application development tools. Other approaches to rapid development include the adaptive, agile, spiral, and unified models.

Rapid application development was a response to plan-driven waterfall processes, developed in the 1970s and 1980s, such as the Structured Systems Analysis and Design Method (SSADM). One of the problems with these methods is that they were based on a traditional engineering model used to design and build things like bridges and buildings. Software is an inherently different kind of artifact. Software can radically change the entire process used to solve a problem. As a result, knowledge gained from the development process itself can feed back to the requirements and design of the solution. Plan-driven approaches attempt to rigidly define the requirements, the solution, and the plan to implement it, and have a process that discourages changes. RAD approaches, on the other hand, recognize that software development is a knowledge intensive process and provide flexible processes that help take advantage of knowledge gained during the project to improve or adapt the solution.

The first such RAD alternative was developed by Barry Boehm and was known as the spiral model. Boehm and other subsequent RAD approaches emphasized developing prototypes as well as or instead of rigorous design specifications. Prototypes had several advantages over traditional specifications:

- Risk reduction: A prototype could test some of the most difficult potential parts of the system early on in the life-cycle. This can provide valuable information as to the feasibility of a design and can prevent the team from pursuing solutions that turn out to be too complex or time consuming to implement. This benefit of finding problems earlier in the life-cycle rather than later was a key benefit of the RAD approach. The earlier a problem can be found the cheaper it is to address.

- Users are better at using and reacting than at creating specifications: In the waterfall model it was common for a user to sign off on a set of requirements but then when presented with an implemented system to suddenly realize that a given design lacked some critical features or was too complex. In general most users give much more useful feedback when they can experience a prototype of the running system rather than abstractly define what that system should be.

- Prototypes can be usable and can evolve into the completed product: One approach used in some RAD methods was to build the system as a series of prototypes that evolve from minimal functionality to moderately useful to the final completed system. The advantage of this besides the two advantages above was that the users could get useful business functionality much earlier in the process.

The RAD approach also matured during the period of peak interest in business re-engineering. The idea of business process re-engineering was to radically rethink core business processes such as sales and customer support with the new capabilities of Information Technology in mind. RAD was often an essential part of larger business re engineering programs. The rapid prototyping approach of RAD was a key tool to help users and analysts "think out of the box" about innovative ways that technology might radically reinvent a core business process.

The James Martin RAD Method

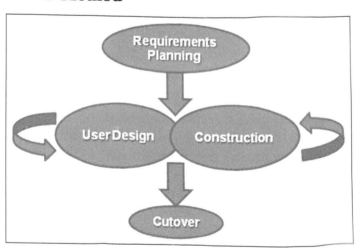

Phases in the James Martin approach to RAD.

The James Martin approach to RAD divides the process into four distinct phases:

- Requirements planning phase – combines elements of the system planning and systems analysis phases of the Systems Development Life Cycle (SDLC). Users, managers, and IT staff members discuss and agree on business needs, project scope, constraints, and system requirements. It ends when the team agrees on the key issues and obtains management authorization to continue.

- User design phase – during this phase, users interact with systems analysts and develop models and prototypes that represent all system processes, inputs, and outputs. The RAD groups or subgroups typically use a combination of Joint Application Development techniques and CASE tools to translate user needs into working models. *User Design* is a continuous interactive process that allows users to understand, modify, and eventually approve a working model of the system that meets their needs.

- Construction phase – focuses on program and application development task similar to the SDLC. In RAD, however, users continue to participate and can still suggest changes or improvements as actual screens or reports are developed. Its tasks are programming and application development, coding, unit-integration and system testing.

- Cutover phase – resembles the final tasks in the SDLC implementation phase, including data conversion, testing, changeover to the new system, and user training. Compared with traditional methods, the entire process is compressed. As a result, the new system is built, delivered, and placed in operation much sooner.

Pros and Cons of Rapid Application Development

In modern Information Technology environments, many systems are now built using some degree of Rapid Application Development (not necessarily the James Martin approach). In addition to Martin's method, Agile methods and the Rational Unified Process are often used for RAD development.

The purported advantages of RAD include:

- Better quality: By having users interact with evolving prototypes the business functionality from a RAD project can often be much higher than that achieved via a waterfall model. The software can be more usable and has a better chance to focus on business problems that are critical to end users rather than technical problems of interest to developers. However, this excludes other categories of what are usually known as Non-functional requirements (AKA constraints or quality attributes) including security and portability.

- Risk control: Although much of the literature on RAD focuses on speed and user involvement a critical feature of RAD done correctly is risk mitigation. It's worth remembering that Boehm initially characterized the spiral model as a risk based approach. A RAD approach can focus in early on the key risk factors and adjust to them based on empirical evidence collected in the early part of the process. E.g., the complexity of prototyping some of the most complex parts of the system.

- More projects completed on time and within budget: By focusing on the development of incremental units the chances for catastrophic failures that have dogged large waterfall projects is reduced. In the Waterfall model it was common to come to a realization after six months or more of analysis and development that required a radical rethinking of the entire system. With RAD this kind of information can be discovered and acted upon earlier in the process.

The disadvantages of RAD include:

- The risk of a new approach: For most IT shops RAD was a new approach that required experienced professionals to rethink the way they worked. Humans are virtually always averse to change and any project undertaken with new tools or methods will be more likely to fail the first time simply due to the requirement for the team to learn.

- Lack of emphasis on Non-functional requirements, which are often not visible to the end user in normal operation.

- Requires time of scarce resources: One thing virtually all approaches to RAD have in common is that there is much more interaction throughout the entire life-cycle between users and developers. In the waterfall model, users would define requirements and then mostly go away as developers created the system. In RAD users are involved from the beginning and through virtually the entire project. This requires that the business is willing to invest the time of application domain experts. The paradox is that the better the expert, the more they are familiar with their domain, the more they are required to actually run the business and it may be difficult to convince their supervisors to invest their time. Without such commitments RAD projects will not succeed.

- Less control: One of the advantages of RAD is that it provides a flexible adaptable process. The ideal is to be able to adapt quickly to both problems and opportunities. There is an inevitable trade-off between flexibility and control, more of one means less of the other. If a project (e.g. life-critical software) values control more than agility RAD is not appropriate.

- Poor design: The focus on prototypes can be taken too far in some cases resulting in a "hack and test" methodology where developers are constantly making minor changes to individual components and ignoring system architecture issues that could result in a better overall design. This can especially be an issue for methodologies such as Martin's that focus so heavily on the user interface of the system.

- Lack of scalability: RAD typically focuses on small to medium-sized project teams. The other issues cited above (less design and control) present special challenges when using a RAD approach for very large scale systems.

References

- "A Brief History of devops, Part III: Automated Testing and Continuous Integration". Circleci. 1 February 2018. Retrieved 19 May 2018

- Reading-software-development-process, zeliite115: courses.lumenlearning.com, Retrieved 22 April, 2019

- Unhelkar, B. (2016). The Art of Agile Practice: A Composite Approach for Projects and Organizations. CRC Press. Pp. 56–59. ISBN 9781439851197

- Laukkanen, Eero (2016). "Problems, causes and solutions when adopting continuous delivery—A systematic literature review" (PDF). Information and Software Technology. 82: 55–79. Doi:10.1016/j.infsof.2016.10.001 – via Elsevier Science Direct

- Dr. Alistair Cockburn (May 2008). "Using Both Incremental and Iterative Development" (PDF). STSC CrossTalk. USAF Software Technology Support Center. 21 (5): 27–30. ISSN 2160-1593. Retrieved 2011-07-2

PERMISSIONS

All chapters in this book are published with permission under the Creative Commons Attribution Share Alike License or equivalent. Every chapter published in this book has been scrutinized by our experts. Their significance has been extensively debated. The topics covered herein carry significant information for a comprehensive understanding. They may even be implemented as practical applications or may be referred to as a beginning point for further studies.

We would like to thank the editorial team for lending their expertise to make the book truly unique. They have played a crucial role in the development of this book. Without their invaluable contributions this book wouldn't have been possible. They have made vital efforts to compile up to date information on the varied aspects of this subject to make this book a valuable addition to the collection of many professionals and students.

This book was conceptualized with the vision of imparting up-to-date and integrated information in this field. To ensure the same, a matchless editorial board was set up. Every individual on the board went through rigorous rounds of assessment to prove their worth. After which they invested a large part of their time researching and compiling the most relevant data for our readers.

The editorial board has been involved in producing this book since its inception. They have spent rigorous hours researching and exploring the diverse topics which have resulted in the successful publishing of this book. They have passed on their knowledge of decades through this book. To expedite this challenging task, the publisher supported the team at every step. A small team of assistant editors was also appointed to further simplify the editing procedure and attain best results for the readers.

Apart from the editorial board, the designing team has also invested a significant amount of their time in understanding the subject and creating the most relevant covers. They scrutinized every image to scout for the most suitable representation of the subject and create an appropriate cover for the book.

The publishing team has been an ardent support to the editorial, designing and production team. Their endless efforts to recruit the best for this project, has resulted in the accomplishment of this book. They are a veteran in the field of academics and their pool of knowledge is as vast as their experience in printing. Their expertise and guidance has proved useful at every step. Their uncompromising quality standards have made this book an exceptional effort. Their encouragement from time to time has been an inspiration for everyone.

The publisher and the editorial board hope that this book will prove to be a valuable piece of knowledge for students, practitioners and scholars across the globe.

INDEX

Printed in the USA
CPSIA information can be obtained
at www.ICGtesting.com
JSHW051416221024
72173JS00006B/1367

9 781647 261108